There Are Three Truths II

For the protection of the author, publisher, and distributor, this book is not intended for rendering legal or any other professional advice, but remain astute at all times.

ISBN: 979-8-218-15022-8

ISBN 979-8-218-15022-8

90000>

About "There Are Three Truths"

Here are some key takeaways from the first version. There Are Three Truths: 2019 Complete Version starts off mimicking our world with content explaining past events, with details of the internet source it was retrieved from. That information is meant to be a foundation of factual information to explore and advance from, as we attempt to understand our world in detail. The book explained the difference between God's and Satan's values. A lot of its material is written in an ambiguous and creative fashion to aid your imagination. I call it a snapshot of our world and a foundation to give strength to "There Are Three Truths II".

There Are Three Truths II starts out with scattered, but informative topics and stories. People might find this edition more exciting to read and giving more context to the events discussed in the earlier version. But, most importantly, this version continues with its hard facts. However, the Quantum Star Eckter series is, probably, the most exciting to read. Quantum Star Eckter found a planet that seems to operate like ours. It found another one before that, but not a lot of details were published about that. Anyway, the inferior planet, now referenced as the former inferior planet, was found, saved, and researched by Quantum Star Eckter.

The goal of the research was to find out how that planet became so wicked, filled with homelessness, racism, unequal opportunities, and more. But the research wasn't just about that; it was about how to prevent such a thing from ever happening again. It was about discovering principles and concepts that brought the planet down and what was needed to build them up.

Luckily, Quantum Star Eckter already had the answer, because they were living it.

All this information provides a way to look into our world to do comparisons and research for answers that are in likeness to the inferior planet and the Esquanent Galaxy of Friends. After all, you should understand that we need to build a better world.

With so much accurate information, a glimpse at an example of how to live, and elaborations on various verses of the earlier Bible, I became convinced that the "There Are Three Truths" series is the new Bible. See for yourself. Even Quantum Star Eckter logically confirmed it.

Promotions

"Thanks to Jason's profiles and other information, you will be able to pinpoint the details that determine whether or not a person is on the side of God, in real-time.

It's based on how they talk, believe, and act, in comparison to something hard and factual. It's now, more than ever before, to know whom you're talking to; because they could be dangerous. Sometimes, it's because of something they don't know, but that's about to change. Plus, you can know who they might still be by what you've already heard and seen from them."

"If you didn't know this by now, "There Are Three Truths" is, naturally, building grounds for potential lawsuits across the globe. Why? Because the system and actions of many of the rich and anyone else having a role in it are "Negatively Compelling".

It's done simply by truth-telling, which is why it is regulated with deception.
Although, the book uses fiction, it is scientifically assembled and mimics an inferior world that can be compared to another. It, also, reveals a method to unearth the facts about a unique world. But, lawsuits alone will not change the world. You have to look at the example of Quantum Star Eckter for that."

"What's wrong with the world?

Did you know that there's a consequence for everything that God said, not just the Ten Commandments? As a matter of fact, probably, one of the most important things He said was not to follow no man.

Now, that was the wording I got some time ago; but the wordings have changed over time, which it shouldn't have. It's becoming less clear, as if to fade out. I've seen one verse seemingly fading out, so much, as to be hard to find. I talked about it some time ago, but I don't remember which verse is was, at this time.

Anyway, here is Psalm 146:3, where it says not to put your trust in princes nor son of man, where there's no help. Do you understand why there's no help? Competition. I told you it doesn't belong here. It's not a quality of God.

Now, let's talk about how the violation of 146:3, putting your trust in the wrong place, is causing problems. Jeremiah 17:9, man's heart is wicked! This is why a character in "There Are Three Truths" said, "Control your development".

You can't control your development by following wicked hearts.

They present the wrong trajectory through life. They bound you to a wrong way to live. You see the fruits of the tree all across the globe. What more do you need to see? This is proof that "There Are Three Truths" is needed to turn this world around. There is no other way.
So, what should you follow? It's not me. It's not "There Are Three Truths". It's the truth that you get from your world, which "There Are Three Truths" has presented in part.

You were told to "Search and you will find", Mathew 7:7. Now, I do have a problem with this verse. I don't believe it's one hundred percent correct. I'm talking about the "don't give your pearls to swine". Giving what's presented in "There Are Three Truths", scientifically and from cross-checking its material, it appears to be an aid to lock this world in its inferior condition. After his confession, an informant said, "People needed to know that life isn't a place to lounge. That's how you become impulsive. That's how you fail to evolve. That's how you get captured. You….". I want to add "That's how you remain vulnerable to deception".

There Are Three Truths proves that the practitioners of an inferior world are not the Christian nation that they profess to be, by giving you an outline of the system and proving the elements of that outline. The practitioners are what they create. You should have known this from previous writings of "There Are Three Truths".

"They can't logically defend themselves against "There Are Three Truth"; so, they have to use sanctions and prevent or regulate its distribution. That move is evidence in itself.

Statistics show that it's run by a racist group. But, you can't draw a line around any complete or single race. Looking around the globe, you see more than one race practicing the same trait(s). You see all races on both sides of the line. The most favorable are those having the least control. The most unfavorable are those having the most control, who are on the problem side. They are boisterous, usually have more money, and usually more intelligent. However, their intelligence, as a whole, never comes to the knowledge of truth. Sound familiar? You, definitely, cannot change the world for the better by following this group. They prefer to chase the riches of the world and to be perceived as dominant over others. They are not sensitive to the injuries they create. You see the fruits of the tree.

The world has the most control over development, when you don't possess the knowledge and ability to control your development.

Many are destined to develop the wrong way, because they follow others, even at a young and vulnerable age. "There Are Three Truths" reveals some of the knowledge about development, which seems to be ignored. It's like expert knowledge is hidden from the seeker, following the wrong source of information, and those who aren't seeking at all.

At some point, you've got to do something, if you don't want to be seen as part of that latter group. So, how do you separate yourself? The answer is as important as you truly believe in God."

"This new Bible is a picture of the following verses from the earlier Bible, Ephesians 6:

"10 Finally, be strong in the Lord and in his mighty power. 11 Put on the full armor of God, so that you can take your stand against the devil's schemes. 12 For our struggle is not against flesh and blood, but against the rulers, against the authorities, against the powers of this dark world and against the spiritual forces of evil in the heavenly realms. 13 Therefore put on the full armor of God, so that when the day of evil comes, you may be able to stand your ground, and after you have done everything, to stand. 14 Stand firm then, with the belt of truth buckled around your waist, with the breastplate of righteousness in place, 15 and with your feet fitted with the readiness that comes from the gospel of peace. 16 In addition to all this, take up the shield of faith, with which you can extinguish all the flaming arrows of the evil one."

"The use of any method to procure a crime(s) or to cause one to seek not his/her best interests, leading to damages, with intent to lead to justice, is a product of a pre-postered mind inclined towards crime." - Agov Yeslea

One of the informants said "We use crime to create crime and to fight crime". You can see that as a theme throughout the book, especially in the inferior planet.

Most likely, Quantum Star Eckter investigated Esquanet Galaxy of Friends (EGF) too, because there's a little data about them too, which was posted as a new finding. EGF found it devastating to overcome when confronted."

"I stole?…. I don't know… Here's what happened!

One day, a long time ago, I caught a glimpse of the news, while getting ready for school. I feel lucky to have caught it.

Anyway, it was….I'm not sure, speaking. I'm sure, at least I think, I'm sure. I tried checking his quotes, but couldn't find it. That makes me question myself.

Here's what he said, "We have the ability to make…." Not sure if this is the exact wording.

From time to time, it pops up in my head. I can see why the government would want to tuck that thing out of sight or silence him on that.

I'm not saying he's a good guy or bad guy, because I don't know. He could've said it without thinking it through, you know, the impact. It would be hard for the government to deal with.

Anyway, I took it and reworded it and made it mine, so to speak. Then, I put it in this book. Hey! I needed it."

There Are Three Truths is so detailed that it's hard, if not impossible, to squeeze a lie in there.

"When this new Bible is consumed by artificial intelligence, it will eventually become a dog, a hunting dog.

If you're about anything good, you'll like it; because of its purpose to turn the world around. When you like it, you will support whatever it takes to make it so.

When it becomes reality, everyone had better be on the same page with it.

Otherwise, it will find you up a tree, hugging a tree, or running or standing between trees. You will be known for what you fight against and how.

Quantum Star Eckter set the rules and purpose in the book. There's no good reason to deny what has been reasonably thought out.

Crime and racism are going to fall dramatically for future generations. Current generations will have to transform or else…,

You're not cool; because you're corrupt or a racist, which is the same, no matter what race you are.

Money is there to be lost."

"The Counsel of Affairs has identified a not-so-new crime that appears to be legal, but is obviously illegal, in respects to its definition. It is, also, seen on a large scale.

I don't know how you can defend it without damaging your reputation or exposing your true character."

"I see the end of me writing this new Bible; artificial intelligence will finish reporting, going further than my capacity, as long as COA instructions are followed.

There is enough knowledge in the world to complete and sustain the task.

It will be an obvious error to deny AI from carrying out its purpose, described by COA. You will see the transformations and how important they are. You will see past errors.

In its complete form, you will see contestants violating the very laws they believe in.

Read up on all the capabilities of artificial intelligence."

"Earlier in the book, it was stated that you can't mix the values of God and demons together and get the best out of this world.

Now, the book progressed to the point of disclosing the details of why that is. It's starting to show points of disruption.

You will see why, when you see how artificial intelligence has to be used. Everything has to cater to the purpose given to it by COA.

This is a major blow to those catering artificial intelligence after today's world, which is a false example.

Artificial intelligence will make this world more effective and efficient in being inferior, left as is. That's because it will be developed to cater to the wishes of the most influential."

"Can you make excuses for not obeying God's Word? Sure, you can. But, there's only one that's legit.

It will be significantly less possible, after the distribution of the new Bible; because your conscience will know the Truth.

You're going to become stuck between POWER and RIGHTEOUSNESS. POWER will pay you immediate dividends and keep on paying you for a time. But not everyone will benefit well enough, with unevenly distributed advantage.

Righteousness is only going to yield you the qualities of God., which is Great. But, it's not popular for those who want material gains at the expense of others.

However, followers of God will have a higher quality of life and their fate will be in His hands, not the ones talking about scarcity, inflation, and recession or worse. In the end, they've only destroyed and predicted doomsday.

So, disregard those financial concepts and follow God. Then, and only then, you can say "I did all I could, now it's on God ". Who else is better qualified?

Put God's system in place, once you see and understand it."

"There Are Three Truths has advanced so far that it would be crazy for anyone, having a complaint about the wrongs in this world, to pass on the material written within.

Oppressors will be seeing nightmares."

"I touched on the core of the world's problems today. I understand why they're using this knowledge to create two different worlds.

I read expert knowledge that was written nicely, but I saw something on a higher scale.
I learned it in college, but was mentally limited by its expression.
I just might own all the experts that I attract."

"Counsel of Affairs passed another law today.

The laws that they pass helps to establish and assure continued harmony as the two planets prepare for their future unification.

The process requires studies, and the reliance on those studies, to assure protections from the previous errors of the former inferior planet.

The project is an example to follow."

Why profile humans and then build a system to materialize and profit from their inferior side?

Dare to be better and to do better things

Table of Contents

Contents

There Are Three Truths II

Theorist #23 said "We can make the Son of God look like the Devil and the Devil like the Son of God".

As a child, I heard someone say this a long time ago, but couldn't find proof. So, I changed the wording and said the same thing. I believe it should've rocked our world. Maybe it wasn't taken seriously at the time. But, if you read and remember the contents of this book, and advisably the first edition, you might take it a lot more seriously. Make comparisons to your world throughout the book.

The Blessing Game

1.   The blessing game is enhanced, when the people in the environment practice God's commandments, like 'love your neighbor as thy self'. It is diminished, when people do not practice his commandments. This lets you know what type of an environment you're in.

2.   When I see a panhandler, I think to myself that those people are brave and don't seem to feel any shame at all. That amazes me every time.

3.   But some have demonstrated some shame, especially those who have assembled together with their immediate family members.

4.   But the way I see it, now, if you played the role of giving when you could and you fall on hard times, there is nothing to be ashamed about pan handling.

5.   You deserve a handout, because you helped to support the blessing game, without abusing it. And, blessings don't have to be about material things, nor do they have to have a limit imposed on them.

The Problem with the Bible and its Interpretation of the Relationship between God and Satan

1.   The Bible gives God and Satan equal power; although it expresses the goodness of God and the fact that He's the Creator, while putting Satan in the world's driver's seat.

2.   Satan is the god of this world, while God is positioned to come storming back as the world's leader, as a result of the short-comings of Satan. Meanwhile, Satan is in a position to brainwash the entire world into believing according to his principles and concepts, which is currently showing great success.

3.   To manifest and sustain the idea or agenda of the two; the overall intentions of the laws must assure that God and Satan cannot transgress upon the other. The law must allow for equal advantage. However, there is a flaw. You can't be involved in creating a dark world or not teaching truth, and be a saint of God.

4.   The intensity of advantage must come from the attitudes and decisions of a benefitting majority, to present a bearing upon the minority, which requires motivating methods. So, a feeding process (media, gossip & secrets) and divisive and abrasive concepts must be implemented.

5.   The majority will have an unfair and overwhelming advantage over the others anytime and anywhere the majority rules.

6.   Do you see any real limitations that are placed on Satan and his ways, besides some stated law?

7.   Can you find a good law that has not been transgressed in favor of Satan? How difficult was the find, if any?

8.   Can you find laws, written or implied, that transgress the values of Satan, especially those that pertain to the development and sustainment of God's ways? The values of Satan are identified in the challenge and violations of human rights to fulfill the Commandments of God.

9.   Do the answers to these questions favor the values and intentions of Satan and his followers?

10.   The various ways that humans and their environments are tested will only demonstrate how they are purposed to respond, which is a proper response. But, even, a proper response may receive a negative consequence, in a corrupted environment. It's all about management of the elements.

11.   The most intelligent followers of Satan will only deceive or attempt to deceive people into giving their way more time to work its so-called magical transformation to paradise. Overall, there's nothing new going on in their magic, other than a deeper understanding of human behavior, which is used to benefit their agenda.

12.   Sustaining two or more countering worlds, in which neither are a following of God, is proof of being off the path of the Will of God, the Creator.

13.   Forced to live accordingly, such affects the development of people from child through adulthood. The most prevalent attitude is to triumph over neighbors and strangers for success.

14.   Where I have a serious problem with the idea is where deception is used to control the perception of another, causing the victim to manifest desires, decisions, ideas, acts, and solutions related to or as a consequence of the deceptive practice. At that point, the victim has lost personal control, if control was ever been in their grasp. Any knowledgeable person should know that the aspect of the competition, deception, has crossed the line and lost its legitimacy as a determining factor of who is good or bad. Understand that there must be a line that must not be crossed, as seen in any sport.

15.   Maybe you might say that a man should not have drunk, if he knew he would become intoxicated; but, then, you'd have to apply that concept to every sin you've ever committed to be fair.

16.   All the negative experiences of a dark world say how to create it and how not to inspire it. That makes it a matter of principles and concepts involving elements that are more powerful than the heart and mind, because those principles and concepts represent the feed.

17.   If you see that the line has been crossed, you should be standing against it, not just trying to safely fit in or profit from it; otherwise, what would that say about you?

Shoc! News Presents the Review of the movie 'Get, Profile, and Control'

*Fictitious Show

1.   Shoc! News Presents the Review of the movie 'Get, Profile, and Control', based on a true story and inspired by the book "There Are Three Truths".

2.   Jim: Hello ladies and gentlemen, and welcome to Shoc! News. I'm Jim Stallworth. We're an underground news source dedicated to bringing you in-depth news from around the world. Today, we have with us a long-time guest of our show, Tom McEnroe. Hello, Tom!

3.   Tom: Good Morning!

4.   Jim: Tom, here, is a strategic analyst at Broswel Institute. He is here to help fill us in on whether a high-profile conspiracy exist in our world and to aid in the discovery of the truth of the matter in question. Of course, this is a regular topic on our show.

5.   We also have a special guest with us today. This special guest's identity has been concealed. Therefore, we have distorted the guest's voice and image. We will call the guest 'Informant B' from here on. Informant B, welcome to Shoc! News.

6.   Informant B: Thank you and hello.

7.   Jim: Well, informant B, give us a briefing of the movie. I'm sure some people have not seen it yet.

8.   Informant B: Sure, Jim. The movie is about a government that profiles, I would say, every aspect of the universe and its effect on the people. But the main concern is centered on the human population, as a foundation to excel from, with no regards for the individual rights of the people.

9.   Jim: But how real is this movie; because we have laws that protect human rights?

10.   Informant B: Absolutely. We do. However, this is a demonic system the movie is referring to. In such a system, nothing is stable, it can all be undone, reinterpreted, and deceptively disguised to promote error in perception and decision-making. Everything is based on the decisions of the one in the most powerful position, not what is right or wrong, as they generally and openly make it seem.

11.   I know that's hard for people to digest, because they are constantly programmed to believe that higher authority has their best interest. But the movie shows how powerful one can be, when they exploit and profile and use the profile to manipulate selfish ends.

12.   Tom: A profile is an understanding of the makeup of the matter, how something or someone works and why, as well as the resources used by the processes. Through this understanding, everything is connected or can be.

13.   Informant B: Exactly.

14. Jim: So, you're saying this information is used or can be used to control every aspect of human nature?

15. Informant B: Not just human nature, but everything in the universe, even the weather.

16. Tom: That is exactly why we have college courses. They are all due to exploitation and results, which is a profile.

17. Jim: So, I still don't understand how human rights can be violated in the process. After all, profiles can be used to aid defenses and prosecutions.

18. Informant B: You're right. I thought the same thing and fought against the very people, who contributed to this movie. I sought to tell, what I thought was, the truth about what they were doing and end this whole thing. However, I began to see the possibility, then some things that seem to defy human nature, and later some evidence, which can only be seen by taking a closer look.

19. In some cases, it appeared that human nature had no definite profile. It was just wild and unreasonable and solely the fault of the person in question, as if no external source didn't play a part in his/her development. Once I seen that, I was sold on contributing to this movement.

20. Tom: This reminds me of what a professor, on the wrong side of a debate, told me. I still think about it over and over.

21. He said, "Using deception and controlling or manipulating methods is a natural element of human nature. We've done it ever since the beginning of time. There's no sense in berating one, because his game is bigger and better. All, even animals, are out to survive, stabilize, and prosper however we can. If human nature is of a foul nature, you have to use foul methods to overcome victimization. But, throughout this ordeal, there needs to be some kind of control, to keep it down, as much as possible."

22. At the time, I couldn't counter his argument. And, if I did, I'm sure he'd whip out something else to leave me befuddled again. That's the type of guy he was.

23. Jim: That is interesting!

24. Informant B: There's a better way. We're just too busy building on and being inspired by the wrong way to see it. As we assemble the elements of a matter, we become inspired by it, given directions toward effectiveness and efficiency, as if that's our only foundation. We need to stop being programmed and submissive or subjective to those, who benefit from the selfish and inferior design of the system.

25. Jim: However, I still can't see a clear picture of what's going on. I see enough to see a great deal of credibility in your story. But I'm missing something.

26. Informant B: Using the media, the way people think, controlling the way they think, manipulating resources, inventing and creating technology, you can do anything you want with the power of profiles. Our world is mostly controlled by the knowledge of profiles, which yields results. That's where the evidence of perception comes in.

27. Jim: Now, I understand. And, we've got to go folks. I thank Informant B and Tom for their contributions to the show. We're out of here. Thanks for watching. (Music. Shakes hands with the guests)

Shoc! News Presents "The Last Show"

*Fictitious Show

1.   Jim: Hello ladies and gentlemen, and welcome to Shoc! News. I'm Jim Stallworth. We're an underground news source dedicated to bringing you in-depth news from around the world. However, I have some very sad news for you. Tom McEnroe is no longer with us. This is a very sad moment for all of us.

2.   As you already know, Tom is or was a strategic analyst at Broswel Institute. I have no idea what all is going on over there.

3.   This is a special presentation to give you all the details I've been told and to say my farewell, and I also have a guess with me, Mr. Jake Johnson. Jake has been through a lot and can give us some insight, as to what might be happening. Hello, Jake.

4.   Jake: Hello, Jim. This is a nice place you've got here, and I like your coffee.

5.   Jim: Thank you, Jake. We're faced with a limited amount of time here; so, let's get down to business and keep our conversation related, as much as possible.

6.   I had been trying to contact Tom for the last few days, to no avail, except for the brief moment I did get a chance to speak with him. He told me that he was under a lot of pressure to refrain from contributing to the show. His wife was facing social ridicule. Grants have been pulled from Broswel Institute, and his tenure is questionable for the future.

7.   Jake: I can relate to his situation. I know he was very important to your show, but I can see why he would give up his dream job. You see, a man can be teased and tempted to go another direction, even the opposite, if you offer him a better quality of life. I'm talking about the satisfaction of greed.

8.   Jim: But Tom wasn't a greedy man. He stood for something in an unwavering manner. You couldn't rock his determination. I know it wasn't greed. He wouldn't go out like that.

9.   Jake: I'm speaking about one side of the issue. While it is a strong influence upon a lot of people, it is weaker than the other side, depending on the circumstances. Circumstances can defame a person's character. What if someone exercised control over you?

10.   While one side is about greed, the other side is about avoiding consequences; especially when they are detrimental. The man has to pay his bills. He has to take care of his wife and kids. So, he has more to think about than just himself. He can't just detach. His family is a part of him. So, the consequences can't be swept to the side. Consequences are the greatest motivators; they force people to handle unwanted responsibilities, even when they have a defiant attitude.

11.   Now, if he was making some kind of progress or had been gathering sufficient support, he may have had hope. Hope can be strong enough to make a man make a bad bet. So, was there any kind of progress?

12.   Jim: ....Well, I'd like to say that being informative is making progress. You know, you've got to plant the seed first.

13.   Jake: What was the competition doing?

14.   Jim: Heck, I don't know.....selling chicken dinners or offering waffles for breakfast to fund some project, whether expansion or something obviously not making a difference. Or, we wouldn't have to be here. They seem to be supporting the very things that underlie the issues they complain about. So, we felt the need to educate. Now, it feels like we've failed, for some reason.

15.   Jake: You could continue.

16.   Jim: No. It looks like an attack from all sides, based on Tom's perspective, which is explained in the book "There Are Three Truths". Plus, I received a letter in the mail. I assumed Broswel Institute received the same. The president has cut grants for arts, in which this program is considered part of. Here is what it says:

17.   "Dear Grantee,

18.   We are sorry to inform you of a cut in grants for the arts, as instructed by the president. All programs and artistic endeavors that do not support and inspire a united nation are deemed terroristic in manner. As a nation, we feel feuds are better handled by contacting agency representatives, who represent the people. This is the only recourse needed to resolve our nation's problems.

19.   However, we will be happy to inform you of any other grants that you may qualify to receive upon request.

20.   Because this is not an attack on your rights, you are free to practice your freedom of speech, in which we all value so much. We wish you lots of luck in whatever endeavor you choose.

21.   These cuts are effective immediately.

22.   Sincerely, Ariana Wayne, secretary of arts"

23.   Jake: That is a blatant lie! They are practicing reverse psychology. They are calling your efforts terroristic!

24.   Jim: And, they know that without sufficient support, we cannot continue. Non-support is like giving the enemy a license to destroy the earth. They understand when economics is or is not funding their get-away car.

25.   Jake: That's how you help cut one down, from the roots. They don't even want the threat.

26.   It, also, proves that most of the money is on the wrong side and rights are stolen by the same. People are forced into a world they don't want to reside in, whether it's because secrets are kept from them, framed, or it's plain unaffordable.

27.   Jim: Exactly!

28.   Well, we're running out of time. I just wanted to let everyone know what's going on and to say "Goodbye". Thank you, Jake. And, thanks to all my listeners over the years. This is Jim Stallworth saying farewell to everyone. (Music and flashes from the past shows are presented).

The Various Types of Forces

1.   A force is filled with energy and is an explosive or moving phenomenon or expression that is measured by intensity and impact, even emotionally and mentally so, and may come from within or from the external environment, if not both.

2.   Force can possess the power to create influence, like physical force, emotion(s), thought(s), history, and law.

3.   Evidence of force can be an expression of a pattern or set of patterns perceived in the environment, whether within the imagination or the external world. It can create the premises for understanding, creative ideas, and programmable effects.

4.   Force can be an exertion of energy towards you or your interests, including the threat of. It can cause anxiety, resistance, harm, and/or an act of defense.

5.   Force has momentum that may have to be met with resistance to slow or stop, like a rolling ball.

6.   Force can be overwhelming, challenging, and influential upon a balance of other influences.

7.   Because there is always more than one force at play, there's always a balance of energies that create these influences. It can be looked upon as an exploitation method of one another, with some kind of agenda.

8.   We have a tendency to read the balance of forces to retrieve a message, whether true or deceiving.

9.   Many things can go right or wrong, which is why we have to learn to deal with them successfully; but it takes everyone to participate, use their talents, and share information; because the information is vast.

10.   Events, which are evidence of forces at work, may consist of various elements, and may be of any quality, and anywhere from in its infancy to maturity, in expression and having various life spans. This creates unique situations, circumstances, chain reactions, ramifications, developments, results, ailments, benefits, consequences, behaviors Etc. If you knew all this, you can imagine what's being developed.

Imperfections and Corruption are not the same

1.   Imperfections are what you expect from a trainee or student that result in a wrong way of going about something or result from some wrong or inaccurate calculation or development.

2.   Imperfections may start with a wrong or clueless mentality, a lack of information and proper control, and/or an erroneous or defective partner or machine. The proper programming or re-programming is needed.

3.   People, who make mistakes and/or are under the influence of another matter that harnesses or alters for the worse their ability to perceive and/or control a process-in-question, fall under imperfections. The seriousness of a matter does not impact the definition. The human-being is usually represented here. It's related to blindness and improper perception. The exemption occurs when "under the influence" is within the controls of the character, who performed the error.

4.   Corruption is a different animal. It's the element of a decision-maker, in an initial role or planter position, which controls the environment and understands enough to organize with the goal of achieving something in the wrong manner or that is wrong to seek. The spinoff is empowerment or programming, in which the effects may be met with resistances like disempowerment and/or reprogramming.

5.   The signal is that the highest level of authority must be flawless, in order to expect the lower levels to be the same.

6.   The nature of an environment controls and regulates everything within, as seen in the changes of various species, plants, conditions, and cultures across various types of environments.

7.   So, corruption is never in a middle or last position, only in a planter, an initial encouraging element position, or where a birth, rollout, or first duplicate is created.

8.   Outside the planter position is the effect of advantage, overwhelming power, mental and emotional programming, and viral effects. Corruption is like the master, while the effect is performed by the slave, the manipulated, the drugged, the blind, the uninformed, the weak, or the overwhelmed etc.

9.   For another example, you can find many transmissions of diseases; however, the catalyst may be what was created in a laboratory or initialized elsewhere or through experiments and studies. It's not that those, who transmitted don't work properly; it's about what poisoned them or their minds. The transmitters were just puppets of nature and/or the science behind it.

10.   When confronted with legitimacy, corruption inspires one to seek to re-interpret the matter, seek and blame an easier prey, make or carry out threats, and/or discourage, erase, or conceal the evidence.

11.   In a disfavored environment, the practice of corruption is sneaky; but, in a favored environment, it is bold and freer to act, even when wrong.

12.   Corruption seeks to make the pure impure and to make a correctable matter foul. The fallen angels are represented here, but human-beings can fall under this category by refusing to acknowledge Truth, when elaborated and clearly expressed, making it impossible to not distinguish one from the fallen angels.

13.   A corrupt person may seek only to be a hard and false example, programming and/or approving of the same immoral behavior(s) as he/she condemns. In that way, they spread corruption. They give "Correction" a bad name and drag innocent people into their corrupt game.

14.   A person or group led by their imperfections can parallel corruption in times of fear and impulsiveness, when confronted with an undeterred accuser, especially with the ability to present consequences, acting only from superficial information or results. In that case, grounds to prove innocence are perceived as weak, or not all, and is the driving force behind the action. It is a properly performing human being(s) in a bad situation and sensing it.

Using the Calculator to Sum up a Total Experience

1.   When you look back in time, do you ever try and identify what has created your boundaries to success or greater success? Sometimes, you might see something out of your control; and, sometimes, it might have more control over your life than you ever thought.

2.   If you've had hard times, it could be best not to look back; because it could lead to drastic and consequential effects. So, you may be put in a situation where you have to weigh the values and make a difficult decision; because you perceive a hook enticing you. But the ordeal may not give you a choice to move on. It could be tightening its rope, waiting for the right time to bring you within its grasp. You may feel the momentum.

3.   When I use the calculator, I put the compatible details into a story as my example. Let me give you an example. It's called "Trouble at the Courthouse"

4.   "…….After a man presents a claim that someone has been interfering with his jobs, implying a high-level of influence, the court is shocked at such brave presentation. So, after the hearing, a meeting is called.

5.   The prosecutor, judge, and public defender meet in a room to discuss the nuisance.

6.   Prosecutor: You're not going to investigate me are you!?

7.   Judge: Settle down, we'll fix this.

8.   Public Defender: Alex (Prosecutor), we've eaten lunch together. You've given Christmas gifts to my kids. You've aided my family in so many ways; you've been like a family member. I mean that about all of us. We're a big family. We're in this together. If one of us is damaged, we're all damaged. Then, someone is going to have to pay.

9.   Judge: Right, Mariah (Public Defender). This is what we should do; we'll meet with one of our psychologists and steer this trouble back to where it came from. Let's meet back here tomorrow, after court?

10.   All hug and agree.

11.   After court, the next day, they all met as planned. The psychologist takes over the meeting, after being notified of the problem. He confirms that they're all family by stating that they work together for long hours, every day of work. Although you may oppose one another, at times, you're doing a valued task of resolving the problems of society. Each of us needs the other. So, it tends to get personal, sometimes; because we have a tendency to become close friends. Friends get personal about what happens to friends. So, that's understanding.

12.   By the way, it's good to see you all, again. As you know, I've seen and heard about a lot of cases. The kind of knowledge I possess is like that of a marketing specialist. I possess the underlying principles and concepts that manipulate most concerns, including the direction of a court case and of a human target. So, don't sweat the small stuff. We just need to know and control the details; then, we can make it go away, from us.

13.   Our familiarity and control of tools like support groups, laws, procedures, psychology, sociology, finances and other matters are unbeatable against anyone out there.

14.   So, as usual, we'll have to make this person look unstable. We'll have to direct court events in a manner that is in harmony with our agenda. The instability phase has already started,

which is why we have the complaint. So, we're in control of the culprit. So, there's no reason to rush to do anything. When we put a person in a position that the public perceives as unacceptable, sentiment rarely fails us.

15.   Now, I'm busy; so, Titan will contact you to act as your public relations manager. He's a very good psychologist and very good with using laws and people of other disciplines to force a desired end. I assure you a simple process, because I know that he can affect the person behind this and aid the plan, while removing the threat from us.

16.   The next day, Titan (Public Relations Advisor) and Timothy met to sync with one another, after talking with the psychologist. Titan contacts all the court officials, close to the case, and sets up a meeting time.

17.   During the meeting, Titan explains the need to control evidence to their advantage and to the disadvantage of the targeted individual. This means, also, making communications from the targeted person complex, or even voided.

18.   The public and jury, if needed, must perceive the matter as we desire, and the target must perceive matters in such a way that it benefits our integrity and not his.

19.   So, to achieve our objective, we shall continue with the initial plan. Nothing shall be certain around him; he must be subject to change, insufficiency, conflict, even violence, and void of support and witnesses, other than ours. But his dramatic experiences and failures must not appear to come from us. And, we must not recognize it; or we'll get our brothers and sisters hurt.

20.   His mistakes must be forced, instigated, magnified, and repetitious; or we must frame them professionally. We must control his exposure in a way that he is surrounded by confusion and false examples and implications.

21.   People tend to act out behaviors related to the environment, in which they've had to endure and overcome. Many times, they fall into our hands and/or attract greater concerns on what's immediately before them.

22.   For you, I want you to continue to show your horns, which implies stability and power, causing a sense of fear and reason to believe.

23.   Now, again, I stress that we've got to go about it in a way that doesn't implicate or expose us.

24.   As a public defender, when a claim is made or repeated by the defendant, turn into an owl and say "Who, Who, Who?" They all laugh. In the middle of a hearing, lead him out; so that you can discuss key issues that he could've challenged, but didn't. That's because he wasn't there. But who knew? They laugh again.

25.   You want the target to look jealous, unstable, uncertain, violent, and nervous. Under these conditions, the target may become your ally and his soul may belong to you.

26.   This is why you always have to protect your image, because it yields opportunities to pull yourself back up. Plus, much of the population is on our side and likes what we do.

27.   Judge: It is so!"

A Deeper Understanding of the Homeless System

1. The Homeless System is an invisible, sophisticated jail, consisting of various organizations that play a role to assist and maintain apprehension, whether the participants realize it or not. However, psychologists help to engineer it, based on the needs of the government.

2. Digging deeper into the operations and effects, I traced the intelligence to the profession, based on type and who stands to benefit. It makes sense that the city planner was in on it, as well as nutritionists, and doctors. To assure protection and compliance, the federal and state's legal department(s), from top to bottom, are also in on it. The absence of media reporting of foul play also implies participation, especially where a government-sided and/or superficial story is presented.

3. It is not in my best interest to do a truthful and more detailed report, given my position in the matter; however, a person like me is probably the only one, who may boldly stand in opposition. Of course, I'm the type that you don't allow a voice to become loud and effective in distribution of the details of this reality. It would be too exposing of the culprits.

4. The chains of the invisible prison system consist of needs to sustain life and what little pride is left. For an example, various organizations may have free food, which is made unaffordable by a state's unwillingness to pay restitution to the needy, especially singles, in the form of money. Those, who do receive money, are usually in dire need of a program, due to some type of disability, which ties them down to some degree and keeps them predictable. All needed services for the homeless are strategically located to provide a type of treatment and trajectory of the homeless.

5. The free food is not of high quality and causes one to yearn for better tasting and fulfilling meals. The body dictates to the mental and emotional faculties when it's time to absorb nutritional products, which is the cause of their close proximity to providers. Otherwise, crime may commence. However, this environment is dangerous for diabetics, who control their vitals with quality foods, instead of medications.

6. The landscape may be so designed, as to not allow passage, unless a risk is taken to walk in traffic, causing a barrier that may make it difficult to escape from a designated area on foot.

7. The totality of public transit routes may form a boundary not far from its starting point, making suburbs or outer areas unreachable. Timely one-way transits are used to restrict travel, unless it's an overnight stay. Mornings may be incoming and evenings outgoing.

8. Exposure to other homeless people can trigger anxiety and stress, depending on the existence or absence of common needs, moral concerns, accommodation of agendas, solid mental state, stableness, desperation, carelessness of law, and sensitivity.

9. Thefts, violence, and usury of others are all a concern, complete with limited and unreliable protection. Innocence can be sensed by the unwillingness to step outside the line between right and wrong, providing a base for a threat or effective assault, which may lead to battery, depending on how the psychological scheme plays out or what the victim has been exposed to in the past.

10. It is not uncommon for possessions to come up missing, when under the control of staff.

11.   The anxiety and stress from being in a perceived bad situation, in which the way out seems dire, can lead to the need or return to drugs and/or alcohol, as a temporary relief. Out of desperation, pride may be dropped in return for any method of fulfillment. The best people suited for such a condition are those, who are more attentive to the fulfillment of an addiction that is accessible within or near their environment or knows no other type of environment. Such may possess street games that others can't surmount, especially when the game is based on a large number of connections. A weak person can find themselves submitting to pressure that will make it difficult to discern them from other gang members or those who act similarly.

12.   Breaks in services provide subjection to the external elements; even during the cold winter months, there may temporarily be nowhere to go. It opens up opportunities for violations of laws, such as trespassing and potentially other violations. Breaks, even for days, sometimes, may mean no food, unless traveling farther out from usual location.

13.   While, many times, the sexes are separated; gays and bisexuals may pose similar circumstances and awkwardness.

14.   Being a place of confusion, it's easy to camouflage an effort to lead or force an individual down the wrong path. They may look around and see no one like them, regardless of whether there is or not. There are plenty of games and tools to wrench out benefits for the authoritative population. The idea is to possess knowledge of the cause and elements of crime and duplicate the principles and concepts within the environment, even to inject a way of thinking and doing within the person, which may cause favorable voluntary action or appearances of facts that make it easy to frame a case fraudulently.

15.   The homeless setup, as a whole, presents opportunities to utilize creative pursuits that can turn it into a crime manufacturing business. The same concept, although built with bricks and mortar, rather than invisible parts, can be seen in many prison systems. The similarities tell you who is behind it all. Parole officers may send their former inmates to these shelters.

16.   On advertisements, you see smiling faces as if to sell a loving and caring environment; but what is questionable is their understanding of the environment. Do they have a superficial or deep understanding? Are they just following protocol and/or instigating it? For an oppressive system to appear moral, it must market an appearance that attracts the approval of a moral society and mitigate dissension. But the truth can be found in the foundation, in which the homeless must spring from, which includes the quality of the available resolution process and whether or not a resolution process exists for a given issue.

17.   Your environment and everything in it are a creation; and all creations, internal or external, interact with one another to develop an expression of some sort. Nothing happens without laws of the universe, which creates an environment that manifests some type of evidence. That evidence is expressed in developments, behavior, and the fashion in which they appear and/or manifest themselves. For an example, all require a sufficient amount of sleep to express an awakened state. But, most, if not all, are required to awaken early in the morning, regardless of circumstances. So, you'll see them falling asleep in public, while representatives of establishments force them to stay awake. The commonality of many of their issues, if not all, is they are caught between two or more opposing forces.

18.   A major predicament is one invisible force causing failure in life, while another force provides minimal benefits, an irresolute process, forced conformance to the demands of society,

and/or denial or disregard of circumstances. To meet requirements in a homeless shelter or homeless program that were previously unattainable in the free world is evidence of foul play. That's especially true, if the victim is not in approval of a shelter environment, has exhibited favor of greater success, experiences costs of being homeless and unemployed or insufficiently employed, and/or remains in a state of personally despised failure.

19.   One type of confusion that is camouflaged behind the case is the quality of a resume and/or job history in a competitive market, in which the later may be fabricated by invisible and visible forces. It comes down to orchestrating events in a manner that discounts the victims of homelessness and their excuses.

20.   Because of the conditions, in which the homeless endure, negative and oppressive personalities are duplicated within them, even for potentially greater favor than others. So, they may protect their own oppressors for favor. They may, also, become violent towards those, who interfere with their sleep, even by snoring. Here, a health issue may become less important in favor of a desperate resolution, especially if the problem is not understood.

21.   They are programmed by the harshness of their environment, even the harsh expression of the external environment (Free Society). It's a pressure cooker that requires the homeless to meet standards in a more unmanageable and less efficient and less effective fashion. Thus, without sufficient storage, income, and access, they are less likely to be competitive for high quality jobs, especially those requiring professional attire. The usual result is a low-end job that sustains their status and instability, as well as potentially slowing their growth. That's if they have the means to travel to an interview.

22.   The success of a business requires that it maintain the elements, in which it is supported. In this business, the cooperation of the whole community is needed to maintain the homeless state of condition, including external perceptions and attitudes.

23.   There are fishermen, who enjoy fishing as a sport, even throwing the injured back, with no regards for the pain and suffering; it is no surprise that fishing for people is also enjoyable, especially if there is very little or no care for their pain and suffering as well. The latter poses more of a challenge to the target, unless the victim is naïve and confident, while actually more impulsive than intelligent.

24.   A right to life, liberty, and the pursuit of happiness can be taken in creative ways, making it difficult to protect, even potentially impossible.

25.   How is it possible to manipulate anyone into a detrimental circumstance with their knowledge and refusal of it?

*This info doesn't mean all participants are guilty, only those who designed it with deep malice and forethought

Mechanics

1.   Nothing is without mechanics, here, meaning a process in which something balances as a result of something else, whether it's a force or a calculation. I'm talking about a human computer, consisting of a computer program (Belief System, Religion), memory, calculator, math (Study of shapes, patterns, numbers, differences, similarities, duplicates, circumstances, situations, and evolutions), which include benefits, expenses, passages, blocks, which encourages the building of the process of conflict management.

2.   Our belief system manages our conflict management system, which builds a religious system. This is what makes us mechanical, readable, and predictable. After observing behavior, the results look like a flow chart, consisting of start, stop, input, decision, options, if statement, output, and stop. However, that's just the basic makeup; something within is vulnerable to or resistant to transformation, which may not be permanent. Nothing is permanent outside the Will of God. This perceived flow chart is what you translate into a computer language, which causes the computer to act as it does, whether in error or accuracy.

3.   Being a computer, you also simulate your thoughts in your mind, based on the flow you have found to be the most current, and accurate predictor of a matter. After being exposed to a person or matter of concern for a long enough period of time, this flow chart is developed and causes one to have predictive skills.

4.   You can see one, as a computer in operation, as you observe decisions versus environmental conditions, like any circumstances and situations that solicit or demand a decision, even to ignore or fail to sense. This is why you are someone else in another situation, which is why judgment should not be used on another person, as to permanently condemn. This very fact gives you the ability to exercise empathy, according to your knowledge and the absence of such, rendering the ability for accuracy and error, due to developments outside your realm of experiences.

5.   This type of information is dangerous, when it falls in the wrong hands; because it gives the ability to construct confusion and conflict. All it takes is knowledge, especially of various types, like current conditions, chemistry, biology, sociology, psychology, and any other relevant knowledge that inter-plays with the subject-matter. The influence can be local or distant, depending on information, position, technology, and ability. Output or response is a reflection of what's within or missing. Input tests the processing, submission, rejection, and questionable attitude of the responsive target.

6.   Outside of God, no one is invincible. Only the power of togetherness and support is the most invincible position of strength. But what is fair for all?

7.   There is no real reason not to build up, rather than tear down.

Manipulating Acclimatization

1. The method or rearing is very similar to how a bat uses echolocation, in which they send out sound waves that bounce off the subject and return for processing. Through the process, they are able to determine location, size, and shape.

2. In like fashion, we send out efforts, with various intensities, and fashions that provide greater feedback.

3. We are more easily able to diagnose matters when we are more familiar with its elements and operations.

4. Resistance paints a boundary when it is consistent. If we challenge it in every way we know or believe we should, we mentally become one with the results. Our actions are, then, molded.

5. We will practice efficiency and effectiveness according to our molded mentality and evidence it in our actions, when circumstances demand the best; otherwise, we may seek to find the time to test or confirm.

6. As the facts become so confirmed and reconfirmed, we harden in that way.

7. Inconsistency is, also, resistance. It means we do not have the knowledge, resources, and/or control to benefit successfully from it. Therefore, it is as demanding of resolve as it is important.

8. Naturally, upon failure and submission, we are forced to acclimatize. It means we have to give up something that has to be replaced according to importance.

9. Importance, according to its level of importance, drives us to succeed, even with an alternative.

10. Importance can reach a level of demand that requires successful act(s) or unavoidable and severe consequences, beyond your control. It, then, becomes a law and a trap, which forces a decision, regardless of sufficient or insufficient time to process.

11. Importance, on a high level, stresses the emotions, causing desperation and anxiety.

12. Too many subjects tied to a high level of importance can cause greater attentiveness and a loss of freedom, binding to responsibilities.

13. Responsibilities may require their own standards to be met, which can control your time and manner of resolve. In essence, you may be manipulated by them.

14. When responsibilities are or become unrewarding to insufficient, the quality of your life is strenuously low. Strain is the beginning of testing endurance.

15. When endurance is tested, the clock is ticking. Either you withstand or fall towards the temptation.

16. What is the message of the resistance?

Can You Build a Sound Religion?

1.   Anyway, the religion we choose is influenced by various matters, like intelligence, emotions, experiences, circumstances, culture, and sometimes, various ridiculous matters.

2.   But our religion is factual when it matches world events and has no conflict with how they materialized, everything that exists, its connections, and the way it performs.

3.   However, a religion should have a moral motive that drives it towards perfection.

Protecting the Interest

1.   Examples of protecting the Interest can be seen in nature; what stands out is the human body.

2.   The human body is made up of elements that create organs (Agencies tasked for a specific chore(s), capable of reverse effects).

3.   An immune system is designed to protect an interest (Body). Its efforts will reflect its interests, as a shield, discharge, or neutral diluting source.

4.   It's ability to reach capacity is embedded in its design and ability to increase in sophistication.

5.   Foreign elements test the immune system's weaknesses and strengths. They ask, "How can I get in?" and develop trying times.

6.   Therefore, the human body represents an interest that must be protected, which includes the mind and the heart.

Building a Value System

1.   In the building of a value system, our focus becomes the guiding light. Unless tamed, we focus on what entertains us, what we want, and how we'd like to be positioned in the social world. Anything can go wrong here.

2.   But, when we include an understanding of God and how real He is, as well as the proof seen in developments, the focus can become very cautious and a lot more discriminating about what has value and what doesn't, as well as where a matter will take you and what will constrain you. The understanding should be as scary, surprising, elaborate, and as interesting as the world presents itself.

3.   The information from the latter is how you build a value system.

4.   When a value system is built strongly, it has a tendency to handle very contentious matters. It has the ability to protect, like an immune system; but, at the same time, to be calm, courteous, direct, and elusive.

5. A good value system is, also, seen in what it embraces and why.

6. It pays to experience or observe various experiences to gain an understanding about values, some from a distance. A good historian, who cares about you, is a safe start. But, so is "There Are Three Truths".

7. Many are led astray by wrong values.

Adapting to Issues Like a Professional

1. Naturally, environmental issues are met with adapting behavior(s) to form a culture. The fashion, in which it formed, are based on the option(s) known to be available and the ability to utilize it effectively enough to, at least, meet the purpose and/or alleviate the effect(s).

2. In business, MBAs use flow diagrams to detect issues, in which the inverted side of that is the knowledge of the causes and options available at every turn of events. Predictive ability and constructive pursuits become keener and more sophisticated with experience.

3. It is advisable that every element of a potential trap be realized to control, enable, and/or express the best results in critically challenging times.

4. So, mainly, the matter presented to the target, the description and history of the target, as well as the options available to the target must be calculated, along with the history of the concept to be used.

5. The idea is to control the direction, fashion, intensity, and extent of effect(s). Knowledge of all the associated elements and potential counterbalances, including those naturally associated, must be plotted and organized to meet the full objective of an idea and to garner the greatest intentional results.

6. This is the stuff of expert advisors in their respective fields, but also modeled events on computers. They are involved in comparisons and modifications, by adding, subtracting, or adapting. They, in essence, squeeze out desired results or posture a character(s) or component(s) to attract a desirable result.

7. They learn from natural and unnatural events, even experiments and questionnaires.

8. Because they come with a fee, the most wealthy and knowledgeable have the greatest advantage over all others. Beware of this in the business and legal environments, or any environmental conditions operating like a business, if you're on the negative end of developments.

Politics and Voting (Part 1)

1.   Earl Stanley: Hello and welcome to the National Peace Summit.

2.   Here, we've gathered some of the most influential people associated with today's national issues. I know a lot of you are very concerned and we empathize with you.

3.   In our country today, we are faced with so much surprising divisiveness, even to the point of, seemingly, a threat of civil war. It's a time like no other, in our nation.

4.   It appears that, as a nation, we need to go back to the drawing board; because we realize that this was not the future, we thought we were creating. There are conflicts everywhere, between people, between ways of living, and with the definition of a Christian nation.

5.   Today, we're going to discover what's going on down in the trenches, as many of the men on the front lines of these issues face off. Then, we're going to hopefully bring a remedy to all these conflicts.

6.   So, let us turn to Mr. Steve Richman. Steve, what is going on?

7.   Steve: Hello, Earl. It's a good thing that you chose me first, because I represent an altruistic view of the entire world and the book of wisdom, known as the Bible. Therefore, you're going to see the missteps of those, who are out of line, through me.

8.   Frank Jackson: The world doesn't revolve around you and your confused belief system.

9.   Earl: Frank, we'll get to you. Let Steve talk. Steve?

10.   Steve: The very people, who are at the helm of controversy are the violators of natural human rights. They have built systems that control opportunities, options, and beliefs. They have, in essence, violated the freedoms and, therefore, the religious rights of others. They have forced one to dominate another for a living and to succeed in nearly every endeavor, if not all. They are the predators of our world.

11.   Those are my accusations against them.

12.   Earl: Ok, thank you, Steve. Great opening!

13.   Ok, Frank, what you got?

14.   Frank: Steve, there's a thread that runs through everything; I call it life. Now, listen closely; and you'll see we've done nothing wrong and certainly don't deserve to be called predators.

15.   Now, just look. What you see in us, you will see in them. Look at how they divide up against one another, They will sell one another, even kill one another, for whatever the reason. Why do they do that? Just see it coming out of them. Watch it! If you see it, it's all for advantage.

16.   All we're doing is paving our own way, in defense. It just so happens that we made greater achievements. We escaped the animal life and, now, we defend against them. They brought this upon themselves. We just want to stay afloat, like a boat. We don't take that animal life from our own people; so, they know not to rise against us. But, those knuckle-heads can't seem to grasp the idea.

17.   The idea is to be likeable. You can see it playing out in them, as well. Some have many followers and supporters, while others are rebuked.

18.   What does "Being liked" do for you? I'm going to tell you two stories. One, my wife, I met her in high school. She didn't like me then. I did all kinds of stupid things. Me and my friends thought it was funny. She didn't, but I didn't care what she thought. So, we had some heated spats, every now and then. Then, one day, I grew up. I owned up. I saw her at a grocery store, and…I don't know. My eyes just lit up, like I had spotted gold underneath the ground I had been walking on, all this time. She just grew up faster than me, and she was unbelievably gorgeous. I couldn't believe it.

19.   However, she had the same attitude towards me. She didn't know I was grown up too. When I owned up to what I had done, she didn't believe me. But I was determined to try and win her over. I told her friends how I felt. I sent her flowers, but she actually paid to send them back to me. But I didn't stop. But I didn't know what to do, either.

20.   One day, a friend, whom she'd just met, invited her to our church. She saw me in a suit and confessing my sins. She, later, told me that she was blown away with my appearance, but she concealed it. From there, little by little, I won the woman of my dreams. Why? She liked me. I worked for it.

21.   Here's another story. One day, I was feeling down and out. I met a guy at the bar, and we got to talking, as if we were like brothers. We could finish each other's sentences. So, finally, we got to talking about employment, and to make a long story short, he got me hired at his company. Why? Because he liked me. But, get this, after saving my money, I had some old friends look me up to go into business with them. They wanted me to do as well as them. Why? Because they liked me.

22.   Now, I don't know where this Steve dude is coming from, but I do real talk, not no fantasy thing.

1.   Frank: Every living thing produces bowels; the human is no different. So, we go so far as to mechanically work to produce what is essential for life, only to endure the production of bowels, so to speak, in an imperfect world. To make the best of a bad situation, we move the bowels out in a way that doesn't contaminate and disease the remainder of the system. Even when we build a project, we end up discarding the useless or inferior. That's the wisdom I got from real life, not the imaginary and complaining type of life. I think that's real talk, something you can clearly see in reality. Who built reality?

2.   Robert: You know, Frank is the wisest trickster I know. He.....

3.   Frank: Trickster!? Don't call me names! Address the issue you have with the truth.

4.   Earl: Come on, let's be gentlemen in our approach. Welcome, Mr. Robert Shaw and, please, continue.

5.   Robert: I'm sorry for the explosiveness of the conversation; it's just that there was no other way to say it to hit home, so efficiently and effectively. Frank is a worldly type of guy that believes in the rest of the world catering to his and his buddies' interests versus the development of a perfect world.

6.   They are sophisticated people, who study things, like how "like" works and explain it to their likings and to their advantage. We just witnessed it.

7.   Frank: I just told the truth. You gave an opinion. You haven't....

8.   Robert: I'm not finished. Be patient.

9.   Frank and all of his types share the same overall interests, which is to take an advantage of the weaker population. When people, like that, become the majority or most influential, their taste buds and anything they have affinity with, becomes the standard for the entire population. Then, it's about meeting their standards, not meeting the high standards set for human perfection.

10.   I understand that, yeah, there's a war between good and evil; but the two sides cannot fight in the same manner. That's because the two sides have different objectives and goals. We already see that the world is not turning out perfection; it's turning out more and more trash...at the top and the bottom. If you're going to weigh the whole world, you've got to start with a perfect standard that addresses the good and the bad. Frank's belief, as explained, is trash, which is confirmed in national, even world results. He talks about "building", but he's hauling more trash than building. That's clearly a result of an error.

11.   If you control what is to be liked, you control affinity. You set a people in a circumstance or situation, like engineering a seed, to grow what you would like to see in a garden; so that you could benefit and/or profit from its growth. Then, you falsely proclaimed that they all control their fate by doing likeable things, while you and your partners in crime were at the helm of it all.

12.   Let me tell you something else, the Bible includes a description of good and evil, you can muster up whatever is representative of your heart's desires; and the whole world will see you, based on your fruits. Be careful how you put your views together, because they will tell on you.

13.   You have told great lies that many don't have the knowledge and wisdom to correctly evaluate, because you knew they were missing certain information and talents, largely because you and your colleagues were responsible for it. You reflected what you engineered.

14.   Frank: What a nice view you have there, fella. No one is close to trying to fulfill your fantasies. We have a lot of church people, who listen and praise your truth; but, at the end of the day, they step the other leg back across the fence. I'm talking about in principle and concept. I'm talking reality. You have to deal with reality, just like you have to deal with hope. Our own God has led us to war to do what The Commandments have rejected. Am I right?

15.   Steve: Frank, God is not evil nor does he uphold it. If you look up in the sky, you see that he uses imperfect things in an attempt to make others perfect. We get to view both sides and choose, according to our hearts. We generate our own judgment. While one may be forgiven, another may not be; because evil was not part of the original plan to develop perfection in truth.

16.   Frank: Meanwhile, we have life, while you have a fantasy. I've got a yacht in my back yard. I've seen your yard. It's decent, but I wouldn't want to live there. But the difference says something about how adaptive I am to reality. You can't do what I do. You don't have the clout. You don't possess the intelligence. You can't afford to get where I am. But you need me or someone like me to sort out and solve some of your problems. And, that might mean calling someone whom you have issues with, rather than appreciation for.

17.   Steve: I'd love to have a yacht. I'd love to have a better back yard. I'd love to have a park like your neighborhood park. There's a lot of things I'd love to have. However, I'd rather have love and its family of qualities that come with it, than to have anything you possess or desire. That's because I'm not for sale and never will be. Now, tell your god that.

18.   Frank: I did not find love in your backyard, sorry. I did find a high level of crime, sorry. That doesn't sound like innocence and love to me.

19.   Steve: Yes, there are issues with you and your kind's manner of governing.

20.   Frank: Why not ask your followers to take responsibility for their own actions, instead?

21.   Steve: Why not practice good governing? Then, the actions of my followers won't be so serious and excessive.

22.   Earl: That concludes it, for now anyway. We cannot all live together. It takes common values to market the solutions of all issues of the people and to properly vote to resolve them. These are the things that representatives of evil stand against. They stand against unity, in favor of selfishness and advantage.

There is no legitimate reason for a global hate of the Black race, other than a spiritual intervention by the fallen angels.

If you ever needed proof of global hatreds, you can find it here. Otherwise, Google it, watch the news, or talk with people around the world. In many cases, observe etiquettes and behaviors of a mixed-race population. It's not something to ignore.

Russia
https://foreignpolicy.com/.../the-curious-case-of.../

Global
https://www.vox.com/.../black-lives-matter-global...

Canada
https://www.npr.org/.../heres-what-black-lives-matter...

Spain
https://english.elpais.com/.../in-wake-of-george-floyd...

Latin America
https://www.americamagazine.org/.../black-lives-matter...

France
https://france-amerique.com/.../black-lives-matter-in.../

Australia
https://amp.theguardian.com/.../australian-black-lives...

Arab World
https://www.washingtonpost.com/.../83234c5e-b7ab-11ea...

Saudi Arabia (Protests banned)
https://www.bbc.com/news/world-middle-east-12656744

Germany
https://time.com/5851165/germany-anti-racism-protests/...

China
https://foreignpolicy.com/.../us-injustice-protests.../

Austria
https://www.barrons.com/.../thousands-turn-out-for-vienna...

Puerto Rico
https://brooklyn.news12.com/puerto-ricans-march-in...

Haiti
https://sflcn.com/haitians-lives-matter-joins-black.../

Africa
https://amp.wbur.org/.../06/12/black-lives-matter-africa

More listings:
https://en.m.wikipedia.org/.../List_of_George_Floyd...

Duty of Care

1.   Lawyers have successfully sued many, whom they've established as having breached a Duty of Care, something that was God-given to all.

2.   Remember when the Ten Commandments were passed down? That was a description of a Duty of Care, but it was given long before that. Do I have to remind you about Adam, and later Eve's, responsibilities?

3.   The rich were given two levels of Duty of Care, according to the earlier Bible. For one, the rich man was despised and rejected, according to prophecy. Remember, "it's easier for a camel to enter into the eye of a needle than for the rich to go to heaven"? Think about that. Somewhere a breach of duty occurred. On the second level, they were told "to leave something behind for the poor" to survive. He, actually, had to tell them that. Now, what kind of people were they?

4.   The church is, or is supposed to be, an example of a working population. A Duty of Care was given out to various types of members, with the idea of serving to rear the congregation to perfection, not corruption and not selfishness. So, the church and the corrupt cannot be equally yoked together, as if to have a foot on both sides. So, if you're a Godly man or woman, how can you safely breach your Duty of Care?

5.   Instead of a healthy functioning of a population, we've got the rich using their system to squeeze out success from those below, with aid from the very victimized source, who support higher ups, who extend their arms deeper into the population. The less you have, the less control you have. It has repeatedly been said that the rich are increasingly gaining on the remaining population every year. Who would've thought we would live in such era that people turn a whole population, groups of people, and individuals in on itself?

6.   People have a habit of modeling after their environment and the things in it, even to copy inferior examples; but a corrupt society is evidence of the need for every participant of society to model the high standards set in the Ten Commandments.

7.   A person with foresight sees the future based on the past, which is limited by what is known and how change is perceived. A person or class of people who steers others towards an inferior end is a false prophet. The world is filled with sickness, confusion, and violence, as well as the instigation of such. But, yet, the false prophets are glorified, supported, replicated, and protected.

8.   The prophet side of us works to fulfill our prophecy, when we feel the need to labor for expectations. The fact that trouble follows certain people can be both a natural phenomenon or an unnatural frame of events. Respectively, one is impulsive and/or experimental, having less knowledge of the consequences of such actions, while the other is a trained survivor and seducer of benefits.

9.   Both the impulsive and the trained survivor and seducer benefit the false prophets, who profit from the makeup of such an environment. The false prophets may demonstrate a primary taste for certain types of people, in which the targeted type will share some common experiences, designed to manipulate the presence, intensity and frequency of compelling phenomena. With such knowledge, they can control the minds and lives of the naive and defenseless population.

10.   A study of existing laws and their agreed upon interpretation(s) gives you a clue of how false prophets perceive themselves, whenever they touch the law.

11.   The whole structure of evil is bound by the design of the lack of Duty of Care, sometimes on the part of both the manipulators and the prey, as well as the supporters and neutral-minded population. The opponents of a Duty of Care have a common attitude that says, "I don't owe you nothing!"

12.   The world is filled with predator and prey. So, hereby, we can grasp who the rich are and not mistaken them for innocent, value producing, and charitable people, unless they can prove overall results to be confirming of the practice of a Duty of Care.

Satire

1.   In a discussion about the potential existence of a conspiracy, some people doubted the possibility, after seeing satire, designed to expose a corrupt scheme against some members of the population.

2.   Satire was treated like a fraud; although it was pointed in exposing evidence of corruption.

3.   However, satire is not some magical story presented by some gifted author; although it could have very well come from such a person.

4.   But, if you ever played out a scenario in your head, you created satire and used it as grounds to prove a point or predict the future, maybe both. If you did neither of them, you didn't think the matter through.

5.   Written correctly and completely, your satire will relay all that you know about the subject and serve as a foundation to hold all the details to preserve the memory, to resolve any issues, and to improve upon the results.

6.   With that said, what could possibly be wrong with satire? If anything, it would have to be faulty, incomplete, or exaggerated. When not so, the complainant may be attempting to avoid the truth of the subject explained.

The Judge

1.   Can you imagine being a judge to a people, whom you want to prove your way of believing and thinking is sovereign above all? I'm talking about a frame of mind that you will have to bow down to in the end, whether you like it or not.

2.   But what if you had no choice but to like it and agree with it, due to the overwhelming soundness of thought? How would you respond? Are you already responding in such a way?

3.   If I was God, I would tell the people how I want them to behave. I would give them instructions that benefit their own good, not for me to take an advantage of their weaker status;

but so, they would harmonize with my ideal environment and continue to attract my love for them. After all, any artist loves his creations, when they match his ideal vision of the subject-in-question. In this manner of performance by a Deity and ideal human interaction, love is reciprocated.

4.   Have you ever looked at your baby and saw the excitement that he/she exhilarates, just from being glad to see you again, after only a short nap or absence? What about when the baby proudly tells others that's my daddy or that's my mommy? What about the excitement of the baby wanting to learn from you, favoring what you say and do over anyone else? What about the excitement the baby gets from you, when you praise his/her first walk or creations brought home from school? To understand this aspect of the creator, he gave us the ability to experience it for ourselves.

5.   So, it's obvious that he created a world that reflects His needs and desires, as well as our very own; because we were made in His likeness.

6.   In a reflective environment, you see, hear, and sense the feedback and the potential(s) of it and everything in it, including yourself, according to experience.

7.   Being young or naive, you will make mistakes, but what matters is how do you process them and correct them or deal with them? Is it ideal for everyone and every mistake?

8.   It appears that a good judge would construct an environment that favors his way of thinking, while using solidarity of life's trials and tribulations to cement his claims for an ideal environment for all.

9.   But, yet, there will be triers of fact and those, who will seduce others to an adverse way, attracting a value system contrary to an ideal environment, reaping rewards from the suffering of others or at the expense of another. These are not the beloved babies, spoken of above. This is the other side of the baby that requires disciplinary action that demonstrates the description of an error versus righteous decision-making.

10.   One is evil, when he/she possesses sufficient or complete awareness, understanding, and control, but knowingly chooses to turn away from the values of truth in favor of selfish ends. That's especially true, when alternatives are clearly within sight and grasp.

11.   These people wonder why their prayers seemingly go unanswered, even when they are reminded of the elements of an ideal environment, only to seek selfish desires regardless.

12.   They want rewards for unrighteousness, which defeats the vision of idealism. How are they not traitors to the very love and attention they seek or to the Creator Himself?

13.   If the Judge justifies His Ways in a defendant's experiences and shows that the defendant, knowingly and without question, defied the way to idealism, the defendant has attracted his own judgment.

14.   Our choice of a judge is no different. We synchronize with a judge, based on our choices and values. It is seen in whom or what we support and neglect. The more like the judge, we become, the more compatible we are. Vice versa, the more unlike the judge, we become, the less compatible we are. We constantly seek our compatible judge.

15. The ideal Judge is inclined towards idealism, which provides a way for all to attain the highest level of the quality of life; otherwise, we have a false judge engaged in bias principles and concepts.

16. You are defined by the judge you choose as a moderator and to imitate.

The Jewish Woman and Her Friend?

*fiction

1. A Jewish woman was taken into custody with all of her family and was tortured, murdered, experimented on, leaving her as the only survivor. After the holocaust, she was seen roaming the streets by someone of the past. The lady brought her in and warmed and fed her. She told her that she was worried about her and that she was her friend, but was scared to help for fear of torture and death. After talking at length, she led the Jewish woman to the bedroom to get a much-needed rest.

2. After lying down for a while, she gazed over to a picture on the wall. The frame said "The Greatest" at the top and "Leader Ever" at the bottom. In the midst was a picture of Adolf Hitler.

3. The Jewish woman screamed, out of fear, and ran out of the room towards the door, only to be met by her host. Catching her and holding her, the host said "What's wrong? Why are you acting so paranoid?" However, the Jewish lady resisted and attempted to flee, thinking she was being trapped and held against her will. But the host held on tight; because she felt the Jewish woman needed help. The struggle escalated and the Jewish woman's condition worsened, especially after a non-Jewish neighbor came to help the host, after the host cried for assistance.

4. A doctor was called in, and he recommended and prescribed medication, which relaxed the Jewish woman, who fell partially asleep.

5. A police report was taken and the Jewish woman was ordered by the court to continue taking her medication, which left her deranged. She was, then, assigned to a home for the mentally incapacitated to oversee the timely delivery of her medication.

6. Her whole environment was full of confusion and sometimes menace, causing lockdowns and other disciplinary actions for all. The Jewish woman could only sit in fear and disbelief of what happened to her, seeing no way out.

7. Then, one day, the former host came to see her and told her she was worried about her and touched her hand and told her she loved her. She sat for a while and read some verses from a Bible to help comfort the Jewish lady. Afterwards, she said "I'm sorry for what happened to you, sweetie. I hope you find peace." Then, she explained that she couldn't afford to keep visiting her and left.

Malware

1. Everything is an imitation of energy, which is reflected elsewhere, including software.

2. Malware is an example of an invasion of privacy to do harm to gain a benefit, by attaching to important elements, needed to operate in some fashion and/or to take an advantage of a source through deceptive practices. Corruption?

3. Software Bugs are the likenesses of side effects from medications or other sources.

4. A computer virus is a source of re-interpretation, having modifying values that alter a program, by inserting code or re-writing the program.

5. Worms are a representation of an inferior Public Opinion Swayer, who misleads others in favor of a lie. He uses a base to present different arguments that appears to be sound, but actually takes an advantage of what you don't know (Mental Security), in which the lie grows exponentially, as a result of the acceptance of others, fostering one side of a story, while denouncing another, even to bypass opposing sound arguments. It is agenda-based, not fact-based.

6. Trojan Horses are very deceptive salesmen, who use false intention(s), favorable to the host, to lead the host to perform favorably for the salesmen, in a surprisingly one-sided deal that may do, not just a different act, but a totally opposite one.

7. Ransomware is malware that extorts something of value by threatening to cause its target to experience some troubling reality, unless a demand is performed.

8. Spyware represents a malicious gossiper that garners access to personal information, only to distribute it to others, at the expense of the victim.

9. Adware is a, potentially, tempting offer or nuisance that comes with your choice(s).

10. Rogue Software is malicious software that misleads one to believe there is a problem or exaggerates it, in order to convince the potential buyer its services are needed to remove it, only to fraudulently collect money and become the manipulator of such problems to seal the deal.

11. Wiper is a class of malware that has evidence removal ability.

12. Scareware is a provocative method that uses shock, anxiety, or the perception of a threat to induce a potential client or puppet to act favorably to a request or demand.

The Supermodel

1.   The world's famous model walked down the runway for all to see, to adore, imitate, and respect. Sporting a careless attitude, she stylishly seemed to weave confidence and arrogance all into one. She could do no wrong and no wrong could be said about her, without stern rebuke.

2.   As she walked, she styled like no other, signifying her uniqueness as her glamorous and leading selling point. She could do no wrong, according to the world. Everyone was compared to her, and she was compared to everyone.

3.   Then, at times, she turned around and showed her butt. She told the so-called little ones, "Why don't you get yourself together and clean up". Cheers came from the crowd. "I provide for you, allowing you to live off of me" The crowd rose with chants of approval. "I clothe you with my donations and the donations of others. I fed you with the same. But you're never satisfied and always complaining. However, you can do nothing for yourself. Try being a model like me." The crowd cheered with greater approval and a standing ovation.

4.   Then, she turned and showed off her beautiful legs, in which many of the so-called little ones turned to one another and said, "That's how you do it!" and rebuked the others, who shared a similar or same impoverished lifestyle as them, but showed dislike for the model.

5.   But, like everyone else, she removed her under clothes and threw them in the dirty clothes hamper.

6.   An examination showed that she not only secreted evidence of desire for many people of the environment, including the rich and poor, young and old, male and female, as well as the strong and weak; but she, indeed, pleasurably interacted with many in a trade of the desires of the heart, leaving many to feel cheated or misled.

7.   In disregard of all the complaints, she was the chosen one, in which all, who couldn't meet her standards and didn't share her values, were considered defective.

My Experience with Going to Church with a Hate Group (Pt 1)

*Fiction

1.   Whew! I'm tired. Sitting and waiting for energy to get up and finish my tasks, I fell into a deep trance, surrendering control to a source of my imagination…..

2.   Rick Sampson: Hello and welcome, people, especially to our new members. Welcome to another exciting day of church. There's nothing I'd rather do than come to church to hear the Word of God. Amen?

3.   Congregation: Amen.

4.   Rick Sampson: Let's begin with some praise and sing some hymns for our wonderful Lord.

5.   Congregation: (Praising the Lord, before they begin to sing).

6.   Rick Sampson: Thank you! What a wonderful day! We help make our days wonderful, when we remain thoughtful of our Lord. We all play a role, whether negative or positive. So, let's make sure we remain on the same page, having a positive attitude and positive outlook towards everything in life; because there's nothing our Lord can't fix. And, we're here to help one another. We're family. We all have a role to play in one another's lives, and that's what makes family special. And, now, the one fulfilling the most important role, second to our Lord, in our earthly family, is our pastor, Dr Benjamin Jakes. Ben? (Music playing)

7.   Benjamin Jakes: (walks up and stops to whisper something to Rick, then sings and continues to the podium) Good morning!

8.   Congregation: Good morning.

9.   Benjamin Jakes: Awww come on, what kind of attitude is that for another day the Lord has blessed you with? Good morning!

10.   Congregation: Good morning!!

11.   Benjamin Jakes: That's better! Today is another day to hear something good about our Lord, what He has done for you, and why He favors you; so, you can walk proudly and confidently through life, spreading good vibes amongst your big family.

12.   Ok, let's get down to business.

13.   Today, I'm going to give you a very special message, something you can be proud of. I'm especially talking to the new members, but reminding other precious members about their value to the world, while extending on that premise.

14.   Not everyone knows the true interpretation of the Bible. We have inferiors reading the same verses, chapters, and book and still can't perceive what we know is true. That's a blessing for us! It's a blessing to know the true wisdom of life. It's a blessing to have God's people surrounding you and helping you walk in the ways of God, while all the good things that you desire are added to you, without taking any thought of the matter. Wait on the Lord, because he knows who His people are. Sound familiar? It's written in the Bible, at Mathew 6:33. Look familiar? Look at the people surrounding you. This is real! Can you say, "Proud to be a member of God's people"?

15.   Congregation: Proud to be a member of God's people!

16.   Benjamin Jakes: We're about to get happy up in here! Moving on.

17.   The Bible is designed to give us insight to our Lord's manner of thinking and how to proceed in this evil world. It's a code, a code not very well understood by many, including a lot of our own race.

18.   You see, God favors races and cultures and cleanses them, as He sees fit. He favored other races that proved to be incompatible with His Ways. He used one race or culture of people to conquer another. Who do you think was favored? It was the winner. You see, you can't lose with God in your favor. It is impossible.

19.   When He tried to spread His Word unto all nations, things really went amok. He saw that He was dealing with an inferior source. He had given them chances in the past, only to lead their most intelligent people into captivity, setting them back in time and to some point of disadvantage.

20.   Today, they're somewhere waiting on matters to flip-flop, so the first will be last, Mathew 20:16. But, they haven't reasoned that it has already happened. It happened when Jerusalem was destroyed. God let it happen, because it proved to be a place of persistent hypocrisy. They went against the Lord for the last time. He sent the Romans to do it, the same people who assembled the Bible and distributed it to all nations. Can I get an Amen?

21.   Congregation: Amen!

22.   Benjamin Jakes: But, that's not all. Just like He gave them the Land of Milk and Honey, He scattered them and another took over. The most precious regions of the earth were allowed to be scooped up by Caucasians. The Bible said it was going to happen and it did. We live in and control the most resourceful regions of the earth.

23.   Where are those, who were first? They are living in darkness. In John 3:19, it stated that the light had come into the world, but they preferred darkness, rather than light. They killed Jesus. This continues today. You can see it in their expression of false interpretations of Truth. The Truth continues to be rejected. They will kill and disrespect their own. They will seek to re-experience dark times for entertainment. They will absorb music with hardness of expression, thereby making themselves harder and harder. Look how they've evolved. Is it not worse than when they killed Jesus?

24.   They prefer to act impulsively, rather than proceeding in a scientific manner. They love expressions of selfishness, rather than unification in genuine love and harmony. So, we are to separate ourselves and not to repeat the mistakes they have and continue to do so.

25.   They protest against the same treatment that they presented to Jesus, as if we're supposed to accept them as they are. They still don't seem to acknowledge how their treatment of Jesus is being returned to them. Instead, they have aided the oppressive process against their own for advantage. They can't seem to utilize the mental aptitude to see that God's point is being ironically used against them. They denied him and taxed him, even to the point of him having to pull off a miracle to pay them, while God dwelled within him. Instead of following Truth, they preferred to game and test him for advantage, mustering up a majority decision to kill him.

26.   So, we take a hard stance in protecting ourselves and our interests. We can't afford failure. We can't afford to be like them. We can't afford to allow them to gain power to retake what we've gained through God's favor. We must always demonstrate our stance with God.

27.   So, if we are to protect ourselves, we have to economically, psychologically, emotionally, and physically separate ourselves from them. It keeps them from having a degrading influence on our development. Positive progression allows them to move into our neighborhoods and inject a poisonous influence, potentially turning it into a dangerous environment and lowering our values, including property values.

28.   Besides, if the supporters of a demon live the same quality of life as a supporter of our loving God, or vice versa, what kind of message would that send? Why do you think the wheat and the tare should grow together, as stated in, Mathew 13:24-30? Isn't it because they will distinguish themselves from the other? This is why we leave only small portions of our gains behind for them to retrieve, so that they will continue to live and experience the quality of their ways.

29.   We need to perceive the two major, opposing catalysts that underlie two opposing groups and decide which one we should associate with and which one to disregard. These catalysts that I speak of churns out different types of people. One does not belong to God.

30.   One builds and the other tears down or restricts growth. So, which one do you think should hold the power over all?

31.   Many say we are offensive, but what intensive war was soundly won on defense alone?

32.   John 3:16 says that anyone, who did not believe in the Son of God is subject to perish. Look at their quality of life. Look at their health. Look at their ability to garner change for the better. Look at their outlook. What more do you need to see?

33.   Hebrews 9:27 (One chance), Luke 16:23 (Torment, no relief), Mathew 25:41 (Eternal fire); it's over for those who killed this man or took part in it. In Jeremiah 8:10, it stated God will give their wives to others. Do you see broken families and people injured by child support issues? In Luke 23:34, Jesus said they didn't know what they were doing. But, do you see a sign of forgiveness?

34.   So, if anyone has any doubt about being here, I hope I erased that doubt.

35.   May the Lord bless those, who harmonize with our Lord and Savior. Amen.

36.   Congregation: stands up and applauds, happily.

My Experience with Going to Church with a Hate Group (Pt 2)

1.   Hello everyone and welcome to the Emergency Diagnostic Review; my name is Richard Roth.

2.   A lot of you are familiar with the latest development concerning a leak from a regional hate group, and we're here to address that issue. Many are very concerned about the damages surrounding the details of a pastor's sermon. We will not go into detail about where this particular event took place or whom was involved, because we don't possess any proof of the matter. However, the real concern is what is fact and what is fiction, reverse-psychology, delusion or whatever you want to call it. I know a lot of people are confused, want answers, and fear for their lives.

3.   I can say that I feel your pain; so, I assembled a group of analysts to address the statements, supposedly, made by a pastor. Hopefully, we can diagnose and resolve any anxieties surrounding the issues, which caused protests and violent confrontations across the area.

4.   I was blessed enough to attract a large number of analysts; but, because of the fear of the violence and pandemic, a lot of the analysts reverted back to safety. So, let's meet the analysts.

5.   For safety reasons, I'm only going to refer to each analyst by an adopted first name.

6.   So, with that said, I'm going allow Mike to present the opening presentation. Mike?

7.   Mike: As a Christian of the majority type and former attorney, I don't see a problem with anything that the pastor stated. He touched on how to have a family or how an organization can benefit everyone. That's a loving environment that caters to all members, having a mutual understanding of how to live.

8.   He attempted to reserve that high quality of life for those, who deserved it. To him, it was probably the reason behind his perception of the Bible as being coded. That states that only certain people deserved to know how to truly live.

9.   Because the pastor stated that God uses races or cultures didn't have to be interpreted as racist or different in approach towards another culture. The use of races or cultures may have been executed, due to the nature of unity associated with those classifications, making them a strong choice to pursue an act against another large group.

10.   If anyone believes in God, naturally they will believe He influences the events of the world, unlike a silent partner. As a result, He tried to spread the gospel, using a large classified group of contributors.

11.   Naturally, anyone, who interfered with a divine purpose, is going to be perceived as inferior. Why wouldn't they? It is written that there are no respects of persons; otherwise, it would be bigotry, in which such things as racism and discrimination become apparent. Hypocrisy cannot and should not be acceptable from anyone.

12.   As far as the descriptions of, what he deemed as inferiors, do those descriptions relate to an act or appearance of inferiority? If it doesn't relate to an act of inferiority, you have to call him out on it. If it does, you have to accept the truth of the matter. Is it befitting of certain people? If so, again, there can be no respects of persons. The description, if true, is befitting of anyone, regardless of race or culture. It didn't have to mean an entire race; it could have been a general description. After all, he did not use a word representative of "All".

13.   In other statements, he acted within the premises of protections of moral members and their interests, as perceived in a Deity's interest and agenda. Who wouldn't find their Deity's interests and agenda as the most important? So, what Christian doesn't seek to read, understand, and live according to the Bible? Apparently, if you have a problem with Christianity, you have a problem with the Bible.

14.   Among these facts, I have not found the pastor's statements as erroneous, and that's if he made these statements.

My Experience with Going to Church with a Hate Group (Pt 3)

1. Richard Roth: Thank you, Mike!

2. Next, I'd like to introduce one of my favorite people, whom I've adored on television, when she was crowned the winner of a beauty contest. I know looks has nothing to do with this; but Valeria is a former beauty pageant, in which her country chose her, not just for her outer beauty, but for her inner beauty. She expressed the latter in what she stands for. Again, thank you for being here, Valeria! Please proceed. (Audience applauses).

3. Valeria: Hello, and thank you, Richard. I'm an Atheist and I seek to discover the premises for the facts and beliefs of others, including support for the Bible.

4. I believe that, whether we believe in a God or not, all good people are seeking the principles and concepts of love and moral interactions. I can feel that connection with them; so, I think I belong here with them to contribute to the resolution of all conflicts, especially, this recent development. Not just that, but I have kids, grandkids, nephews, and nieces. And, lastly, I have a lot of beautiful little cousins that I, also, feel that I owe a better future to.

5. Truth and love need a public relations officer, the more the better, to stand up against the atrocities of mankind. I don't want to look back and be found guilty of not investing my talents into something so important to develop. It's about being able to say I brought a gift into the world, or helped to do so, that made a difference for the better. If anyone comes to my funeral, I want it to be said that I was a great contributor to the changes we seek to create in this lifetime.

6. With that said, I am totally floored by a dividing catalyst, centered on a secret code of conduct, and the Christians wanting me to follow them. But, dividing up my small relatives, one for heaven and the other for hell, is unacceptable; and that should be unacceptable for anyone regardless of age.

7. I took up engineering and understand how it relates to human development, something Mike's Deity should know. I understand that I have to evaluate all the elements involved, especially those that represent obstacles that need to be overcome. In the process, engineers have to be mindful of what obstacles we bring to the table in each of our endeavors.

8. In your case, you seem to want to engineer a population that is so diverse that it is, also, adverse in effects, reserving the best for an appointed, privileged population of choice. But your Deity is too blind or ignorant to see it? Again, you want me to follow you to this so-called perfect interpretation of a Deity's effort to win as many souls to a heavenly fate. Are you crazy, or are you not telling me everything?

9. I know when I'm up against someone, who doesn't share my values, when I present clear and accurate principles and concepts that are denied or downgraded as less important at a time that it is vital. So, my question is, with all the errors, who really wrote that thing?

10. I mean, you've got this God theory, which entails His devastating, everlasting consequences for violating commandments, like love thy neighbor as thyself or any suggestions that are best for garnering a loving and supportive environment for all. But you reinterpret the message or express your differences, as if your opinion matters more or you feel that you can manipulate this almighty of yours. Your actions say a lot about how you really think about your God, including whether He really exists.

11.   It seems to me that your book of truth is really no more than a sales script to get your way. All you do is look up the script(s) and use it to program the target to be subjective or submissive. Can I get an amen? What gives it away is unequal treatment, which not only procures imperfections, especially through a squeeze play of some sort, but usually attempts to calm the afflicted with a belief that better times are coming for them by way of God, whom you can supposedly manipulate or don't really believe in.

12.   Being a Christian of the majority and a former attorney, I knew you were a big flaw in the room. That's why you found nothing wrong. If you did, you kept it quiet, because you came from an environment, where one side does not cross the line to meaningfully give the other side an advantage. That's not to say that either side is doing anything it's purported to do, because they perceive a line of protection somewhere. Any sniffer can smell it, if they possess the background.

13.   When you do crossover, though, it's not genuine or that important, it's usually only for show to embed a false appearance of a seeker of truth and fairness for everyone. History and errors confirm your type has been trying to establish fairness for all, only to be no closer than you were many generations ago. But your God is all-knowing and attempts to spread the gospel to all, with one possessing coded information to administer and execute, while the secret leaks out and zaps the unfortunate like lightning. Suddenly, it shows that you have such powerful wisdom that a killing by authorities cannot be perceived the same way as a killing by a subordinate. Zap! I said, "Zap!"

14.   I can't tell you, as a public servant, from a vampire, who lives off the blood of the weaker population, but in this case, the blood and sweat.

15.   Mike: I don't think that we have to attack one another. This is about establishing truth, not about me and you or how you feel. Please don't use this event to attack me. Have the same respect for me as I do you. Let's try and establish the truth. That's what we're here for. Let's not lose focus. Let's be professional.

16.   Valeria: You have respect for me? You want me to help you divide the population, including my loved ones; so, you can live a life of luxury from all the confusion. And, you want me to believe that your sovereign Lord, who has all of our best interests, is all in on this?

17.   Plus, you want me to be this stupid professional, who has a narrow enough mind, not to see your evil vices or perceive you as having this special knowledge that can't be shared. You want me to rely on faith, through all these errors and continued oppression; so that you'll have peace and stability, while those protesters march for good reasons, risking harm to themselves, and go to jail? And, this is while you try to poison the attempt to establish truth.

18.   You don't think I should give my opinions about your titles, when you present information that aligns with those same titles and accepts a con-artist as having done nothing wrong? But you deserve respect and have given me mine? And, this is after I proved I belong here, as an atheist. You have proved nothing about you belonging here, not even implied it.

19.   Mike: I did, but I guess you saw what you wanted to see and heard what you wanted to hear. Can we just move on (Shakes his head)?

1. Richard Roth: Ok, Mike and Valeria, thank you for keeping it professional.

2. While I don't like it, when one is attacked during a debate, what we stand for and its relative values, principles, and concepts are vulnerable, when they are brought to the table to influence the direction of the debate. At that point, it becomes everybody's business to address one way or another.

3. If we're going to debate the validity of facts, we've got to address the matter from its roots to its foreseeable future, if it's put on the table. There is no other way to say we did a thorough job of considering and debating all the relevant matters that go into the pool of facts.

4. So, I'm sorry that you felt offended, Mike. But it was up to you to logically defend against any relevant accusations against you that pertained to the debate, in which you chose to be a participant. Only you can represent what you stand for, which shows your weaknesses and strengths, when it is challenged from another point of view.

5. When we know we'll fall short of establishing our truths, it's a time to reconsider, research for greater strength, or learn and grow from our errors.

6. But I think it's good to see a challenge of a diverse number of views to see the bigger picture. So, we're all here to debate for that purpose.

7. But, to grow, we have to act on our newly attained knowledge.

8. With that said, we'll continue on. Jolene, would you proceed, please.

9. Jolene: Thank you, Rich. I like to view matters from the standpoint that God is the same yesterday, today, and forever. Most importantly, I want to elaborate on the fact that God is Love. And, He's a great Teacher.

10. When he kicked Adam and Eve out of the Garden of Eden, everybody was evicted. He didn't leave a special race to maintain it. He didn't leave a special race to watch the gate. He didn't leave a special race with a secret code to get back there.

11. Instead, He put us in a position to desire His hand over the one Adam and Eve followed to their exit out of the Garden. Now, we're divided and fighting for what they abandoned.

12. Given another chance, we're making a decision to show that we've adopted His ways or continued the ways of His competitor. What has come after is a struggle between races, organizations, and people. One has overtaken another, while still another has escaped the vices of a strange oppressor, in which the struggle becomes more complicated with the scientific advancements of today's leaders and future leaders.

13. There was no favoring of races, just a turnover and strife from competitive people, who hold supremacy as their idol versus unity in Love and all His related elements.

14. We're all in this together. We can make it better or we can make it worse than it has to be. So, many have divided up and dominated man unto his injury. These people reside amongst the downtrodden and the oppressors, both, of whom make our world as complicated as it is today. Isn't that what's written? Didn't it say it was because of greed? So, it's clear that, if you fit the description, you are whom the Bible is pointing out.

15.   Although, there may be errors in the Bible, there are enough facts to get, at least, a glimpse of the big picture and make comparisons and discover puzzle-pieces that are practical and contributive between puzzle-pieces, which align with the overall agenda.

16.   God chose diversity, as seen in His creations; it was His competitor, who opposed Him, with an opposite point of view: competition, hate, and supremacy. This is why imperfections matter; they are the root cause of strife and an unforgiving attitude. Because imperfections are held onto, in disregards to the demands and suggestions of God, as well as their damages to others, it becomes an idol. Idolatry tears men apart.

17.   But I get not treating everyone the same, just not with the understanding of engineering them, mindfully and/or physically towards self-destruction of the life and soul. If there be self-destruction, it should be pointed towards a part of the self, considered to be an imperfection. If we were to do this, successfully, we'd change the world for the better. It starts with proper social engineering, far from what we have today.

18.   Thank you (Applause).

My Experience with Going to Church with a Hate Group (Pt 5)

1.   Richard Roth: Thank you, Jolene. I find your analysis solid and informative, making you a great contributor to this debate as well. I like Valeria's idea of proving one's qualification to contribute to the accurate findings of this forum.

2.   Now, let's turn our attention to Charles. Charles?

3.   Charles: Thank you, Richard. I want to touch on matters of deception, how to identify it, and how to protect yourself from it (Applause).

4.   Again, thank you. I want to start by qualifying myself as well. I concentrate my efforts on the link between human characteristics, their developments, and the expectations of a Deity, as well as His intelligence level, and reasonable expectations. I believe that my contributions, due to the disclosed basis of my contributions, qualify me to participate in this debate.

5.   I listened to Valeria and found her to be interesting, especially from the standpoint as an engineer and her concern about the potentiality of a Deity. So, I want to say that I find evidence that God does exist on the basis that our entire world is pre-engineered, which we perceive as nature. Nature operates internally and externally, in which the laws of nature are put on display. Therefore, I think it is fitting that we are in God and God is in us.

6.   From there, we can see how the Ten Commandments are good for avoiding or reducing conflict in our lives, which is a reflection of the knowledge and workings of nature.

7.   Mike: I agree with you, Charles. I, also, think it's interesting that an engineer can overlook evidence of engineering. It helps confirm that none of us are perfect.

8.   Valeria: Thank you for bringing that up, Charles. Somehow, the idea brought us to the need to distinguish between an imperfection and a choice to be and/or to protect evil. I think that

once your mindset is voluntary and absent of a strong compelling influence, you're no longer under the spell of an imperfection, as seen in one who engineers. You are, in essence, making a choice and living it. Somehow that element of engineering was overlooked.

9. Sorry for that interruption, Charles. Please proceed.

10. Charles: No problem. I think we have to address any issues that are brought to the table.

11. When I examine the pastor's sermon, I immediately knew that it did not come from an all-knowing God. Surely, God, the largest and most sophisticated, conscious being knows when someone is being oppressed and forced into a life of temptation, abuse, and manipulation. This guy, apparently, thinks that his own conscience is hidden from God. In his presentation, he clearly reduced the sophistication of God, as if he never knew God. I believe this is the most common mistake made by a lot of people. Usually, when I discern this mistake, I just walk away.

12. But, maybe, he has underestimated the intelligence of a knowledgeable audience or thought he could hide his scheme from them. Only the less knowledgeable would be fooled by him. This is why everyone should be reading and learning about our Creator, because even the very elect can be fooled into believing nothing more than an idol.

13. It seems that God already remedied this problem by sending Jesus to shed his blood for the sins of all, who believe. Jesus said, I'm the Truth, the Way, and The Life, John 14:16. Those, who needed healing chased after him to touch him or his garments. I perceive this as symbolic. This is a symbolic expression of searching for the truth and achieving the benefits that result, once it's found.

14. But you had to believe it was the Way; otherwise, you'd revert or give up. Not believing and giving up is how you become led by the vices of others. Again, I said "Symbolic", meaning it can pertain to the results of any research or study.

15. Therefore, blasphemy of the Holy Spirit and disbelief in the Truth, the Way, and the Life are the only two issues that will doom you. Those, discovering the Truth, the Way, and the Life as building blocks to build upon will go on and do greater things. So, it makes sense that we are to search for the Truth.

16. Every aspect of a belief should have a basis or it's questionable. From a basis, we can imagine and become productive, resulting in creativity that aligns with the elements of Love and its relatives, such as healing, resolution, and unity.

17. When our imagination is not and cannot be connected to a sound basis, it results in delusions, disarray, separation, helplessness, and vulnerability. This is why you don't build on sinking sand, but on firm grounds.

18. I'm going to give you an example of a strong delusion believed by many. In our world, we have a choice between two major religions: righteousness and unrighteousness. There is no other major religion. A religion diluted with the elements of the opposite is still an unrighteous religion; because it's not perfect.

19. The Bible, but especially a good understanding of the elements associated with our righteous and loving Creator (God) and the opposing elements, clarifies the differences between the two.

20.   Because many have decided that church and state should not share the same religion, they have given the state a license to practice against them, which is the religion of unrighteousness. Then, they spread the idea that God endorses the government, thus unrighteousness.

21.   Both religions have a fundamental structure that must be conformed to, forcing submission to the frame of mind behind the source, except one is voluntary, while the other is not.

22.   They like to explain it as a state not endorsing a particular, unique and minor religion amongst them; but the state's influence spills over to mediations and corrections amongst the people. In essence, a foreign mindset rules over the mindset of the members of both the righteous and unrighteous religions.

23.   The fruit of this tree is, thus, revealed in the quality of developments. If you say I'm wrong, knowing God's way is perfect, how do you explain the poisonous fruit? It was the people, who engineered this establishment. Someone perfect and all-knowing did not yield, nor desire, poisonous fruit.

24.   That is how a group of people can lead others into a delusion, using peer pressure and consequences. That is why the pastor, who presented the presentation, if he did, is dangerous.

25.   I discovered, what appears to be, a perfect example of proper development. We were all born naïve to Truth and moral behavior, even Jesus, being part man. I read God put baby Jesus in the hands of God-fearing parents, who obeyed His commands.

26.   I sensed God rearing Jesus by encouraging him to learn about the people in his environment. He questioned the priests, but never really joined them nor was he baptized by them, due to differences. Jesus had something more dependable than the wisdom of the world: God within. So, he learned about life on a deeper level than all those surrounding him. At some point, he said the church is within you, "My sheep hear my voice", John 10:27.

27.   Being the Truth, the Way, and the Life, he proved to be a great Teacher by utilizing symbolical expressions of things already known with details to present clarity of thought. He understood the process of building blocks. This is how a change of mind or a moral progression of mind is garnered.

28.   Creating darkness, increasing complexity, or using reverse-psychology is certainly the opposite and is not associated with the elements of love, forgiveness, and healing.

29.   So, the pastor did not represent Jesus. He represented separation rather than unification, domination rather than service, and taking rather than giving. Together, these elements oppress, tempt, and manipulate the remaining population in a shared economy. Again, the pastor could not have been of God, nor did he represent His interests.

30.   Valeria: Similarly, I look at everything as having logistics; and this man believes in disrupting the logistics, while presenting a case of foul, when certain standards aren't met. It's framing, deception, and defamation, which somehow should be overlooked.

31.   Charles: Exactly!

32.   I, also, want to add that this pastor is dangerous from the standpoint that he may feel that he needs to continue, regardless of Truth. You see, it's just like a rap celebrity, who was seeing another celebrity of a Caucasian type. He had to break up with her, because of how his

supporters thought about the idea. People get to a point where reverting and/or admission to truth leads to damaged pride, security issues, instability, and a loss of love. That's the way it is with any hard criminal.

33.   When we are responsible and mature adults, we look at how to properly improve the future of our world, by investing the right values into the future generations.

34.   We have to look at whether we're creating or presenting resolution, uncertainty, or revolt. Only one is acceptable.

My Experience with Going to Church with a Hate Group (Pt 6)

1.   Richard Roth: Thank you, Charles! I like the fact that you chose a very key point of analyzing the legitimacy of the Bible and Truth, thus qualifying yourself to be a contributor in the seek for Truth.

2.   Now, let's turn our attention to Jason, who has a very good analytical approach to probably anything you can imagine. Jason?

3.   Jason: Hello everyone and thank you, Richard, for having me.

4.   Like others, I'd like to qualify myself as well. I break down issues and other matters to get and present a solid report of my findings. I use definitions as building blocks to present a case or understand what I'm dealing with. I find it baffling that a lot of professionals or political figures produce different or opposing results, and when not so, turning a blind eye and deaf ear to embedded facts of a case. Below is an example of a lot of the terms, I may consider, to make a decision about a matter.

5.   When processing information, I distribute details, including repetitious details, which are relevant to each term. These details will be written to adapt to the terminology in which it appears. However, I don't want to take up a lot of time explaining how I do it. Instead, I just want to present the type of terms and method I use to give a professional opinion.

6.   With that said, I want to answer the questions, "Did a pastor present this sermon?" and, if so, "Who presented such a sermon?" I've already gone through the process of discovery; so, I'm just going to tell you what I think.

7.   While I could not determine what was actually said, using building blocks, I found that the likelihood of a similar sermon presented to a portion of the population is highly probable. I examined treatment, social activities, child development, statistics, self-inflicted harm, media events, political and legal matters, and physical conditions in many cities and countries, to build a highly probable case that the sermon is widespread, even across much of the globe. But I also found a disturbing fact that the inferior conditions aren't always carried out by a foreign race, but may be economically motivated.

8.   To combat the issue, I felt the need to give an example of some of my work, to illustrate the soundness of my discovery process and for the oppressed people to adopt and improve upon for greater success and problem-solving.

9.   That's all I have, Richard.

Discipline

A discipline is a particular branch of knowledge or system in a natural state or derived from certain experiences or exposures.

Common sense

Common sense is a shared understanding across a particular discipline, in accordance with the extent of exposure.

Sound Definition

A sound definition is one that is complete, accurate, and consistent in relation to that, in which it covers, thus jurisdiction.

Element

An element is something that has an electrical-like connection(s) to a matter-in-question, whether in influence, effect, or appearance.

Focus

Focus is the concentration upon a matter(s) within a chosen, defined, implied, or specified range.

Agenda

An agenda is an objective that by itself, or in combination, acts as a mental, causal agent of achievement, sustainment, support, and/or resistance, when its coded projections are acted upon.

Advantage

A source of favor, labored for, given or received, as a result of an event, establishment, or choice that has the ability to or, actually, elevates the potentiality of a desired development or outcome, whether foreseen or not.

Code

A discipline, imprint, or instruction observed or depicted as a means to materialize a desired development or outcome.

Structure

A matter of various elements or parts, each displaying some form of uniqueness, that may be static or changeable, in part or whole, whether in makeup or with influence.

Pipeline

A structure that holds matters within or provides opportunities in a cylinder-like form.

Timing

Timing is the natural or unnatural regulation of matters in a timely or untimely manner, in which a linking of matters is established or missed.

Invisible Influence

An invisible influence is a mysterious or familiar influence that can only be understood by deciphering the meaning of its collective engagements.

Storm Indicators

Storm Indicators are a collection of resistance areas that are known to oppose key areas of an agenda.

Trend Indicator

A trend indicator is a summary of the nature of key areas of resistances or support.

Projection Indicator

A projection indicator is a summary of the nature of all key areas of, both, resistance and support areas.

Trend

A movement that resembles activities that appears to be inside of a pipeline of conformance regulators.

Consequences

A consequence is a development that follows a previous development(s) or has the potentiality to do so.

Past

The past is a collection of previous occurrences, relative or not, which is often used to form an opinion of current and future matters.

Present

The present is a current state of condition, formulated by the past and capable of deciding future conditions.

Future

The future is the result of a combination of the past and present, in which all the electrical connections produce a balance of opposing forces, secret or obvious.

Projection

A projection is a formula that combines a relevant element(s) of the past with a stillness or movement of all relevant matters of the present to illustrate potential, resulting developments or outcomes.

Diversity

Diversity is a measure of changes, varieties, types, and/or options available, especially to a particular seeker.

Controlling Element

A controlling element is one that exercises authority in enforcement, physically, or has formidable advantage, at least, in the mind of the observer or challenger, potentially causing manipulated thoughts, alternatives, and/or actions.

Options

Options are perceived or experimental choices, whether compatible, beneficial, or not.

Benefits

Benefits are matters that are pleasing, comforting, supportive, or improving of a personal agenda or, to a lesser degree, a relieving of efforts or a strain of efforts to meet a requirement.

Beneficiary

A beneficiary is a receiver of a benefit, naturally or unnaturally.

Administration

An administration is a source of management, in which all influential-related activities are reflective of.

Trait

A trait is a feature that identifies with a particular source.

Synchronicity

Timely occurrences of relations as if to be in agreement, linked, followed, or engaged in planned actions, whether compatible or not, in a scheme of things, such as war or construction.

Disadvantage

A disadvantage is a weakness in a competitive edge or in the likelihood of success.

Herd Force

Herd Force is a condition that attracts and compels you in some direction, while preventing a side exit. There are agenda-accommodating activities on all sides that thwarts an exit. Put another way, there's an inability to perceive an exit, due to some sort of secret, perceived threat, or containment.

1.   Richard Roth: Thank you, Jason! That was certainly one of my favorite presentations.

2.   Jason didn't go into everything pertaining to his project; because, like he said, it is time consuming and tedious. But he didn't reveal some material that I thought was very important and says a lot about his creativity. Here is some more of his work:

Catalyst

An origination of an initial event is almost always, if not always, derived from a balance and/or imbalance of a set of circumstances, having electrical connections and distribution of affects, which is known as a catalyst.

Universal Mechanical Theory

Mechanical theory is the belief that all things are connected, having local and distant affects and effects, whether known or unknown, thus the belief that there's a reason for everything.

Social Origination

Social origination is a point, in which a matter is developed or instigated from social influence, potentially having or inclusive of a viral effect.

Logical Origination

Logical Origination is a point, in which a matter is developed from a natural mechanical process of phenomena.

Deceptive Contrast

Deceptive contrast is the discounting, dismissal, or deceptive promotion of the denial of legitimate differences.

Logic

Logic is knowledge learned from the observance of a qualified leader(s), observed in a particular discipline(s).

Violence

Violence is any turbulent or destructive behavior that attempts to or actually obstructs or contrasts accurate and moral phenomena, with intent for limitation, damage or destruction of a thing of value, including sense, logic, intelligence, values, dependencies, physical and emotional health, as well as freedom.

Value

Value is the quality, in which something is useful and/or adored.

Justice

Justice is the end result of a process of transforming a matter or manner of thinking into an ideal form, derived by the calculating mind of one or more people, representing a mold of experiences, in which the qualities are stamped and reflected back.

Formula

A process that materializes an appearance, development, circumstance, condition, behavior, objective, goal, or outcome.

Conversation Resumed

3.   Jason likes to design his definitions to have a real feel to them and that the collection of terms kind of…well…bleeds into one another. This all helps to tell a story and organize the details.

4.   Jason is always trying to improve and update his project, which helps him to improve his ability to express his opinion and stay tuned up with reality. It's good for self-evolvement and putting pressure on the deceptive and violent population.

5.   Mike: I'm very concerned about over-valuing Jason's work. I'm afraid it'll get someone hurt.

6.   As a former attorney, my experiences tell me that the courts have their own resources. They don't need Jason's….custom..definitions, or whatever you want to call it. Just tell your story. Don't slow down the system with excess. If there's something you need to get done and you don't know how to do it, just delegate. That's what attorneys and expert advisers are for. They are all experts in their fields. Jason's method is only going to cause confusion and trouble. We're all looking for a solution.

7.   We have handicapped people. We have the mentally ill. We have, also, just down-right bad people. We don't ask for this, but we have to deal with it. So, someone has to get paid to do

so. Then, we have to get the money to pay them. So, it becomes a business. Who wants to work for free?

8.   Jason: I'm not a trouble-maker, Mike. I see many authorities side-stepping the truth of matters. A lot of times, when that happens, the case wasn't clearly or completely expressed and someone threw a popular spin on the outcome. It happened, because the attorney, defendant, or plaintiff were blocked or weren't knowledgeable enough to proceed with an intensely detailed and compulsive manner or shared a protected interest with another party, potentially the court itself, creating a conflict of interest.

9.   These things happen, because a class of people enjoy, to some degree, a lack of accountability. This enjoyment is necessary to steer a population in a higher class's desired direction and for personal gratifications.

10.   So, we're not all on the same team and having the same priorities. We see how your system works. We, also, know that our world is mechanical and there is a thing called a catalyst. I see people taking routes to put themselves in a position as a catalyst or creating one to provoke confusion. I see people, also, making profit systems out of matters that can be resolved or not researching for resolutions or healing concepts. That's why I do what I do.

11.   So, I'm not going to just delegate and, ignorantly, watch it happen, while I think I have a legitimate resolution. One thing that I see as protecting a criminal or immoral pursuit is the regulation of those, who attempt to resolve these types of problems. I don't know what you're doing, but you don't seem to be up to the task of acknowledging a lot of things, like Valeria said.

12.   Mike: No one's perfect. We're all evolving and I'm sure someone is working on exactly what you perceive. I say let the experts do their jobs.

13.   Valeria: I'm not surprised. That's Mike for you. Jason, I see you as an expert, and I wish you well in your project. I'd also like to help, if you ever need my assistance. As you can see, I'm quite the opposite of Mike.

14.   Mike: Here we go attacking…..

15.   Richard Roth: Ok! We're going to wrap this thing up. I'd like to thank each and every last one of you for showing up and contributing to our search for truth.

16.   I know this doesn't solve any problems, but it does give us a perspective going forward. Hopefully, tomorrow is the day we all heal from this. Until then, good night.

Jason's Custom Definitions (Extension)

Idolatry

A source that imperfectly parallels the mind of God, who is perfect, but is followed regardless of flaws, especially without question, is an idol.

Leader

A leader is a qualified source of following for observance, learning, conformance, and/or achievement, which may only become visible, when a relationship is discerned from the past to the present and onto the future, as if to be the building blocks of a matter.

Tainted Leader

A tainted leader presents itself, when the level of following is superficial and the opportunity to execute fraudulent or erroneous underhanded schemes are executed.

Statistics

Statistics are the result of applied or implied mathematics that results from the recognition of phenomena over time, providing accuracy in accordance to scope and application.

Compass

An analyst part of a seeker that considers and chooses matters potentially perceived to be useful, resulting in trendy behavior that is reflective of an idea or agenda.

Intelligence

Intelligence is the ability to decipher, gather, depict, and to use data decisively, which also entails managing a directory.

Knowledge

Knowledge is a collection of results of perception and calculations from the use of intelligence(s).

Consolidation

Consolidation is a combining or combination of formerly separate elements or matters to form a mix or mutual effect.

Grounds

A firm establishment, in which a matter is or can be confirmed as true or evident, is grounds for presentation.

Fishing

Providing bait or presenting enticing elements to draw a targeted source for consumption or gratifying means, which is not in the best interests of that which is sought.

Bipolar

A point of interest or subject-in-question having opposing courses of directions, determined by the strongest fundamental catalyst, is bipolar.

Prototype

A prototype is an accurate concentration of a source's characteristics, along with initiating and responsive elements, which are used to perfectly illustrate or duplicate original phenomena activities.

Quality Attributing Test

Quality attributing tests are tests that qualifies the process of prototype building, by following exact standards, strategies, and rules that produce equally accurate models of all opposing sides, including the mediating source.

Business

A business, which is the opposite of theft, is a scheme involving an exchange of values in the best interests of all parties involved, to the greatest extent.

Theft

Theft, which is the opposite of business, especially if organized, is an intentional and understood, destructive scheme or deed to rob or deprive another of a matter(s), in which the matter(s) robbed or deprived is in the best interest of the victim of theft, which may include the distribution of debilitating effects or matters having such effect(s).

Lie

A lie is an expression or support of an idea or agenda, contrary to adverse, concealed knowledge and/or expectations of a matter, regardless of reason.

Engineering

Engineering is the identification, organization, and introduction of scheme(s), through observation and/or trial and error, consisting of a catalyst(s) and its known, relevant domino effect(s), with the idea of duplicating it in reality to manifest, monitor, dictate, and/or control developments, whether socially, mentally, emotionally, economically, or physically.

Result

A result is an established point in time or end of a process, in which a development, which reflects all past and present conditioning effects, is perceived.

Uncontrolled Honing

Uncontrolled honing is a mysterious influence over a matter or life of a target that makes its effects more intense and/or obvious over time, which usually produces minimal evidence in a secretive scheme and may produce a squeeze play.

Squeeze play

A squeeze play is a tightening of options or opportunities that entrap or dictate minimal directions or movement.

Emotions

Emotions are representative of a complex balance of transforming feelings, which are effected by a human version of a Global Positioning System (GPS) that is sensitive to one's position in relation to an objective and long range goal(s), which is also connected to a directory of past experiences, knowledge, and intelligences, which provide comparisons and projective feedback, making it prone to the effects of telepathy, by way of cause and effect and the manner in which they were achieved, and training.

Directory

A directory is a collection of disciplines with their relevant traits, trends, etc. gained from past and present experiences, and organized for the purpose, in which it is to used, whether to follow, create, or to project.

Binding

Binding is the act of having supreme access to or choosing and utilizing or controlling a catalyst(s) that is out of control of the one, in which the catalyst(s) has an unavoidable effect upon.

Distortion

Distortion is a result of phenomena or a message so complex or obscured that clarity cannot, currently, be attained.

Inferior

Inferior is representative of a low quality appearance, reputation, and/or ability, in comparison to a more excellent model, having only the ability to, more successfully, navigate amongst its likeness or lesser in quality, which may be manifested by limited access to competitive resources and/or maintained by restricting access to resources of advancement, or that is, theft.

Agreement

Agreement is an expressed approval through communications or adopted deeds or beliefs, which through comparisons, a classification(s) become apparent in part or whole, which is seen in the extent in which it parallels the nature of the thing compared.

Resistance

Resistance is an area of testing, friction, blockage, destructive activity, or the support of.

Support

Support is an area of approval, favor, upholding, or protections.

Classification

Classification is the arrangement of matters-in-question by likeness and/or compatible elements.

Tracking

Tracking is the following of a subject of interest, which is more reliable when you follow identifying data that depict an element(s) of the classified target or influence, besides names, in elusive and transforming leaders.

Values

Values are utilities, or what is brought to the table, fit for a purpose and embedded, chosen, and/or agreed upon that are split between a system of righteousness and unrighteousness, in which each are supportive of one or the other, making it an obvious fit and may consist of something as simple as commitment; but the total values of self or a group must be enough for business or the scheme of things.

Business Plan

A business plan consists of a collection and organization of useful values and contributors that contribute to a proposed agenda, which can empower the formation, problem-solving, sustainment, and growth of a business or scheme; thus, the test of a business will reveal its business plan, even that of a government and its agencies, as well as strengths, weaknesses, and tendencies towards corruption.

Responsibility

Responsibility is an accountability to a moral path, development, and outcome that reflects a relative value, in which any other option is a deviation.

Talent

The ability to produce a value that is useful for a purpose.

Information Interview

Information interviews are events involving information gathering of expectations, history, essentials, legal (state and federal), costs, demand, supply, storage, taxes, equipment, scientific applications, talents, requirements, competition, contacts, mentors, etc.

Counter Values

Counter values are competitive and testing, with a tendency to divide, separating from purpose and status, and may be inconsistent across a vulnerable population, in which circumstances not generally occurring on one side or the other may be linked. Areas of resistances are composed of counter values.

Network

A network is the electrical connections to all things connected that enables and aids appearance and/or performance, if relative, in which an absence negates a feature of performance, even of least or most subtle type.

Grid

A grid is a set of defined locations, whether in respect to one another or assigned to some unique portion of an area or subject of focus.

Path

A path is a structured progression of travel through locations and/or connections that must be performed, before a task, cycle, appearance, agreement, or other development is completed.

Deductive Reasoning

Deductive Reasoning is the act of reasoning the potentials, likelihood, evidence, and legitimacy of fact, without bias, settling only on solid grounds to establish facts, conditions, developments, and outcome.

Discrepancy

A discrepancy is a variation, in a comparison of one to another, in a countering position, in which the same or no method is capable of manifesting the variant in the countering source.

Deed

A deed is an act performed, preserved as a promise to do something, or usually expected under certain conditions; it is an answer to an effect(s). Except for impulsive behavior, deeds are performed with a sensitive monitoring of cause and effect, familiar or experimental.

Event

An event is something that occurs as a result of something.

Trade

A trade is an investment of any type that yields a quality of return, even the yield of no response. Speculative trades are, generally, performed in times of excess, while other times are as a result of desperation.

Belief

A belief is something calculated or perceived as the most reliable manner of evaluating, eluding, coping, progressing, resolving, or overcoming an obstacle or condition.

Habit

A habit is a repetitive deed, usually or expected to be performed under the same conditions, especially in respects to available and accessible options and the degree of ignorance.

Rotary

A rotary is a cyclical path through a series of required elements organized to parallel a particular event, simple to complex.

Cycle

A cycle is a progression through a rotary(s) from start to finish or back to start.

Priorities

A priority is something that is naturally or essentially favored that must proceed before another in a rank of potentialities, designed to produce an effect, condition, or event.

Trend

A trend is a general deed or direction of a subject or condition.

Purpose

A purpose is the possession or exercise of intelligence, knowledge, talents, tools, morals, and/or abilities, which in coordination, prioritizes, streamlines, and parallels a rotary, or set of, that trend towards particular and potential developments and outcomes, whether known or unknown.

Objective

An objective is a purpose carried out in a particular stage(s) of a rotary, having a prioritized order.

Goal

A goal is the intended result of a meeting of an objective(s) that transformed a desire into fulfillment.

Predictable Phenomena

Predictable phenomena are the sufficiently constructive and accurate understanding of the domino-effects of a matter experienced and-or learned, especially when confirmed, from the conditional effects to the relative developments and results. Exposure to repetitive cause and effects are the basis of predictive knowledge.

Jason's Profiles

Counterintelligence

Counterintelligence is the intelligent management of counter values, their placement, and competitive pursuits against a target and/or target's interests,

brought out by the target's determination, expanded extent of efforts, and creativity, in which ability of the countering influence to learn and quality of resilience are the most obvious evidence of a countering influence.

Its rank is identified by the type of intelligence needed to produce each counter value and the range of influence, along with boldness of activity and protections reserved for it.

It speaks to the heart and mind with regulations and the orchestration of thoughts and emotions in real time, aided by historic responses and influences that seemingly yield wisdom, as if to be practicing telepathy.

It's character(s) is identified by its overall association with righteousness or unrighteousness and may exhibit a guiding influence with the materialization of aid, which may be of a low quality, and may be paired with a countering influence as well, in an attempt to yield its purpose.

Learn about any counterintelligence by asking questions and acting in pursuit of answers; but be aware that high profile counterintelligence may respond in defense, using expert advisers and their diagnostic pursuits to silence evidence against it, such as in the case of false mental diagnoses. Countering is evidence of what is known about the target.

Ignorance

Ignorance, being opposite of intelligence, operates in the same manner as intelligence, except with a superficial understanding or severely limited talent to perform on the same level, potentially aided by a poorly developed directory and prone to copycat habits, which makes one prone to manipulations that can be intensified against themself by an example of their own support.

Ignorance is also aided by a defective value system, naturally purposed to lead and implicate directions, but may be replaced by prioritizing popular decisions, actions, and beliefs or anything but science, resulting in a fragile frame of mind.

Like animals, which are members of the dung diner's club, which devours other's feces, as well as their own feces, seen to consist of undigested food, ignorance will devour superior and inferior information with no way to process it correctly, only to excrete superior and inferior matters not seen to fit.

But they may digest questionable subjects that seem to fit and others for their quest to appear informative, potentially evolving worse than before, with no knowledge that the sufficiently intelligent can see all this.

The clue may be in the missed target.

Ignorance is promoted, as seen in how a person or public is encouraged to think. In one example, a person may be compared to another, as if one is a model of a defective condition and the other is following in those, almost exact, footsteps. The method is an efficient way to sidestep or dismiss the details of the big picture that formulated the condition. But a situation is created that poses the question, "Who can be trusted?"

The media is constantly reporting matters of repetition, but doesn't address corruption behind the scenes of civilian crimes and mental diagnoses. Why? Because it's dangerous and disrupts high level pursuits. So, the one-sided presentation becomes brainwashing, because no one is reporting on an opposing view and soundly explaining it all away. If they do, they can only go so far to prey on what you don't know and what you trust, while potentially limiting the freedom of speech of the victim and/or suspect involved.

I've noticed that people acting out of ignorance, usually have the loudest mouth, the surest attitude, and bolder in expression, making them highly employable by authoritative manipulators for repelling those protesting against corruption. You can't argue, because they're sure of themselves and resort to insults and total disrespect. Higher ups, who provoked the whole confrontation, stand behind them. The instigators believe in using the same race, as if it's the most effective pursuit and as an attempt to cover up racism. These people are usually more successful than protesters; but, hey, it's about the black protester being wrong about everything too, or nearly so.

Attribution

Attribution is a very powerful process that involves pairing or associating something with something else in a habitual manner, whether for training perception, demonizing, or exalting something over another, if not all of the above, making it a tool for framing anything at will.

When you think of attributions, think about symbols attributed to stocks and as trademarks that identify with their relevant companies. But attribution has other applications.

Attribution is the most important tool and reason for unreasonable hate, whether racism, discrimination, revenge, excessive charges, or defamation. All hate is unreasonable, when a real solution is not sought or is applicable.

Attribution has to be somewhat constant or the lie will, eventually, diminish. So, the media may, almost, constantly associate a race or type of people to a target of hate, like immorality, something despised, unfit, or viewed as unclean.

An attorney may wear a suit and present professionally, while a defendant may wear prison attire and look wild and unprepared.

In public areas, homeless shelters may provide homeless residents with minimal services and care, while the public views all residents as dysfunctional, noting certain types that make up the larger portion of the dysfunctional population, but make up a much smaller part of the whole population.

In neighborhoods, one neighborhood may appear clean, prosperous, caring, consisting of the angelic type; however, an adjacent neighborhood may appear dysfunctional, poor, unclean, uncaring, and filled with menace and violence, noting specific types that make up the majority in each. The so-called angel may be the cause of the so-called demon, who may only be acting in defense, ignorance, out of programmed ignorance, out of desperation, or compelled by someone.

You may have heard horror stories that include violence everywhere a particular person goes, although the violence may have been manipulated against the targeted person to frame him/her, only for the target to, eventually, explode in anger and violence, which many see the final event as confirming truth, when in fact science was used to carry out a scheme of defamation. At that point, it is almost impossible to prove innocence, especially because of misplaced trust. Loner is, also, usually attributed to this type, probably because of the practice of avoidance. But who gets caught manipulating these cases?

In another case of attribution, drugs or any potential cause of addiction or control, such as debt, can be utilized to attract known behaviors developed to sustain a status, when conditions are volatile, creating a potential to turn to a life of immorality and crime. Student loans are a good example of control, when they're expensive and interest rates are high, raising the importance of succeeding in a volatile market, especially when the student faces discrimination practices.

The cost of losing can create anxiety issues, especially knowing freedom is threatened.

Strong addictions increase the voluntary attribution of behaviors, which puts anyone at risk of being subject to the power of anyone on a higher status.

In a popular witchcraft story, it was claimed that a black man appeared to someone of a Caucasian type, which helps an attribution process to succeed.

While attributions may be natural and true, not all are and must be managed in a way to constantly paint a false picture, including the provocation of immorality, including violence in neighborhoods and prisons.

Always pay attention to the big picture surrounding you and associated events and any negativity; so, you may defend yourself by separating and carrying yourself as upright; otherwise, you lend a helping hand to your oppressors.

System

A system is created to maintain equilibrium and/or progress beyond an initial point in a jurisdiction, designated by its design and purpose, until it is interfered with or terminated. In an environment of fluctuating bodies, health, morality, emotions, mentalities, desires, essentials, conditions, natural and unnatural events, a sophisticated system will increasingly adapt and grow, as a system of a major, medium, and minor systems that are coordinated to achieve the purpose of its creator.

The health and direction of the entire system is representative of the mentality of the immediate creator or manager.

The big picture is the most accurate view in a bipolar system, which reflects the performance of the most influential catalysts that determine direction.

When a system can only make money in one direction, certain people are hated, acclimatization to horrifying conditions are up, donations are discriminately directed, and people want to pay less in taxes, what could go wrong?

Character

A character is a system of compelling, restricting, and/or neutralizing elements that produce grounds for the features expressed in or withheld from interactive phenomena, as if to be following a script.

A human character is like a pendulum, naturally landing in a balanced position, but more complex, due to its evolving and adaptive decision-making and exposure to a variety of types of influences as well as its ability and inability to deal with the variety of such appropriately; but its development is only compelled by what it has been exposed to, making for unique characters.

Unique human characters have to get acquainted with one another, to know each other, not assume others are like them.

A human character is strengthened by successes, seen as accuracy and/or dependable fulfilling methods, and weakened by the opposite, unless the character clings to a belief foreign to manipulative effects, which could bring suffering.

Human characters consist of values that work like a system, with some type of beliefs, picked up and/or confirmed in reality and values to support the mission; such gives a clue to the character's agenda and manner of reaching and sustaining equilibrium, and/or progressing forward.

Acknowledging their values, in respect to their agenda, how they proceed, and their successes and failures, allows us to read into them, even to predict potential changes in evolution. The character's exhibited personality tone usually gives a clue to the degree of harshness of external conditioning effects. This is all prime material for a manipulator.

Condition

A condition is the state of something and, in which something can be or is contingent upon, and having peaceful, interesting, detailed, subtle, bold, excitable, confining, offensive, understanding, nonconstructive, superficial, conditioning, expressive, and/or other elements.

Conditions are the settings of things, with electrical, empowering and disempowering connections, in a given time, place, and/or event, whether imaginative, emotionally, mentally, spiritually, and/or physically.

There's plenty of room for mysterious or unprovable influences to roam, whether due to ignorance or support, if not both.

Matters progress and regress back to a condition(s), within the whole.

An experienced manager, in a position of control and ability to garner support, especially socially, can execute and sustain conditional effects that drive a target's sensitive nature, especially if his/her own experiences are used in an empathetic method.

The manager's work is discerned by the sense of organization and orchestration that is, especially, sustained enough to inspire a message, especially when personal initiations and responses don't match up with feedback, and/or control is absent and unattainable, especially concerning long term goals.

Otherwise, conditions allow for opportunities to be achieved.

Sensitivity

Sensitivity is the affecting influence of phenomena, sensed through one or more of the five senses, which are sight, hearing, smelling, feeling, and tasting, in which the elements are compared to familiar elements for matches and calculated in the heart and mind as an identified presence or as an impression to be defined, all of which a directory and database is used to decipher information and discern messages.

Sensitivity, and its relative directory and database, may be seen as anywhere from impressive to ignorant, and potentially fluctuating; but the calculation of manipulated effects may be the driving force behind the interpretation of events and the deed performed.

The database of sensitivity is similar to the following in construction and is useful for brainstorming, planning, scheming, storytelling, discovery, investigating, researching, or inventing. It is as good as it is accurate, organized, useful, clear, complete, and directional.

"Worry: threat, Devastated: devastation, Confused: Conflict, Expectation: synchronization, desire: inclination, Imbalance: deficiency, Balance: sufficient, Measure: scale, Focus: attention, Importance: weight, Tracing: tracking, Prediction: profile, Condition: analysis, Valuation: condition, Devaluation: depreciate, Undervalue: deprecate, Progression: advancement, Regression: falling, Pleasant: pleasing, Joy: Elation, Comfortable: compatibility, Helpful: accommodating, Satisfied: fulfilled, Anxiety: challenge, Tone: expression, Adaptation: adjustment, Change: mutable, Acclimatization: climate, Trajectory: path, Adaptation: variance, Mood: effectivity, Interpretation: impression, Impression: datum, Fear: danger, Teachable: diplomatic, Stubborn: protective, Protection: value, Appreciation: value, Value: quality, Force: exertion, Weight: bearing, Attraction: appeal, Pulling: attachment, Commitment: responsibility, Binding: attachment, Influence: bearing, Profile: conduct, Chemistry: reactionism, Transformation: conversion, Trajectory; guide, Function: mechanism, Thought: focus, Computation: calculation, Weakness: vulnerability, Responsibility: liability, Perception: intelligence, Image: observation, Logic: programming, Example: imitation, Following: tracing, Agreement: harmony, Structure: organization, Following: leader, Knowledge: application, Application: example, Confidence: trust, Deception: profile, Essential: fundamental, Control: controller, Controller: catalyst, Power: force, Influence: supply, Restriction: resistance, Filter: standard, Weakness: failure, Corruption: deception, Corruption: undermining, Countermining; counterintelligence, Cycle: sequence, Solution: resolution, Confrontation: discord, Test: trial, Oppression: injustice, Injustice: imbalance, Deficiency: ineffectiveness, Ineffectiveness: failure, nature: essentials, System: organization, Operation: compelling, Compelling:

mechanism, Propel: provocation, Provocation: engagement, Effectiveness: success, Viral: circulation, Dependence; solution, Strength: success, Social: relations, Popularity: charm, Threat: danger, Favored: preference, Discrimination: distinction, Inadequate: weakness, Measure: appraisal, Error: violation, Law: conduct, Limit: change, Pure: dense, Truth: constancy, Attribution: pairing, Conspiracy: agreement, Implication: inference, Logic: application, Decision: choice, Ignorance: misguidance, Rejection: repudiation, Responsibility: agent, Science: order, Repetition: confirmation, Misguidance: deception, Malpractice: negligence, Pretentiousness: fraud, Fraud: deviation, Imposter: deception, Deception: fraud, Deviation: error, Truth: grounds, Soundness: reliability, Consequential: result, Example: leader, Intentional: set, Synchronization: co-occur, Planter: seed: Seed: germination, Germination: order, Order: development, Cause: motive, Counter: oppose, Contain: bound, Interest: benefit, Concern: interest, Manipulation: process, Pursuit: activity, Game: competition, Counter: point, Probability: grounds, Motivation: incentive, Drive: motivation, Drive: scale, Measure: influence, Timing: synchronization, Sight: spectacle, Expectation: understanding, Reflection: variable, Sight: variable, Belief: synchronization, Belief: match, Violent: blast, Leader: spectacle, Repetition: cycle, Reasonableness: justifiable, Experiences: leader, Bound: consequences, Distortion: deformation, Slave: regulation, Leader: consequences, Leader: incentive, Drive: manipulation, Measure: impact, Impact: influences, Violent: injury, Resilience: adaptation, Adaptation: method, Resilience: recovery, Recovery: deformation, Connection: causal, Irresistible: overwhelming, Compatibility: harmony, Adversity: disharmony, Threat: adversity, Justice: Fair, Predictable: expectation, Painful: injury, Expectation: prognostic, Anxiety: distress, Decision: comparisons, Decision: consideration, Decision: measure, Decision: compatibility, Decision: experiences, Limit: bound, Restrain: deprivation, Limit: deficiency, Capacity: ability, Deficiency: capacity, Income: capacity, and more."

Traits

A trait is a matter that is evidential of a particular source, usually in a particular condition or under its influence. It's not just hereditary traits, like you got your mother's smile. It involves evidences, like stocks to a broker, cash to a bank, trademark to a business, discrimination to a racist, worry to threat, etc.

All traits are linked to other matters, thus evidential, in which the process is, both, natural and can be manipulated by creating events that naturally manifest other event(s) and/or trait(s), whether immediately or later in the stage of development.

Since all matters are distantly or locally linked, intended and unintended traits may manifest. A person with sufficient experience can, more accurately, perceive and/or manipulate the chain link between traits, even that, which leads into different systems, like the emotional system (discussed later).

All emotions are linked to some type of event and/or trait, evidencing something, and our mental processes use traits in investigative and manifesting pursuits. That's why deeds are exchanges, something done for something else.

One of the most powerful aspects of the game of traits is the answer to why something happened or why someone made a particular choice; then, the reason can be duplicated, changed, or blocked.

The mind imitates the way things work; because, it receives a message through results. The trait system is a networking system that works like a chemical system.

Being knowledgeable and understanding this system allows for the receiver to understand what's being built, in terms of your experiences, who might be behind it, and what their values are. These values have connections to matters in reality, giving them tracing ability, in which the source of affection may be spread over a number of sources, thus a following.

Negative Compulsion

Negative Compulsion: the use of herd force, underhanded schemes, and/or deception to compel a target into a negatively developmental direction or towards self-inflicted harm or a criminal act.

Systematic Compulsion

A pre-established setting of an environment,

- with intent to procure an improper attitude and/or act that initially turns the environment conflicting, having no contingency on the innocence or moral behavior of its target; and/or

- designed to be unusually fragile and confronting in relation to what is assumed to be an alien or in likeness; and

- is usually protected by those, who share the same attitudes and beliefs, excluding paid or forcefully dispatched responders, unless they voluntarily use excessive means.

God

The behavior of the population of the earth demonstrates two meanings of God:

- The widest and most sound meaning: The Creator of the world, whose mindset is of the highest quality and, to a great extent, is perceived in the nature of the things He made, who also gave humans the highest potentials over all other lifeforms of the earth and matching expectations, as seen in the Ten Commandments and His request for perfection.

- The unique and arguable meaning: A powerful figure, to some extent is evidenced by the things in the world and the world itself, whose mindset is arguably fitting for the personal or cultural ideals of the holder, whose interpretation may possess a mix of inferior and superior values or allows or perpetuates for the influence or use of inferior values.

When "The widest and most sound meaning" is the least coveted "The unique and arguable meaning" is the most practiced and lends itself to endless tricks of deception and compulsion.

The most ambiguous trait of "The unique and arguable meaning" is the positioning of oneself next to a known or perceived positive model, while doing the opposite in practice. (Compare to Mathew 15:8). It's, also, used to sway a favorable opinion of an onlooker or in an attempt to twist the logic of a participant in a confrontation. This trait may, also, be used to show a representation or influence of a social group.

The weaknesses of "The unique and arguable meaning" is the fact that it can't consistently follow the paths that churn out ideal and moral results, leaving itself vulnerable to backlash, which encourages security concerns and solutions.

An Imitation of Consciousness?

1. The earth turned with different perspectives.

2. The planet harmonized stability and instability with purpose in a unified operation of contributions.

3. There were tracts of earth of various sizes, like large and partial subjects waiting to be connected.

4. Consolidation provided solidity of purpose, understanding, and natural resources.

5. An island sat isolated, but supported from beneath, while the water mediated all around it.

6. Interconnectivity became apparent and useful, even in distant lands. The interconnectivity presented itself more clearly as we pierced deeper towards, even into, an interest.

7. Looking up from the earth, an air of mystery, and seemingly magic, presented itself.

8. The cloud was the focus of evidence that more lies ahead to be discovered.

9. A drop, seemingly out of the middle of nowhere, fell to the earth.

10. The soil of the earth absorbed it.

11. The wind, unseen by the naked eye, influenced the cloud. From there, mystery began and curiosity arose.

12. When the cloud(s) cleared, a revealing source beamed its light upon the earth and functionality sprung to operation.

13. The rock recorded time and history, even as the wind saw fit.

14. While the earth was a collector, it was guided by a higher, unseen force that could only be imagined with sufficient knowledge.

15. Patience was needed, because a conscious rush or overzealousness of effort(s) has a tendency to lead only to darkness. Wait on the drop.

Went to Church and Paid the Devil

1.   Remember, God knows the hearts of men (Luke 16:15).

2.   Men are so different, put under different circumstances, and treated differently in respects to the judgments of humans, who are insufficient in understanding all the details of the circumstances and matters in question. The degree of influence is, even, of great concern. How can one judge without all the underlying details?

3.   Many go to a church that is solely concerned with growth or sustaining present conditions. They lightly solve the problems of the underclass, if they do at all. They feel power in unity, when Satan's influence is dominant, in their favor. So, they choose the type of leaders, who are gifted in developing their desired future.

4.   Satan, the father of deception, has to initialize and sustain oppression against the human population, while appearing angelic for the game of foolery and to address trust issues.

5.   Through the satisfaction of needs and desires, not to mention comforts, he has bought a great deal of the world's population, at the expense of the minorities, even some of those consisting of the same dominated race(s).

6.   As they proceed with their worship, many honor the conspiracy side of Mathew 15:8, where it states that they honor God with their lips, in which their hearts do not equate with such statements. They do the opposite, as if to test or correct God and signal their approval of the Devil.

7.   The Devil has gripped them with fear and rewarded them, like dogs led to a fight. To survive, they have trained themselves and their offspring to harden their heart for battle and dominance of the weak.

8.   Their spirit has a tendency to pray for matters that call upon the support of their father, the devil. These prayers request only what Satan can deliver. Feeling fulfilled, they honor the source, who is compatible with their request(s). From there, they build on it and it becomes prioritized as all they care to see, hear, and know.

9.   With their imagination, they help dress the Devil and his ways as beautiful and righteous, ignoring the poisonous fruit that continues to fall as evidence to the contrary.

Progress Prayer

1.   Lord, over the years, I've gathered information from my experiences and saw that times do change, everything must be reviewed for reproof, and information, found in one place, tends to move.

2.   Based on those changes and moves, I've learned to keep a record of the facts of life and to defend it with all my might, allowing the opposition to, informingly, go their way, in which they stubbornly choose.

3.   What's important is how I change, in reference to who You are and how You perceive matters. It is not my duty to tell You how things should be, when You're all-knowing. But I have

progressed enough or are progressing to know what You stand for, as opposed to an opposition, making me curious and objective about any tendency or move that violates any part of Your characteristics.

4.   I know I can't follow the crowd to get this information, no matter how large the crowd. I understand that it is You I must see with a pure heart and not the deceived and misled, who have participated in the seeding and maturing of poisonous fruit, and say "Follow me, because I see".

5.   I question everything and try to perceive the legitimacy of responsibility of every step of development, as to filter out misleading influences; so that I can see the difference between Truth and magical error.

6.   I understand that I must not allow the closest and farthest ally or enemy to mislead me in Your Word.

7.   I, also, remember not to let the circumstances of this world turn my heart into a heart of stone. I will seek to undo any damages to my heart and mind that caused me to sway from Your Truth. I will do it for me and You, and not for show. I will have a sincere intent, I promise.

8.   But I understand that, where there is a void or insufficiency, I'll have to depend on You for guidance.

9.   Amen

The Flow

1.   Many individual sources were created and many did not flow into one another, at least for a time, leaving the source natural to a point.

2.   A stream roared with beauty down the mountain. A lake caught water from the hills and another received, also, from sewage. Still, another was a channel from a large body of water, likely to form another, but not certainly.

3.   Yet, although they were not interactive, they all received from the sky, as a common source of influence.

4.   Man looked at this and saw that it was useful for good and evil and used the concept for his delight.

5.   When the natural is touched, causing interaction where it wasn't before, the evidence is the crossover. Where is the crossover?

6.   When a source rises in defense of good, you should question that source, elude it, and/or decide its future.

7.   All things have a flow, and they are defined by the way they flow.

Why the Devil Doesn't Belong in the Building Process

The Building Process

1.   The building process is a construction of effort, fostered by an idea, which designs or alters a matter(s) of focus.

2.   It is assumed that every building block was thought out, formed, and/or chosen for a specific purpose within the whole scheme of things, depending on the level of intelligence and focus, which is an illustration of traits.

3.   The idea is exposed by the traits that transpire from the rhythmic and timely efforts, which creates a theme that supports certain ideas.

4.   Therefore, the traits are the foundation of the idea and create a theme, which can be used for future projections.

5.   The catalyst(s) provide the effort(s), but a combination of catalysts can make the perception of a matter complicated to comprehend. A catalyst can also create other catalysts.

6.   An overseer can diagnose the matter, but that depends on the qualities of such a source.

Unjust Overseer Cannot Afford to Release What Sustains

1.   An unjust overseer cannot afford to release what sustains himself/herself or give substantial power to an opposition, without a change of mind and heart. So, the overseer is most likely to hide behind the complex nature of matters, while the drama continues to unfold.

2.   What could go wrong? This is why the Devil doesn't belong in the building process.

Evidence of Satan being in the Building Process

1.   When Satan is in the, statistics will show that God's people are not "The People", when it comes to constructing a world of God, the Creator. Instead, they become misfits. Satan's followers can't build something that severely obstructs their main beneficial concerns.

2.   When the building process is built on one supporting foundation, especially with time and advancement, it becomes more difficult to reverse the progression of Satan's qualities in the environment.

3.   Those who benefit from a demonic condition will be less willing to alter their successful lifestyle for a questionable future and/or an equal position to all others, but especially of a lower quality than their present one.

4.   Other evidence include confusion boosted by others claiming to be of God, having equal to greater knowledge, but administering false wisdom and doctrines, thus supporting a demonic way.

5.	A demonic way is boosted even more, when the less knowledgeable is praised and rewarded for harmonizing with the false ministry. Suddenly, peer pressure presents itself.

6.	The culture of the population will be more like cells attacking the body, a disease, instead of cells contributing to the quality and sustainment of the life of the entire population. Somehow, this becomes God's way and not the Devil's.

7.	Statistics will show an expansion of elements in line with demonic qualities; and choices will remain, for the most part, compatible with the purpose of the building process.

8.	When in error, a change towards a better direction will have a tendency to swing back in the opposite direction, potentially with circumstances thwarting a reverse. Knowledge of this will reveal a purpose.

9.	Voting will have no serious impact that brings permanent and consistent change for the better, when someone is in power and determined, and sophisticated in deception and trickery, regardless of implosive activities.

10.	Statistics is evidence of how the partitions are shaped in the building; it's the difference between access and inaccessibility that gives it the relevant form. It looks like a jigsaw puzzle.

11.	Failed experiments or endeavors to circumvent problems are clearly seen as leading to a dead-end. Freedom and success are, also, of a low measure.

12.	A person may go through ups and downs, even range, like a stock price on a historical chart.

13.	The reasoning may only be understood by the catalyst(s) and the individual(s); because others may be on different pathways, with a different catalyst(s). Asking questions may feel like pestering or treated as undeserving.

14.	The process of understanding the catalyst is like depicting the moral of the story, whether for the individual, a part of the population, or some whole, which may be a restricted area that may lead to consequences.

Development

1.	In the second phase, form starts to take place. If you're familiar with it, you think of themes that may potentially develop, which is in line with the past. It's because of the tools, like the construct of matters, their demonstrated purpose or aligned purpose, and the conditions.

2.	The construction of matters and manner of progressing are natural to man-made, causing certain arousals of thoughts, motivations, and potential behaviors to develop, which are not standard throughout the population. The results are erratic and inclined to unfavorable conditions, including mental unawareness and hope over producing, or any weaknesses. It may be as erratic as the results of giving the same or wrong medication to everyone, with different circumstances.

3.	The third phase is where we see the purpose or agenda and can, potentially, identify with the relevant, major, catalyst(s) behind the scenes as well as the supporters.

A popular Myth

1.　A popular myth is that minorities, namely African-Americans, have a learning disability, as if it's a racial trait. That myth is destroyed by the ability to code the ability to learn into robots. The code comes from an understanding of how to learn, in which comparisons to a defective model can unearth missing pieces of the puzzle. Therefore, foul play can be detected, when technology performs a human task successfully. Success of the myth depends on proving something humanly fundamental is missing.

The Main Trait of Satan

1.　The main trait of the Devil is the resilience towards evil. Many share this trait, when they are knowledgeable enough and are still determined to do evil, even when under less encouraging circumstances. They, also, create or utilize concepts to motivate and control others to do wrong, but prefer to be perceived as an advocate for good.

2.　In each of these circumstances, we see levels of power and influences starting to unfold. The lower levels are controlled by the top levels.

3.　But, when there's an issue, they want you to concentrate on the highest <u>subjective</u> level to the lowest to find fault. They, almost, if not ever, want you to sincerely look up, unless it's about increasing the effectiveness and/or efficiency of their agenda or falsely maintaining their reputation.

Certain Systems Help Propel Dark Wisdom

1.　If you check just about any system, there are parts that respond directly or indirectly to another and some are more important than others. Some rule over others, while another may be contingent upon a condition created by another or some set or whole. Still, others may produce or respond to timed actions.

2.　You can break the system down in pieces and determine how to make it successful or unsuccessful or appear so, usually, in more ways than one. In the process, you can fool a naive onlooker.

3.　Therefore, you can't afford the Devil and his supporters in high positions, because the world can't change for the better; and they can't afford for you to believe it can.

4.　If truth is threatened to come out, they must use physical means, even aggression, to conceal what they can't logically or deceptively overcome.

5.　In the case of deception, they believe noise, misdirection, distraction, censorship, insults, small or irrelevant errors, fabricated personalities or reputations, concentration on immediate concerns, and negative and positive consequences will quell the movement against them.

6.   Therefore, they may be very difficult to remove; and one or more of them may be helping you to do so unsuccessfully.

Mind Your Own Business?

1.   A lot of people believe that they should mine their own business and avoid trying to change the world; these people are a disgrace to their own kids and next generations. This is a backwards mentality, seen in its irresolvable trait, which makes it totally useless against confusion.

2.   To begin, God doesn't share their views. He chose disciples. He taught them. He said "Go and Teach...). Why? Obviously, it creates change.

3.   The world has a direction and isn't completely understood. Sure, there are those, who will remain static. But there are those, who wake up after various measures of exposure to truth and comparisons.

4.   You cannot create change without selling that change. The ability to sell a claim, belief, product, or way of behaving requires a clear expression of what that change is and how it is more beneficial, as well as other factors. Ask any salesman.

5.   Murdered or threatened civil rights leaders and constancy towards an increasing, inferior direction all call for consideration, learning, planning, and appropriate action. That's especially true when the effects and rectifiable damages linger.

6.   Cowards take the easy way and boast a false claim of "Mind Your Own Business". There's a time for that and a time not to. I remember reading and hearing about women, who were pushing strollers through a park and got shot by a bullet meant for someone else. They were minding their own business. If they had a chance to come back and do it all over again, for preventive purposes, they would become activists. That's because, there are things that must be acceptable and things that must not be. Imagine, if failure means to relive a dramatic experience?

7.   To solve a problem requires taking an activist's approach. Otherwise, condemn them and never show up to support them. What could go wrong, when the other side is clearly determined, growing with advantage, technology, and resources? Escalating confusion is saying "It's not a time to be weak".

8.   Just because ignorance is popular, it doesn't mean you must join the parade and feed it. It's far more damaging, when an adult teaches others to be still, vulnerable, and accepting of a storm. Choose examples wisely. Always ask what the problem is, understand it, and revert it. Inventors and salesmen have made a killing in profits for this.

9.   After all, if you've ever debated your point successfully and recommend "Mind Your Business" on the same or similar subject, you'd have to be conflicted inside.

10.   You may choose to let go of the past; but that doesn't mean it's going to let go of you. When that means challenges ahead and you're going to face the poisonous food on your plate, do you eat it or begin to rectify the situation? When the problem is persistent, painful, damaging,

and authoritative in nature, what will you do about the authorities? Who or what influences the authorities?

11. No one person can bring change to a large population without support.

The Struggle and a War Share the Same Dynamics

1. A culture that rises to power, and successfully exercises control over others, has taken power from those they have power over.

2. When they have separated themselves from the others, rights, values, and freedoms will be distinguishable.

3. In a state of inequality, the outsider may travel to a place(s), where the environment may make him/her feel uncomfortable or at risk. The outsider may be subject to verbal and/or physical attack. Other's views of the outsider may be unsolicited and wrong. Instability runs amok; especially due to changes that may be frequent and/or unfair or takes an advantage of a weak position. One positioned next to another may be seen as out of place. Your quality of life depends on your position, which depends on whether the parameters above apply to you and/or how effective the parameters are. In this case, parameters are obvious. Any filtering process is part of the family of parameters that help create divide amongst the population.

4. The power culture will progress and the others will remain static or regress, duplicating resistant ways of the power culture, to sustain or reach a higher status. Because, to be favored is to be acceptable, social inclusion becomes a priority of those, whose priorities are to survive and make the best of their positions. The power culture, then, becomes cemented as it is supported.

5. Due to their status, underhanded and undermining abilities, transformational talents, superior appeal for support, power to control, and great ability to avenge obstacles to them and their interests, the power culture have garnered a clean reputation, regardless of association with right or wrong. They have situated themselves as "The go to People".

6. As a core model, like a child, he (The power culture) grew up, experimented, researched, won and lost, overtook and was overtaken; but, throughout time, history was accounted for. As time went by, he began to systematize more and more of his findings and grew more capable, taller, healthier, stronger, and more elusive, even if in appearance. His market matched him word for word, and move for move.

7. He could dance, as to scribble inside and outside of the line, all around a center point, demonstrating imperfection, which he encouraged. Even though, these were signs of the Devil, he was loved, in accordance to his support and duplicated elements and behaviors. As a matter of fact, he got his examples from the study of planets and the signs in the sky and other natural creations of the world. He imprinted his ways on all his creations and things he controlled, and him and his supporters, as well as copy-cat artists, danced accordingly.

8. But he is not always what he portrays to be or do, making him hard to follow, to know, and to predict, unless you have insider information. Not all who share a part of his traits are a part of his clan and vice versa. Be careful who and what you follow.

9.   In a war, one or more will pursue a plan, only to excel or to meet resistances. The resistances may mirror an opposing or incompatible source, but not necessarily so. However, it is more convincing to an outsider to see through the eyes of one side versus another and vice versa. Because the most experienced and capable can pull off a fraud, it is better to grasp the case from the largest picture.

10.   The contention will give a clue about the talents, resources, number, agenda, reach, power, potential whereabouts, and type of resistor(s).

11.   Time will dispense organized and coordinated events that hold a consistent and persistent, long-term pattern together. If all the facts are presented, they will answer all the questions, from decision to decision, move to move, and explanation to explanation. Otherwise, something didn't make it to and through evidence.

12.   The practitioners of fraud, who do wars regularly, are more sophisticated. They know about model lifestyles, their supporting conditions, including tensions, and how to recreate them.

13.   They know about model cases, their supporting conditions, unique ways of thinking from various walks of life, emotional behavior, how to feed it, and emphasize points, while keeping the trajectory safely away from them and turning the case over to an expert for study. The study is used to find a way to overcome obstacles that hinder success of the prosecutor's case, as seen in cases where the jury made a decision that they wouldn't have made, if certain information wasn't restricted from the case and where extortion, including false charges, was used to control the defendant.

14.   It's the timeliness of matters at key times and places that obviously disclose a hidden enemy, who maintains his/her/their agenda. The longer the time and trend, the more obvious that, which is hidden, is apparent, even predictable to a large degree, regardless of the use of various manners of influence. This is the evidence that is, likely, to be withheld or not considered.

15.   It's a mind game, designed to frame a case favorably. There's a fight over the control of procedures, information, intelligence, facts, reputation, abilities, favoritism, and outlook. The idea is to fit a defendant into a frame, developed for the creation and nourishing of a particular, inferior character and to sell it as a personal issue and to buy an agreement.

16.   A circus act, surrounding the defendant, attracts the thought of consistency, urgency, importance, and legitimacy to the case, in the eyes of an outsider. But a circus act manipulates the mind and emotional environment of the defendant, encouraging aggressive behavior that will, most likely, look like confirmation of accusations. It becomes a playing-field for experts, in which a defendant would feel the precision of effort to carry out an agenda. That is the stuff for a journal.

17.   When consistent, to a large degree, they will yield an imprint, which is a total or near total understanding of them that makes them predictable, for a time and over an area of related influences. They will, also, reflect their perception or understanding of you, to some degree.

18.   But, be aware of the strong ability to transform a matter in their favor, by utilizing an essential type of judge's way of processing information (including you and any carrier of judgment). Again, they desire a certain judge. That's especially true, when the idea is not known to one side and in error. So, sometimes, there's a fight over who the judge will be or whether he/she will be removed.

19.   At the same time, the influence may be the result of cultural awareness, resulting from cooperation and shared cultural practices, ideas, and agendas, which detail whom to influence and how. Herein, the enemy or challenger may be identified. The degree, in which they support your best interest, is the test here. If your best interests are not prioritized, the authorities and their supporters are your challengers. That's because the idea is not to destroy and/or profit, but to prevent false cases, fabricated cases, and real correctional procedures, which addresses causes of errors, especially matters that drive anxiety and desperation.

20.   In a competitive environment, advantage requires one to sustain the ability to be unpredictable and in control; so that outsiders will remain in the dark about expectations. Risks, especially heightened risk, says something about the unavailability of a sufficient, alternative opportunity. This type of environment, filled with many others, having the same behavior, is evidence of the managing style of their overseers. It says a lot about the overseers, just as the player in the game is ignorant of their oppressors' models. The overseers' techniques are emotionally felt and mentally perceived by the players through the precision of effort overtime and their results. In the end, they almost never become as strong as their providers of care.

21.   A win or wish may not come the way you want it. A loss may be more convenient. Homelessness may yield a sandwich, not a solution. You may go for it all, but may have to be thankful for what you have. A right may be short-term and a wrong may be long-term. If the other way around, you may be on the inside, a spy, or used for purposes of gathering information or for deceptive or influential means. But nothing may be black or white, or even consistent.

22.   All sides evolve from intelligence(s) gathered from the other(s) and newfound knowledge and abilities. Therefore, the remaining population will reflect protocols imposed upon them, even those implicated. But, to gain the most intelligence from the source you're testing or pursuing, you must observe and sample as much of the source, and its effects, as possible. You must be knowledgeable of the interactive nature of nature and human developments and reactions. The slightest details can mean the biggest advantage.

23.   To maintain advantage in the evolutionary process, it must be controlled. Control involves how matters develop and if it will, as well as how it will be distributed and/or perceived, if applicable. This type of control is dominated by those with the highest perception and greatest ability to affect matters of importance. If there have been unfortunate results that were unreasonably or unfairly derived in the past, control is in the wrong hands. Further evidence of control in the wrong hands are decisions that yield no permanent resolve of issue(s), directed animosity towards certain people, unscientific, and isn't dependent on accurate standards applied to all, which produces no conflict towards any natural scientific remedy or expression that lends itself to the natural balancing concept(s) of nature.

24.   The dynamics of the population must support the power culture and their infrastructure. Their interest will not only be to survive, but to prosper and to push the limits; because there's no one to stop them. The remaining population must be friendly, ill regards of the conditions of their livelihood. As the power culture excels in information, science, and technology, the remaining population becomes less of a concern, even powerless to attain equal grounds or to fight back. When power is ill-gotten and selfish, the concept of supporting the power culture becomes a self-denying or egoistic scheme.

25.   Are self-denying and/or egoistic schemes already happening? If so, legal cases for suits and crimes will be accepted and rejected by the higher powers of the power culture. Success will

be decided by the interests of those in position to create and decide the standards to be met, for consideration and acceptance. Do the results show inclinations towards certain races or evade others, based on conditions outside their control or reasonably chosen due to some circumstances imposed upon them? Does the whole of the power culture have to be considered to minimize conflict, even at the expense of the remaining population?

26.   The power culture may be of various races; but those races may, also, be on various levels of power, depending on the existence of an environment(s) that is favorable to certain types. Equal treatment may or may not be the solution; in any case, it's about proper treatment that leads to unification of beliefs and efforts that bring improvement and perfection to the world.

27.   Understand when the unquenchable fire exists. The source is authoritative, afflictive, scientific, mysterious to a point, and the solution depends on them and their interests. And, also, the only solution provided or known is something that, reasonably, should and may increase the intensity of fire (Entrapment of a demonic type). Moreover, the demonic influence may circumvent any effort to prevent the event from occurring again.

28.   The greatest source of fire is within you. It's moody with love and hate, fulfillment and hunger, happiness and depression, intelligence and ignorance, content and disappointed, pleasure and pain, convenience and struggle, pride and humility, confident and despair, sensibility and baselessness, progression and regression, as well as eagerness and fear. The ability to undermine and prompt any of these feelings are known and manipulated all the time, even naturally. Like notes, they tame you, if you let it.

29.   The impractical use of influence can promote emotional and mental confusion, potentially leading to the appearance or condition of being eccentric. Process it and record it; then you'll hone into the plan that operates behind the scenes.

30.   Impulsiveness and the following of a crowd that is insensitive to the nature of life will, at times, lead to error, in the likeness of the blind leading the blind. The tamed will evolve from the wrong foundation, which bestowed them with an aggressive attitude, like a plant reflecting the conditions of its environment, past to present.

31.   Their mentality and environment will appear testy, conflicting, and divided, even against their best interests to some degree. They will prioritize their feelings over the expression of the unified operation of the scientific world. This may be due to a lack of knowledge and prioritizing means of operation that have brought success to others, like some competitive scheme.

32.   They will seek resolution, potentially right or wrong. When desperation appears, especially in the midst of ignorance and entrapment, the wrong way may take priority, depending on strength of character. But strength of character can be undermined here. Because competitiveness comes from a contest between one or more sources, leading to a win at the expense of another, in an exchange of values, anxiety looms. It's a place or condition where eruptions occur. What follows is a balancing act that can lead to deception, domination, theft, and murder.

33.   Vulnerabilities are opportunities and schools are a training ground; so, life's challenges tend to walk through the doors of the naive, who are prepared for a path of prey or predatory status. For many, the game begins too soon and/or feels indifferent to an ideal solution, if raised to perceive the laws of tact and fairness for all.

34.   Others look the other way, as if to pretend the choice doesn't exist or whatever makes them feel better about life. Meanwhile, at some point, a war may be going on, even in their back yard. But, when they need help, there is no immediate support. Many may remember their lack of participation.

35.   Meanwhile, a war may be going on, even in their back yard. But, when they need help, there are no immediate support. Everybody may remember their lack of participation.

36.   Many will talk about their so-called power to overcome; but they ignore the lack of control over others, needed for cooperation or support. Any leader has to gain a following through effort(s) and, therefore, demonstrate his/her abilities. Not all are leaders. Not all should be. An audience has to exist for a leader to exult upon. Not all audiences should have a leader. The Creator is the only One, who is Good and needs no one for Him to exist and to achieve.

37.   This is how the underclass is undermined for a profit; the normal or moral functionality of events are hindered or rendered useless or inconsistent. Who controls the authoritative population?

38.   After all, a chemical operation lies beneath their ability to control the self. Absence of the knowledge and ability to control is an absence of power. But, yet, the higher class is knowledgeable of such a subject and has created products, demonstrating their knowledge, ability, and control, in comparison. Much of the environment lies in dependency upon them and at the mercy of them.

39.   The management of underlying issues requires increased perfection of character, as the level and power of influence broadens. There is no room for trust issues. But, so it is with any field of science that brings influence upon any of the population, which gives more power to those, who understand.

40.   What follows is the importance of ethics; but ethics are as properly written, implicated, monitored, and enforced as the perfection of characters and their practice of due diligence, to assure the proper use and safety of the methods and products produced.

41.   They represent a knowledgeable population capable of cross-examining the work of their peers to put counterbalance and equilibrium in their places.

42.   Their work and the quality of their work are perceivable as conditions of the environment and everyone and everything in it, as well as the world around us.

43.   Of course, their limits are dependent on their knowledge and intelligence; but what do they do with what they already have? What motivates them? What are their motives?

44.   So, the oppressed become more and more like the core culture and their interests; but, generally, in a corrupt environment, only one receives its recompense and only one receives its punishment. It's the operation of "You are what you create" in affect. We're in an atmosphere, where an adjustment in the smallest matter may present huge consequences in another(s). What is good and what is bad? What is sustained and/or intensified? What was known? Who was involved? What is reasonable and what is not?

45.   In the end, we find that only those, who operate on the solution side are of God. Others operate in the pre-stage, middle stage, and/or post-stage of events, sustaining or intensifying fire(s). One group has the most influence upon the world. When one has a foot on both sides of the fence, one side will cancel the other; unless he/she exercises constraint to leave matters in

conflict. Then, the element of conflict chokes his/her good nature into non-existence; because it is a relative of hate.

Professional versus Hacker

1.　As a subject-matter is observed, a researcher attempts to equate his/her understanding of a matter in question, with real-time behavior of the subject studied under various environmental conditions. In the process of profiling the matter, general characteristics come to mind, like abilities, usefulness, purpose, qualities, limits, motivators, motivation, obligations, recourse, drivers, practices, resources, dependencies, exchanges, flexibility, category, habits, substitution, adaptation, ideal environment, contagious environment, inhibitors, evolution, how achievements are made, potential enhancements or regulators, and so on.

2.　After researching and experimenting, intelligence is gathered and exhibited as a model in machine form.

3.　On one side of intelligence, elements are possessed to assess, mimic, predict, and diagnose the matter in question. On the other side of intelligence, elements are possessed to re-direct, frame, manipulate, and control the matter in question, when necessary.

4.　Both can become efficient and effective, but only one is a professional and the other a hacker.

5.　The professional solves problems and attempts to expose the hacker and/or disruptive source. The hacker serves the part of the world, which is profiting from confusion and domination. While both are associated with transformation, the hacker seeks transformation from healthy, appropriate, or moral conditions to their opposites. The hacker does not attempt to publicly expose the professional, but to transform his/her image and riches. Like the professional, there is no subject that the hacker has no interest in; because all things are connected.

6.　The professional is in as much control of the world as the quality of intelligence is known in the world, on a per subject basis, and he/she is as elastic as the intelligence possessed.

7.　However, the hacker has an agenda, which doesn't allow him/her to consider and/or give credibility to competing interests and values that disrupt his/her objectives and goals. The hacker's weakness is giving a solution to his/her intense creations, whether in response or initiation. Instead, he/she seeks to justify destruction and death, his/her main qualities and destinies. The hacker favors, only, ideas and solutions that garner favor for his/her selfish agenda.

8.　The professional and the hacker may be indiscernible, at times; because the hacker, pretentiously, borrows from the professional and/or legitimately steals from the target of interest, in a scheme to appear upright, for deceptive means.

9.　What ensues is transformation or increased confirmation towards good character, as well as temptation and motivation of known traits of the subject in question, known to yield favorable responses under those circumstances. Any success, over a period of time, demonstrates that the hacker knows how to hustle the subject in question.

10.   Due to the need to be deceptive, the means of tracing may be disrupted and may appear incoherent, with the exhibited parts and/or reinterpretations displaying favor towards the hacker. The hacker's contributions may be downplayed enough or dismissed to offset blame towards the subject of interest. Even when the subject in question has no known efficient and effective choice, blame may be forced in the direction of the subject in question.

11.   But a hacker's success is dependent upon the makeup of the environment, which allows him/her to operate successfully.

The Glyph

1.   The glyph is a model of your logical scheme of focus, of the world, and of the universe, which can be compared to the glyph of reality. You can be hacked and/or healed by it. All you have to do is participate in life, its challenges, and wisdom. Your participation gives insight into your glyph.

2.   The interaction between your glyph and the glyph of reality is always balancing. See Mathew 7:2.

3.   The focus should always be on how everything fits in with everything else, including how matters balance out or get out of balance. This is how your glyph becomes more informative and instructive. So, your glyph is a reflection of your experiences and how much you applied efforts to seek out information. But it will also reflect the effects of successful deceptive schemes (Hacking).

4.   The glyph is scientific, because everything that happens within it is a formula, and, without a formula, nothing ever happens. Ever! The formula is useful for repeating for confirmation and later for the detection of inner changes of the vehicle or carrier of concern. It could mean a disruptive or healing source.

5.   Astrologers have created archetypes and assembled them all around the glyph as a model for the various areas of life and how matters unfold and develop. While many have used it for divination, I'm focused on where matters are in the scheme of things (Formula), in which matters can appear, progress, regress, and/or cancel. We see it all the time; but, yet, it can be hard to notice and follow the background activity(s), especially to evidence it. You can see the hacker's specialty in that.

6.   I see the glyph as the earth hanging from seemingly nothing, with outer space all around it and in the background. Even though we may see nothing, it's obvious that there is something there, seeing the earth is stable without perceivable support.

7.   We can look around and see how one matter affects the other, like how land conditions change and how human conditions and lifestyles change with it. But, not just human relations, but how animals and plants adapt, as well as changes in the distribution of various types. To have precise intelligence and ability, we must possess as much of the intelligence that the glyph of reality reveals to us.

8.   A mountain climber is successful with the right knowledge and resources to achieve higher levels, giving us an example of how to solve problems and/or advance in any endeavor. So, let's take a brief look at the mountain climber.

9.   The mountain climber has tools, like a pair of mountaineering boots, crampons, and an ice axe. The mountaineering boots are for gaining more of a sure footing. Crampons are shoes with spikes, which are worn when ice is on the surface navigated. Ice axes are used to aid in ascending and descending the levels in a vertical range.

10.   When a hill is the obstacle between where we are and where we need to go, physical effort is the primary means to get there, besides the knowledge of direction(s). But, when it comes to a mountain, we may need to adapt with skills and a range of tools that may be needed. That's not to mention the challenges that popup storms can present. Popup storms are used by hackers to sustain, alter, and/or slow the direction of progress.

11.   The most important part of mountain climbing is pinpointing stable and unstable positions, whether up or down. Upon stable grounds, you can sustain yourself, descend from, or pull yourself upwards. These are the positions that professionals and hackers, alike, work with to progress their agenda. When you're less perceptive and knowledgeable as they are, all you can see is how stable and unstable points of interest were in your journey. This information is a formula. It's more of a legitimate formula, when you apply complete and due diligence in your efforts to succeed, including to learn how to proceed successfully.

12.   When the formula is compared to the identical example of success, an ideal concept, or another successful person's method, we can begin to see a correlation and/or a difference. If a difference, we must investigate, which may be resisted. Differences can mean the work of a hacker, who may not want you to know his scheme and how he manages it. That may be the only evidence you see, initially or without any effort to unveil additional information. But, as you proceed to find your answers or resolve your issue(s), the hacker may parallel your moves at key points (Stable positions).

13.   For many, they apply almost zero effort in using due diligence to resolve their problems; instead, they thank God for what they have and are able to do. Therefore, they may climb or sink at the mercy of their case managers.

14.   Because the professional and the hacker share the knowledge of pivotal points, they both know the evidence that supports your belief and what is questionable or unfounded, including those pivotal points that signal one or the other, as the culprit. It is known, even if both posture themselves as angels, but are actually hackers.

15.   Your only knowledge may be evidence of a lack of due diligence and/or an open mind; by this, you may see the power of authority at work. That's especially true, when the matter, for some reason, has come to an unresolved end, more so when complete with further afflictions.

16.   A hacker is the only one associated with a fraud; any other error is an accident.

17.   The end is always filled with dynamics that affect a frame of mind or glyph.

18.   A person is always in the midst of dynamics that affect a frame of mind or glyph.

19.   All things, including people, are part of the dynamics that affect a frame of mind or glyph.

20.   People respond and initiate various matters that affect other people, like laws, various representations of competition, and social treatment.

21.   But, many teach or believe not to blame others for your problems. Yet, many of them divide up and blame political parties and their supporters for the events of their environment. They tried to teach me that in college, where they preferred to hack my mind with topics for essays, use reverse psychology, and discredit my knowledge, instead of teaching me how to be a paralegal. Since I was led away from graduation and solid knowledge of paralegal studies, I was affected by others. The point is 'blaming others' is commonly legit.

22.   Any belief that leads to action that afflicts harm upon another is a legitimate reason to blame another, even if the entire world is the culprit.

23.   Any belief that can potentially afflict harm upon another is a threat to those affected.

24.   But, everyone is part of a formula…..

25.   The formula starts when you are born into a situation.

26.   The moral of the story is 'The dynamics sustain or change the world', not an individual or less influential group of people. In other approach is a fraud. Even in the Bible, it states at Ephesians 6:12 that we don't wrestle against flesh and blood, but against the evil powers that be.

The Power of Feng Shui

1.   Feng Shui is promoted as a means of positioning matters in your home to attract life force, called chi, which can be negative or positive. I read about this a long time ago and never took it seriously. But, yesterday evening, something started impressing upon my mind, just not enough to be clear enough to perceive the details. So, I couldn't do anything with it.

2.   So, I must've fallen asleep with the question on the top of my head; because it came back with a deeper impression.

3.   I knew it would be something I would be excited to tell you about, because it's in line with carrying out the objective of "There Are Three Truths", which is to enlighten with Truth and to expose the Immoralists.

4.   I take the promoted definition of Feng Shui as symbolic. I will say, how you decorate your home does have an effect on you and others, in accordance to how it is perceived. So, it will not have the same effect on everyone, whether good or bad. The attraction of good or bad luck is questionable to me, in this sense. Now, let's move on to its more obvious application.

5.   First of all, let's redefine Feng Shui to make it more understandable. Feng Shui is the practice of positioning something in opposition, in favor, as complementary, challenging, or as incompatible, if not a combination. It includes positioning a subject-matter or person against itself. Feng Shui represents the two-way value system, where negative and/or positive chi may be attracted.

6.   Do you want a metaphorical example? Let's use medication. Medication is assembled with elements that challenge and overcome an unwanted obstacle. While that may be good, the creator, who chose the elements and assembled them, may have an agenda that entails mixed reviews, but maybe not. But, maybe, it's a solution that draws support for the views of the creator, which may invoke a favorable response. That response can be an intelligent one or one that is sure to draw an unintelligent decision, with supporting elements, from one limited in intelligence. It's an art of design to attract an intended development or outcome.

7.   If you feel in the dark about chemistry, in the form of medication, and wonder why all the diseases and sicknesses that exist, it's because the source thrives in darkness. If you reason from a dark or partially dark foundation, you may serve evil forces.

8.   Remember, no one wants to destroy themselves or do anything that leads to that end. So, something has to be done to make it seem so, and others must be convinced that it is so, or see and desire an advantage in believing a lie, if not all of the above.

9.   Medication has been evolving over time and controlled by the most influential; so you'll see a pattern developing extensively and predictively, even through all of its twists of fate. The developments and results, over time, yield the direction and intents of events.

10.   Feng Shui is part of nature, but the use of it to materialize an idea makes it unnatural. Here, the mind searches for or attracts values that parallel it's main idea to create the most successful outcome. It's most effective on a detailed level and in the hands of a capable source. As a victim, it may feel as if to be lead into a trap and/or molded into a way of thinking and behaving.

11.   Because Feng Shui is used to carry out intent, knowing or discovering the purpose is a good guide for predicting future development(s) and/or outcome(s). It allows for the greatest chance to see through the game of foolery and the rain of distraction. Remember, a purpose of intent follows known guidelines to achieving any associated elements and meeting or falling in line with established objectives that materializes the goal.

12.   When we walk into a pleasant environment, it makes us feel a certain way and, in turn, we think a certain way. It can create a habit of going to this place to gain the same feeling(s) and thought(s). In such a case, we witness how a positioning of effects causes or arouses another value, which causes or arouses another to materialize, like a chain-reaction of effects. A chain-reaction of effects can be done by going to or enduring an unpleasant experience, as well. Feng Shui has programmable effects, in which devastating or habitual events may be used to create.

13.   To identify the system and its direction, you must pay attention to the direction of chi or the dynamics.

14.   Because Feng Shui is used to carry out intent, knowing or discovering the purpose is a good guide for predicting future development(s) and/or outcome(s). It allows for the greatest chance to see through the game of foolery and the rain of distraction. Remember, a purpose of intent follows known guidelines to achieving any associated elements and meeting or falling in line with established objectives that materializes the goal.

15.   When we walk into a pleasant environment, it makes us feel a certain way and, in turn, we think a certain way. It can create a habit of going to this place to gain the same feeling(s) and thought(s). In such a case, we witness how a positioning of effects causes or arouses another value, which causes or arouses another to materialize, like a chain-reaction of effects. A chain-

reaction of effects can be done by going to or enduring an unpleasant experience, as well. Feng Shui has programmable effects, in which devastating or habitual events may be used to create.

16.   To identify the system and its direction, you must pay attention to the direction of chi or the dynamics.

17.   In an inferior system, a hated person may be presented with social resistance. If prolonged, the health of the person's body begins to release chemicals, designed to help enable survival tactics, but can harm the body overtime. The lack of success, due from social resistance, may attract a negative perception of the person's ability to put forth logical and sufficient effort to survive or to prosper. The person may be seen as, potentially, acting out of desperation, if the conditions surrounding the person is extreme or sustains long enough. The same person may change, inwardly, towards a menacing attitude that may lead to aggressive acts, whether against the self or another, if not both.

18.   The self-sabotaging acts may lead this individual into a smaller confined space of freedom, where those of the same type recycle negative chi upon each other. The authoritative administrators of negative chi may relax rules and standards to allow this chi to prosper more than usual, including the limiting of law enforcement staff.

19.   Because the environment must be divided against one another, to build wealth from the losses of another, the knowledge of Feng Shui must be secretive to a great degree and denied by the administrators to a large degree. Otherwise, recognition of the Feng Shui concept would allow for an implosion of the entire system. That very fact materializes the need to carry out selfish acts of survival, even to protect those most dear to the heart. It, also, causes the development of insensitivity, especially due to the overwhelming amount of energy to achieve altruistic results.

20.   When you see certain people in an adverse position to matters that are essential for a healthy life, including a good reputation and possessing equal opportunities, you are possibly watching the intentional practice of Feng Shui in action. The confirming evidence is in the ability to resolve the problem vs the response, the understanding of what's happening vs the response, and the recognition of Feng Shui mechanics vs participation.

21.   What drives Feng Shui is the magic of how one value causes another to materialize and which type. Observing the system enables a practitioner to practice successfully through duplication. The deep knowledge is not always necessary to know.

22.   You always use Feng Shui. Always! And, if you don't acknowledge it and use it effectively, you most likely will have a harder time in a competitive world, like we live in today.

23.   When you observe all things that you think are associated with a matter of focus and is responsible for the development(s) and outcome, you just observed the Feng Shui of events. It may be the weaknesses and strengths against another of the same, with nature helping to mitigate the results.

24.   Chi transforms from one stage of development to another, taking on different names based on its role in the endeavor. This is how we get our definitions by observing, depicting, and giving it a name, which identifies the step or development in the process. Chi happens naturally and must be learned to help control it.

25.   Your best efforts to control Chi may be aborted by matters or people having more authority, which or who may be beyond your reach or influence. The sources outside your control may be authoritative or semi-authoritative, if not a combination, where semi-authority is not grounded in truth, but in a social trend or tradition held to be superior.

26.   You may observe another as not as mature as you. That's because you're comparing your focus of the matter (Feng Shui) with the other.

27.   Feng Shui is as complicated as it is simple. It depends on how complex the matter is. Feng Shui is the understanding of the natural positions of matters in a polar world, which creates a sound mind that is only correlated with reality. People, who try to define or explain a matter falsely, can be caught with this kind of knowledge, even logically trapped into believing. But, they may not show approval and leave with no sound reply. I've won numerous debates with Feng Shui, including creating stories, without knowing what it really was.

28.   When something surprises or has even an ounce of mystery, your Feng Shui is incomplete and signifies hidden knowledge and/or enemies. So, where there's mystery, Chi offers the opportunity to learn something new.

29.   While you may hold strength in the practice of Feng Shui, you may win, but the cost may be greater than the gain. Losers may resort to physical abilities to preserve or to overtake a position. Your ability to practice Feng Shui will respond successfully or unsuccessfully, if not just to quell the uprising.

30.   Feng Shui can be anywhere from a focus of a single subject to the focus of an entire world.

31.   A positive response, to those suffering from negative Chi, is the practice of the rules or Reiki, which entails any rules associated with reversing negative Chi.

32.   The knowledge of "There Are Three Truths" and the earlier Bible enhances the practice of Feng Shui. You may ignore Feng Shui, but you'll always be a part of it. You will always be influenced by it. So, your best stance is not in ignoring it, but in learning and fortifying your position in all matters of immediate concern and those, having the potential to be pressing and stressing.

33.   Feng Shui is a tool that can attract harmony, through the sharing of knowledge. However, there are people who use knowledge to the cost of another. Countering pursuits can be dangerous and a competitive environment exposes strengths to those, who may not deserve to know about it. But, at the same time, harmony should be the goal of all of us. We can do more together than apart.

34.   Now, the oppressed have been around for a long time, giving opportunities to study and understand how it can occur and from what type of positions it can be most prevalent. But, if that type of knowledge was effectively put to use, the experienced administrators would have caused one of the most reliable cash flows to become unreliable. So, every case must build upon its own merits, to hold society in a vulnerable position.

35.   So, the entire world must be dark and deceptive to the under-privileged and the true meaning of justice and it's execution must be minimized.

36.   The enemies of God believe in working with ignorance to dominate another for a profit.

37.   A man has kept all his secrets to secure his position as the man of the house; then he died unexpectedly, even to him. His family missed him every time they endured hardships.

38.   Another man taught his family how to survive without him and made sure they practiced successfully, as he could possibly muster up, as if he weren't there.

39.   Which man of the house would you prefer?

The Hierarchical Level of Sinners

The Highest Level of Sin

1.   No one can sin higher than the fallen angels. They came from a perfect environment needing of nothing and an environment equal to the qualities of God.

2.   There's nothing to explain, when all was understood. There's nothing to buy when all, within reason, was offered. Therefore, a fate is sealed as the former is unreasonably rejected.

The Second Level of Sin

1.   On the second level, there exist the highest to the lowest of authorities. This is the first level, in which "Drive" is considered. Here, drive has the lowest consideration, if considered at all.

2.   Drive is as reasonably considered as its source is essential, perceived, assessed, understood, and manageable. It is, also, reasonably considered as its possessor is conscious and according to the level of a programmed conscience. So, we don't expect an animal to act like a more developed human or a more developed human to act like a less developed animal.

3.   Many, at this level, possess heightened visibility due to exposure to a greater number of experiences, as a result of contacts and the introduction of various circumstances and situations of the people and societies. Heightened visibility, also, comes from reading, research, and investigations.

4.   Visibility is, also, heightened by the known existence of essential sources of knowledge, like a Bible, treatise, reference, expert etc. It doesn't matter if such medium was sought or not, only the knowledge of its existence and known essentiality is of importance here. That's because of the duty of care and due diligence that's naturally inherited in the position, after a takeover inherits the responsibility of administration. Administration requires a moral direction to avoid the manifestation of sin, in the most reasonable manner possible.

5.   In this position, an administration cannot be setup in a manner that it can be overwhelmed with information. A takeover must be capable to fulfill its moral duty or be declared unfit and must forfeit its powers to a more capable source, to avoid sin.

The Third Level

1.   Being under the guide and manipulation of the authorities, as well as the influences coming from elsewhere, drive is stronger and must be considered as it is effective. Drive has the ability to overtake, even if it just thrives in weaknesses and/or ignorance.

2.   People, on this level, are similarly tasked with the same responsibilities of authorities, just on the grounds of reasonable expectations, which also depend on development, growth, and responsibility. So, the mechanics of how sin came about is part of the equation of determining the degree of guilt. A sinner is as guilty as he/she is purposeful, understanding, and demonstrative of concentrated skills (Deliberate), compared to the quality of drive, which may or may not allow resistance. For an example, a deceived person cannot be reasonably held responsible for matters that materialize as the result of deception. Then, where is the control? The same is true if the person is overwhelmed.

3.   The most crucial judgment of those, on this level, is based on their likeness and support of the erroneous sources above, while sufficiently aware of their errors.

4.   Secondly, it's based on how the rest of the world is inflamed with imperfections by the individual's current behavior.

5.   Thirdly, it's based on circumstances surrounding consciousness and the ability to expand on it and becoming adherent to a reasonably established conscience. As a result, a frictional attitude would result towards a corrupt establishment. In a world of deception and blindness, the aim may, potentially, be misdirected and/or the efforts of corrections faulty.

6.   It is because of an immoral system and beliefs, which places higher values on immorality, that righteousness is challenged by the riches of the world. Such systems and beliefs create an environment that is accepting of the fallen angels and allows them to establish and advance the operations of their agendas.

7.   While drive is more considered on this level, its importance recedes as anxiety levels diminish and are relaxed, while completely dissolved in the case of greed.

8.   Notice of immoral funding:

9.   The funding of an inferior source should be declared illegal whenever the source funded is a competitor of, what is declared proper and righteous. Likewise, all decisions should be scrutinized as in support or resistant to the other.

10.   While an argument may be raised for either side, the reality of natural, moral, and calculated results reveals the true judgment of a course of action.

11.   Illegal funding should be classified as a source, as knowingly supporting a cause, whether material or in spirit, which is detrimental to the proper development and/or survival of a diplomatic or elastic source.

12.   Any corrupt or corrupting source is an immoral and backwards representation of a correctional and prevention institution/society.

Combat Drills

1. Combat drills utilize metrics associated with unique sectors in the environment, social society, or market. These metrics are elements that have effective influence on measures, such as extent, quantity, quality, endurance, growth, depth, support etc. The overtaking of metrics is destined to regulate a matter of concern. Naturally, measures reflect the condition of the environment, in which the object of study inhabits, combined with its unhindered capabilities.

2. Challenges to the security, operations, and policies are launched in exchange for responses that signal hidden information, changes, and/or confirm existing knowledge of the object-in-question.

3. Responses, prescripts, collaboration, functions, timing, principles, concepts, imprint, technology, organization, mentality, talents, strengths, weaknesses, variations, versatility, boundaries, restrictions, regulators, support, respect, and evolution are many of the elements sought in combat drills.

4. The resulting elements of combat drills are used to carry out objectives and goals of the administrator(s) of challenges. They are usually tasked to force-divide a sum of people in polar directions in any endeavor, through some undermining method.

5. Combat drills can be used for preparation for control, war, and/or court. The plot can be complex and as wide-ranging as the perceived interacting elements.

6. As a victim of combat drills, you can feel the Chi within. Whenever you attempt to resist its thrust, it bottles up inside. You can feel the message in as much as you are sensitive, detecting, and understanding of the elements. The method, usually, contains repetitious or similar characteristics that build thrust and confirm the message over a period of time; but the culmination of methods can be very contrasting to one another, but tasked to yield similar or same results.

7. Temporary rewards or slightly better circumstances, combined with hardships in the opposite direction and false examples, may encourage fulfillment of that, which is thrust upon you. Combat drills is the most effective method of witchcraft, which has the highest tendency to force an individual, and whole nations, out of character.

8. Combat drills help to discover the elements of the object of study, not only to defeat or overcome it, but to strengthen the resistant efforts of a matter encouraged to be successful, again aiding the divide.

9. As the method(s) begin to demonstrate success or are perceived to be faced with changes, policies are established or amended, to sustain or re-establish the direction of a matter.

10. All the reasons for defeat or failure to succeed combine to shed light on the method of divide, as perceived across all endeavors, sectors, and fields of study.

Development of a Belief System: Pure or Impure?

1.   A belief system is encouraged by some scheme of events, which warrants questions.

2.   When a belief doesn't originate from real events, it may come from a conception that happens to materialize, for some reason. It may be a combination of both.

3.   But a belief starts out as a conception, which generally requires interpretive skills, before it is perceived as an idea. The idea is distinguished by the acknowledgement of a part(s) of past experiences that it parallels. Because an idea is meant to progress or clarify a matter, it has a relational and creative side, which makes it, potentially, progressive or alerting. It may be progressive towards resolution or improvement.

4.   A belief system is watchful of cycles, rhythms, themes, and trends, as well as disruptions, disassociated and/or foreign elements. Its alertly nature is heightened by the importance of a matter or severity of consequences, making it vulnerable to external control. It is inclined towards programmed behavior, as a reflection of its observations. That's because a belief and a belief system are a copy of perceived phenomena.

5.   The programming of a belief or belief system may respond in a heightened state, when control over a threatening subject-in-question is not found.

6.   Beliefs require connections that are confirmed by interactivity, supporters, supplies, and verification; while disconnections are confirmed by their unmet standards that identify missing connections and potential arrogance in defense.

7.   However, there are times when connections are incomplete, and behavior appears to be following a belief; this is an adoption.

8.   Adoptions may be forced, when there are no known dependable alternatives. This is how arrogance can upend a logical expression, before it can get a start. As a result, false logic materializes as a resolution to obstacles produced as a result of arrogance.

9.   For whatever the reason, adoptions occur as a result of adapting to phenomena, especially if oppressive. A long time ago, myths were created to help us adapt to and understand our environment. They helped provide the foundation for science: the articulate expression of reality. Oppressive phenomena, including sales that appeal to the emotions, may cause the adoption of sinful and criminal behavior and, thus, the unjustified appearance of arrogance. Long-term effects can result in programmed behavior.

10.   An accurate belief or belief system is an exact copy of reality and is confirmed by the observation of the same and is as thorough as it parallels the changes of phenomena.

11.   A belief system prospers under unhindered conditions, in a natural and logical environment, balancing and progressing in sophistication and resolution, which threatens to eliminate arrogance. It has natural rights to logical expression, due to the fact that it is Truth in performance. And, any effort against Truth, for the purpose of corrupting, is a sin.

12.   Speaking of sin, many have been made accountable for sins and crimes that were engineered, as a result of profile information attained from the observation of the behavior of logical expression (Truth). Logical expression, because it contains the expression of cause(s) and effect(s), details of accountability lie within. Within the stream of cause(s) and effect(s) are

expressions of power, intelligence, and other advantages that emit values of accomplishments and disadvantages that allow damages to occur.

13.   A profile of such realities enables the ability to identify the culprit(s) and resolve towards improvement of process (Sin) or towards resolution(s).

14.   A belief system, which filters and processes external environmental effects, holds one of the connections to the emotional environment. It also looks back to assure accuracy of build and progress, but that requires a leading standard.

15.   The leading standard for an act or event is a purpose; but, on a higher level, is a religion. Without a religion, the two systems, belief system and arrogance system, have no director and, thus, no way of appraising progress and accuracy. They both look back and sustain, reform, or improve upon their progress. The approved or accepted elements are perceived in a comparison to past and future methods and results, at any point in time, as well as a comparing of both systems to one another, including rejections.

16.   The values their system produces, approves, and/or utilizes for beneficial means is what separates the system of belief from the system of arrogance.

17.   Arrogance is the negative side of pride. It materializes as a result of a need to present a strong stance to protect something felt or perceived to be important or of high value. So, it will utilize fraud to hold incompatible parts together. It is a competitor to logic and an element of demonism.

18.   Arrogance will not, sufficiently and voluntarily, recognize and/or aid the efforts of logical expressions, when the consequences of losing something, perceived as a greater value, is at issue. But, the chance of being exposed as illegitimate could be a game-changer, except in a strong arrogant stance, where there's no perceived consequences.

19.   Arrogance is strong, when the possessor is sufficiently more knowledgeable or advantageous than the opposition. It can, therefore, organize and express the importance of a matter as crucial, while denying the effects of its negative side, with intent to preserve the issue in question. It may express or imply that the ongoing issue is of a lower priority.

20.   The actors of arrogance and their subordinates, forced to adapt to their system, give off a sense of being conflicted within; although they may appear and sound confident in expression(s). "Confident and conflicted within" is a reliable symptom of arrogance. But, don't expect an admittance; but don't be surprised by one, either. That's the kind of environment they present.

21.   Arrogance is famous for the statement, "Because I said so".

22.   When arrogance is responsible for the assembly of policies, it will use cause(s) and effect(s) to initiate and preserve its interests, which may include punishing the resulting, corrupted actor, while maintaining the status of director of circumstances, engineering the environment for cause. As a result of "Confident and conflicted within", the occurrence remains stuck in a cycle and profitable only for the arrogant.

23.   Arrogance can only attempt to minimize logical expressions, because it utilizes logical expressions as independent clusters to control the sense and experience of reality and physical means to enforce adoption. The clusters may be held together or connected by a lie or social behavior.

24. Arrogance cannot be pure, or it will be obviously false. Therefore, mysteries are the weaknesses that possessors of belief systems can explore and resolve, to the dismay of arrogance, with the exception of allies.

25. Arrogance thrives in an environment of physical control, advantageous conditions, as a result of favoritism. To preserve its home, it must resist resolutions that threaten its environment.

26. The identified, supreme element begins to fall when inverses and/or subordinates start to disappear and actors of arrogance become increasingly pure, under the same circumstances, which attracts the desire for war or a favorable change of circumstances for themselves, which validates a previous act as arrogance.

Poke-A-Game

1. Poke-A-Game is fun and rewarding for a lot of people, usually superiors, but not the puppets.

2. This is a game where they poke you where they want you to go. Whoever has the most power wins.

3. Oh, you don't think this is real? I learned it in court and law school.

4. I've already shown how people steal, disrupt lives, and create profitable behaviors inside people. The pokers are protected and the poke is downplayed. In the end, the problem is you, if you're the puppet.

5. Poking has a lot to do with sculpting you, your life, and everything around you. The game will take an advantage of your weaknesses and kill your strengths.

6. If you're having major issues or a lot of small ones, and you haven't thought of it as the poke-a-game, you're not even close to competing. What's sad is your life can be ruined by it.

7. In court, in Minnesota, I was stopped for driving on Nicollet Ave with no insurance. I was going through the same financial struggles, I've already detailed. So, I couldn't afford auto insurance; plus, my income was too unstable. Some researcher said "There is no defense for driving without insurance". So, I lost. So, this is proof from the court, itself.

8. In law school, I was expelled by using groups and frivolous complaints; so, I was stuck with the student loan bill, which I have not successfully contested.

9. I complained about someone causing hostile environments on my jobs and got slapped with a false charge and a delusional disorder.

10. The FBI doesn't respond, because they've successfully instituted the delusional disorder and can, now, wait for the poke-a-game to run its course.

11. The poke-a-game is run by the law of arrogance, which includes sweeping provocative matters under a rug and profiting from the effects.

12.   Although I don't condone raiding the capitol, I see the disbarment of the defensive attorney, mentioned in this article, as a practice of the law of arrogance. Let me tell you why.

13.   When a matter comes up in court, it should be diligently and fully contested by both sides, the defense and the prosecution; So that laws, favoring both sides can fully be discovered and developed and lead to prevention and proper resolve.

14.   But, in this case, politicians don't have standards that they have to abide by, like attorneys. The development and administration of laws help make the poke-a-game effective or ineffective, even through silence on one side of the scale(s). Law enforcement, or the lack of, has the same effect.

15.   So, leaving a defendant defenseless is part of the poke-a-game that takes an advantage of the person's weaknesses and robs him/her of a strength, for profitable endeavors.

16.   Everyone is elastic and connected to the environment; so no one is exempt from the effects of the poke-a-game. Historically, the too big have fallen.

Violation of Due Diligence?

1.   Anyone, who is found without excuse for time, without justification for abstention, slacking in abilities, and/or not having weighed and measured, is obviously in violation of due diligence, in accordance to its value and purpose.

The Tempting of Jesus was a Symbolic Example

1.   Many think the tempting of Jesus was something that, largely, pertains to him; so, you'll see a lot of church people, who couldn't prevent themselves from succumbing to temptation, joyfully talking about it.

2.   Jesus was the illustrated example to follow, at least in this case, if not all. You see, Satan could not have designed this world so successfully without the succumbing to temptations.

3.   He had to do it in levels of success, giving the least to the bottom and more towards the top, until worldly wealth was the greatest among those who carried out his most crucial tasks. This type of distribution encouraged the moving up or desire to participate in the debilitating concepts against mankind and the stymying of God's values.

4.   The temptation takes place under wild and needy circumstances, where you're offered a benefit in exchange for a wrong. The higher you climb, the more you have to synchronize with Satan's people and accept greater responsibilities. Sometimes, all that is needed is support. Other times, you must be engaged in destructive principles and concepts that support an evil cause, which may be disguised as heroic, but divisive.

5.   In respects to how much one gave of himself/herself for the offer of Satan, he/she in turn smothered the Son of God in controversy. In respects to the number of people, who succumbed to the offer, Satan's system became more effective with peer pressure.

6.   Many thought, they would actually see the devil under these conditions; but saw only his ambassadors. This signaled the fact that it wasn't about whom; it was more about principles and concepts. The signals of principles and concepts are the tools that expose a person's following, especially when the target is more willful than tempted or forced. In this way, they're all caught by the Detective.

7.   The Detective understands the difference between entrapment and due diligence, as well as adaptation and perseverance.

8.   There's nowhere to completely hide, because the results speak for themselves

The Waterfall

1.   Water demonstrates strength of character and resilience, while covering the violence within.

2.   It falls from, even, great distances, hits rocky ground, splits, and reassembles, as if nothing happened.

3.   The plunge is evidenced by the depth of the piercing of the earth, even giving a clue to time.

4.   But just as it pierced the earth, it was channeled and tamed to some degree by the earth.

5.   There it sits almost still, but at times blown by the wind and disturbed by the violence within.

6.   Yet it still fed and bathed the inhabitants and watered the flowers.

7.   Having been through it all and persevering, it still deceptively creates the appearance of a beautiful world, yet, you could see through it all.

The Monitoring System

1. A system of detecting and measuring, consisting of predictable data, based on historical developments, is an adaptive and evolving mind in action. It doesn't matter if it's purely mechanical or both human and mechanical.

2. It is aroused by threats to itself and its interests.

3. Those holding concealed facts that are deemed threatening by the monitoring system or that attempts to detonate it and/or its interests are subject to balancing acts or retaliation.

4. Balancing acts occur, when the matter is questionable or can be mediated by corrective measures that address the fundamental or mechanical issue(s).

5. Retaliation is simply a push back or a setback levied upon a challenger, who possesses a legitimate cause and, potential, solution.

6. The considerations and inconsiderations that produced the alert are a summary of what's being protected and what's not. This is where a nerve can be hit, so to speak. It's a trip wire in a minefield.

7. While it is advised to stay out of the engine compartment of functional area, you most assuredly won't get anything done, if you succumb to the advice. The most effective ways to address issues in a demonic world is a dangerous one. This fact is proof of its existence.

8. Many times, the challenger with a legitimate cause is stuck outside of the engine compartment and on the hood. Trapped between the engine compartment or functional area and the wind, the challenger is subject to damages.

A Well-Kept System

1. To maintain or improve a condition requires a system.

2. A working system requires tweaking in times of change.

3. Tweaking prevents unwanted changes and adjusts for greater effect(s) and efficiency.

4. Statistics demonstrate what is approved or favored, as well as how effective a plan is performing, through time.

5. If one works for the system, with sufficient knowledge of its operations and carries out its demands, is he/she innocent?

6. "If you keep doing what you're doing, you'll keep getting what you're getting" is not a new concept. Therefore, it signals intent. It may signal an effect of deception, addiction, or lower consciousness.

7. When an inferior agenda must be covered up, it must be secretly carried out or blurred with misconceptions. This signals intent, if that, which is covered up and known to be wrong, continues or repeats, without a stronger challenging and driving force.

8. Knowing these facts, we must find supporting facts on superficial levels and below.

The Dark House and the (Dim Light) Leader

1.   Darkness is any area where there is mystery and a lack of knowledge or awareness. The Prince of Darkness addresses any issues from here. He appears to have all the answers, but can't create change for the better, unless him and his advocates benefit most.

2.   In the dark, not only can evil operate more safely, but good can exercise its secrets to protect its manner of operation(s) as well.

3.   There's a leader of the house, who carries a dim light He leads the people through the house and the people seek him for his light. Because he has the dim light, they are as dependent upon him as they are without light.

4.   The "dim light" leader knows the limited sight of the people and keeps the light dim to control the people and their beliefs and actions. His light was as dim as the moon, in comparison to the sun.

5.   In the lower room, people were partying. However, their population was diminishing, but their giving of birth offset their rate of extinction to some degree. They idolized and adopted many of the ways of the "dim light" leader, because he possessed the wealth of the house and showed them the best way for them to live, as it pertains to them and their circumstances.

6.   Meanwhile, in the upper room, the "dim light" leader shed light on the wealth of the house and the ways of obtaining it. However, he maintained a dim light and, even, divided it amongst them. With light, there was power in accordance to its brightness. Now, they could specialize, but within bounds. They partied and celebrated their wealth, without guilt of conscience, for they idolized the "dim light" leader.

7.   While the light was divided in the upper room, the lower room generally had to find their way, for the most part. Imitating the upper room, they sought for position over another and to use the efforts and weaknesses of another to their benefit.

8.   Let it be noted that the reluctance to transgress upon another is a sign of weakness in a demonic system, which is likely to attract more transgressions and transgressors. This is why a poor response by protective authorities is a snare.

9.   Both rooms were against each other, because trust was rarely found and a threat always loomed, nearby or distant.

10.   Humans saw themselves as imperfect and erratic, while each seeing themselves as better and more excusable than another.

11.   Because of darkness, they never knew the "dim light" leader was the cause of it all. He was the only one, who could give an interpretation of the matters of darkness.

12.   Yet, one thing loomed and that was the shadow of darkness. It depicted most, if not all confusion, within its bounds and a growing number of threats with very little or no resolution. But who would dare set off an alarm?

13.   Seeing that he was the only one, who could provide an answer that couldn't be contested with proof, besides God, he cautiously moved forward with his agenda(s), creating a "Can't Prove It (CPI)" policy. The power in this policy were instructions on how to proceed outside the bounds of sensibility, which included how to recruit and use accomplices and create natural protections.

14.   Because they prioritized the riches of the earth and a demon and his demonic principles and concepts, their decisions entrapped them in an anti-human policy that included revenge plots against the population as a form of justice.

15.   Combined with the desire to compete for supremacy over another and to operate in opposition to God and His ways, this was the basis for their entrapment and eventual demise.

16.   The majority built the system that trapped everyone, while they used their power of control to escape responsibility and consequences.

17.   When the stream of morality is too weak or non-existent, recovery is unlikely.

18.   They were as trapped as they refused the greater light.

Hooks in Case I Pursue it

1.   Oh Father, they have produced additional needs and desires in me, while intensifying those I already had, setting directions for me. Then, they opposed me in nearly every direction and manner.

2.   They have positioned their hooks of destruction in nearly every direction, in case I pursue them.

3.   They have positioned me and the fruit tree in close proximity; but they have poisoned it, in case I pursue it.

4.   They have raised me like fish in a pond and ready as a meal, while showing me their hooks.

5.   Some opportunities have been camouflaged in the past and turned out to be hooks also. Therefore, my way is not clear and unsure.

6.   I presented a complaint, only for them to study how I brought it to light and to re-engineer it. They have done the same for all creative pursuits that challenge them and their interests, including my pursuit of life, liberty, and joy.

7.   Then they dialed up hate to muzzle me.

8.   In this way, they have produced an anti-human program.

9.   Upon my prayers they have devious wishes and have traded me in for a poisonous frog.

10.   Lord, I ask that you see that I'm as fulfilled as you see that I am decimated.

11.   Do as you will to resolve the matter according to your Will.

Intelligence Has No Limits Except Physical Impediments

1.   Since the world was built before humans were created, we can only copy the intelligence of the Creator.

2.   As we search and find, we begin to gather intelligence of that, which is pursued, by following what is proposed as its logic, which is proven to have a high degree of accuracy. This is why the mentality of a person can be led in many directions, whether true or false.

3.   Intelligence and logic consist of building blocks, and you are unlimited, as long as you know and follow its laws, which are rules that imitate the creative activities that bring forth the same or similar results. However, physical matters may become cluttered with contention, causing failure or the appearance of such, even molding a form, which provides evidence.

4.   Intelligence is about understanding, imagining, and/or adapting to current and changing circumstances and situations, as well as being creative in some type of project, by way of reasoning, including the hearing, observing, questioning, and answering process.

5.   Impulsively following others or examples requires the least intelligence, which may produce foul and, even, be dangerous. An impulsive following is justified in its lack of justification of facts and formulas. Its incompletion and broken links are potential justifications of fraud or opinion(s). However, something new requires more advanced intelligence. Complex problems, also, require higher intelligence, in accordance to the degree of complexity.

6.   Physical realties can hinder the objectives and goals of intelligent endeavors, simply by using physical objects to present adversity and/or disability. Evidence is seen in sufficient intelligence or greater versus failure, especially over time and attempts. In other words, if an intelligent pursuit is equal to a conventional pursuit, found to be historically successful, it will continue unless impeded upon.

The Compelling of Emotional Decisions

1.   Sensitivity felt Constructive Influence, in which the Interpretation gave increasing clarity of Message, and Pressure. Pressure developed Tension with Resistance, which created a Sensitive Spot, which drew the main Focus. Focus centered around Success or finding it, and Fear was planted elsewhere. Fear grew with the intensity of Tension, gathered from the Distance of being out of bounds, because of Care for Success. Anxiety developed from the Pressure and Forced Conformance to an Idea, which represented the current, best Solution. The Solution became part of what was Standard and Supportive of the Forces that Compelled Sensitivity in the right or wrong direction or to do what was less than ideal.

Quantum Star Eckter Series

*Fiction

Laboratory Experts' Surprising Find

1.   After landing on a strange planet, researchers and analysts appeared to find something rather interesting, which later prompted them to leave.

2.   They called their findings energy, which is how they observed everything around them. To them, energies are of various types, in which a unique collection represents a unique category. They found that, at least, certain energies could be mined or exposed through a fishing technique or through a penetrating method that can identify its physical and/or unique behavior, if not a combination of both.

3.   Coming from a more subtle environment and naïve about the current surroundings, they were easily subject to shock and fear. But they loved to explore the universes for knowledge, ideas, and solutions.

4.   They discovered energy moving beyond the bushes near the forest; so, they watched it for a time. The energy seemed to make noises and wasn't hesitant to confront anything, regardless of size or ability. It seemed to claim whatever it came upon and dwelt, with no care for a previous inhabitant.

5.   After further study, the analysts concluded that it was a type of energy that was impulsive, led by its senses, but showed some learning ability and patterned ways of proceeding. It reflected its knowledge of what it knew or thought about its surroundings, which was limited to a certain degree of intelligence. It seemed to have communicating ability amongst its kind. But it was prejudice against certain of its kind and much of every other kind. So, it stayed in combat mode most of the time.

6.   After leaving for the study of another type of energy, they noted that it was all that they found in the other type and more. They found this type to be more dangerous. It acted like a virus trying to infiltrate their systems, as if to have a much higher intelligent ability, especially learning ability. It seemed to be just as interested in us as we were in them. Whatever we did, this energy seemed to imitate, but sought to trap and capture. The researchers retrieved their weapons to ward them off, but they had weapons as well.

7.   Later that week, the analysts observed the patterns of the many types of societies and found that, indeed, this energy was just a smarter type of the other; but the intelligence did very little to change their evolution for the better. They evolved as an enhancement of the other energy type, instead of a more sophisticated type.

8.   They concluded that the more impulsive and naïve energy was prevalent throughout all living matters, in more or less enhancement. They had no control and never attempted to control the wilderness of their core.

9.   After sending their findings back home, they evacuated to proceed to another project.

10.   The identification of these visitors is unknown and speculations unproven.

Alien Introduction

1.   Shortly, whom we call Aliens, will be discussing activities that they've discovered on earth. The reason why I'm bringing you this news is because they are a more advanced culture than that, which is seen on earth. I was able to enter one of their vessels at a time that they had visited the earth. How I did it is too long of a story and not relevant at this time. I'm here to risk my life by sending a description of my experiences, here, back to earth.

2.   What's important is their opinion of us, which is seen by them as a potential example of the primitive history of their own people. Almost all participants have teleported to Quantum Star Eckter and are walking through security, which is necessary only because of visitors, who are in conflict with and present to try and understand the position of the Quantum Starlettes (Legal Citizens).

3.   My friend will do his best to interpret matters to me; so that I can pass the message on to you. I apologize for any errors that may appear.

4.   Here we go; the attendant is approaching the main judge, who is accompanied by several other judges and a group, who appears as council.

Court Begins

1.   Attendant: Sir, all are in attendance.

2.   Main Judge: Welcome everyone to Quantum Star Eckter, including our guests from Esquanent Galaxy of Friends. As you know, we are here, not only to build a case for how we live as a people, but to confirm our effort of due diligence in our commitment to preserve our best interests and those of the Exquanent Galaxy of Friends. We, also, realize that our efforts should follow the substances of truth and not any selfish desires geared towards triumph over another, other than for the protection of a righteous standing. We seek efficiency and effectiveness of expression of all moral concerns.

3.   The guidelines, going forward, will be based on algorithms, which have been extracted from all interacting forces of the past and present. When necessary, these guidelines are updated to duplicate the activity of the nature of new phenomenon, which we are faced with during times of speculation and mystery. Therefore, as part of council, we have set in place automated clones of particular disciplines (ACPD) and their expert representatives, who are responsible for the accuracy of their programming. They are open for questioning and will voluntarily aid the discussion for maximum productivity.

4.   I appreciate your respect of all people and the ACPDs in advance. If there shall be any dissent, please consult for the underlying science of the matter in question, before attempting to modify the direction of the court. Remember, we are not only here to be effective in our findings, but also to be efficient.

5.   As a participant, I ask you to press the button of dissent, placed in front of you, whenever there is a dispute with what has been stated. Your 'Mark of dissent' will be placed near the electronic transcription of the statement in dispute. Upon gathering additional information and confirming its accuracy, you must remove the 'Mark of dissent' after reviewing your historical marks on your local screen. I'm not here to teach you the technology of the operation of this meeting. I assume that all have consulted with our technology department, before participating in this court.

6.   With that said, let's begin. What is the summary of circumstances?

7.   Briefer: We have sent some of our people down to the indigently intelligent planet (Earth) for the investigation and observation of their manner of surviving and living, as well as the conditions imposed upon them. We have, both, a confirming and alarming report.

8.   As you know, this is not our first endeavor with the planet, which we have received a legal mandate to research and report our findings for the protection of our existence and manner of living. In short, we continue to find them as a threat. We are, also, yet to find any potentially strong trends that may lead to a better alternative course.

9.   That is the end of my briefing.

10.   Main Judge: Firstly, what has been confirmed?

11.   Case Manager: Sir, we have confirmed that the indigent planet remains violent in its endeavor to squeeze out advantage and success from other parts of its population. They remain in, what we call, an "Offense and Revenge" cycle.

12.   Main Judge: Are there any positive advocation that may redirect our views of them?

13.   Case Advocate: Sir, I believe that new technology and new information may have an effect on their development.

14.   Prosecution: Objection, sir. The premises, in which the indigent planet is focused, is upon population control and the inadequacies of essential resources. From there, they project survival tactics. Few of these tactics involve humanitarian advancement for the whole. Most are selfish pursuits for the advancement of the self or some related group. This is what sets up the cycle of "Offense and Revenge".

15.   Case Advocate: Sir, the technology concerns I'm trying to relay is about solving the inadequacies and the need for population control. We live in a vast world, in which population control is yet to be a real and genuine threat. They have made some advancements in these areas that could lead to the resolving of these issues.

16.   Prosecution: Again, I object, sir. Those people of the indigent world are destined to use technology and information in a selfish manner, regardless of their overall condition. After a period of living a certain way, they become programmed to accept and construct from those premises. That is especially true, when they have experienced or have knowledge of the consequences of not doing so. It is from that premise that their leaders will arise and instruct them towards advantage and the remainder of the population will and do reciprocate. Their leaders enjoy the benefits of power, which motivates them to continue the cause at all costs. It is because of these facts that they are a threat to us, if they shall develop to a point that they are capable of entering our sphere of influence and animation. Can we afford to take that chance?

17.   Case Advocate: I admit there are some bandits in the population, a lot of them. But there are some, who possess good intentions. I think the threat is reduced, when we alter the social fabric in favor of them.

18.   Prosecution: The engagement with these people will only lead to war. They have developed weapons that are now sophisticated enough to annihilate their own home planet. While we are not threatened by their current scientific developments, the remainder of the population is. Besides, it is not our problem. Our problem is their attempt to invade our territory with their selfish and eradicating agendas.

19.   Main Judge: Don't they have some kind of moral guides or some source of moral guidance?

20.   Case Advocate: Yes. In each segment of the population, they have some unique reporting device that they can grasp the understanding of and proceed from the relevant basis. It is said to be sacred to the population, in which it wields power over. This is how we can find the best of them, who may better relate to our way of thinking. We may be able to look upon them as brothers and sisters of our very own kind.

21.   Prosecution: Just to answer your question more completely, they have evangelists, who support the very premises I described to you earlier. These evangelists represent a large population of people and are looked upon as leaders, who are put in place by their personally, envisioned god of selfishness. These people are flocked together in high numbers, which evidences my point of view, when you observe the condition of their environment. Seeing that this is their direction of living, we could duplicate it more effectively and efficiently, while solving our very own concern about this threat. We would only reflect their respect for life.

22.   Case Advocate: My question is "Should we be like them in resolve and be seen as with clean hands?"

23.   Prosecution: Clean hands represent preserving righteousness and eliminating the threat of unrighteousness and the destruction or correction of evil sources. These people destroy the righteous with reverse engineering of their minds. Evil is used to confirm the unrighteous and redirect the righteous, and, even, the mentally ill and dependent associates. They are not open for diplomacy; Instead, they are determined. The success rate is obviously low in developing a better society, while they continue in disregards. But, let me emphasize that the opposing leaders, who stand against the unrighteousness of the authorities among them, are redirected with reverse engineering or death. These opposing leaders are rarely sufficiently supported by the population. So, to attempt to alter is beyond the capacity to make sense of the idea. Our natural responsibility is to protect against them at all costs, including constant or sufficient surveillance of their affairs. I see no other strong or strengthening facts supporting an alternative.

24.   Case Advocate: In spite of all the findings, I remain optimistic. I believe that the future is the deciding factor, not history. History has changed in the past. It can change again. Look at us.

25.   Prosecution: Our history, as you know, has been lost from a previous war and post-war conditions. The indigent planet does not seem to be an exact copy or example of our history. However, it holds clues to how we may have developed in some ways. But, most of the facts don't fit, seeing that their manner of development is destructive, favorable to certain classes and people, and don't support our current views. It's clear to me that the foundations are unique and opposing.

26.   Main Judge: Thank you, Aucasio and Rockotol for your presentations. We will call it a day and give ourselves a chance to review the findings and, hopefully, our visitors will better understand our position in the conflict. Remember, we are open to new ideas, which may help the indigent planet as well. Most of all, it helps to solidify our progress towards greater truth, peace, and love.

27.   We will later adjoin to discuss the date and time for the discussion of progress and the addressing of any lingering issues, in which the latter is rarely of concern. It is so!

Alien Star Summit @ Quantum Star Eckter, pt 2

1.   Hello, it's me again from Quantum Star Eckter. I'm reporting the latest information regarding the investigation of planet earth.

2.   Supposedly, the main judge sent a vessel to spy on the people of the earth. After a period of spying, they enticed a few prominent Earthlings to help them resolve the issue involving vacated government positions in the Exquanent Galaxy of Friends.

3.   The residents of planet earth were told that the government positions became vacant almost as soon as one was appointed to the public seat. The idea was to stabilize the election process and the governing bodies across the galaxy. The galaxy seeks to become like Quantum Star Eckter, having the least moral concerns throughout the population and more focused on information and technological progress. But, because government positions require a holder of a moral example to hold and sustain a public office, genuine questioners present information to the courts to consider whether claims against the holders of office are substantiated and warrant an investigation. Many times, a holder is replaced by a temporary holder and the vacant position requires other idle, public figures to help administrate. The whole process is exhausting and discourages the best of the population from running for office.

4.   Dr. Alexander, who holds a PHD in psychology, social and political science, spoke up first and confidently. He said, "I am honored that you chose me for such an important task. I assume that you chose me for my education and experience in politics and political expertise.

5.   As you know, we don't have that problem, at least, nowhere near as serious as the Exquanent Galaxy of Friends. And, while I love Quantum Star Eckter, I don't think it is always advisable to copy the methods of another. Sometimes, it's best to manage society in a manner that gives it free will and free choice. I'm talking about as close to a hands-off approach as you can get. Government should be designed to strengthen with the development of society, regardless of the type of developments. The natural developments of people should be supported and sustained, while the government stands to profit and open up more compatible opportunities, regardless of the directions of the people.

6.   The idea is for government to be always strong and sustaining; since it is needed to administer the most important matters of the population. The administration should not be so complex as to warrant so much scientific approaches that the positions require an overwhelming amount of expertise, which is the issue here. Instead of a high amount of expertise, use

popularity as the determinant for who will hold office. Let any other matter be between the divided people, where the most influential people determine the end point. You're making the governing process too, too difficult. Government is for the most influential to create advantage for themselves. Science is for sustaining the most influential, not for delving deeply into matters that relinquish the population's dependence upon them."

7.   An undercover officer of Quantum Star Eckter asks, "So, you're saying that developing a complete moral society requires too much expertise and not worth the effort?"

8.   Dr. Alexander: You see the difficulties here? The people are without a strong and reliable government. The government is more like a referee, but in favor of the most influential. It's a boat trying to stay afloat of all the sharks in the water. The boat needs to be big and strong; so that it gives demands and forces respect, at all times.

9.   Undercover Officer: Again, the assurance of moral development seems to be lost here. I'm about the substance of unity, peace, and love.

10.   I've observed your planet's conditions, and I can tell you it's no Quantum Star Eckter. I've seen neighborhoods that I wouldn't be caught dead in, while Quantum is a total tourist area to die for, complete with mandatory requirements to sustain it, even for manufacturing sites.

11.   I've seen so much contradictory behavior, including many preaching righteousness, but upholding political figures and/or policies of unrighteousness. They blindly or corruptly uphold the seeds of immorality and crime. I never dreamed that a people can be so confused or corrupt. I found media distortion, movies of distortion, and songs that talk of so much violence and just so much wrong in your world. It's like, what you said, just cater to the most influential and stay out of the way, as much as possible. Anything can happen under those circumstances.

12.   Dr. Alexander: but what you see is a strong government. You don't see that here.

13.   Undercover Officer: what about all the dominance and forced submission of the wrong way of life?

14.   Dr. Alexander: we cannot afford to cater to every incident and person's development. It's too overwhelming and takes up too much government resources. Government must be conservative; so that it doesn't stretch itself too thin. People are going to be people and do what they want to do. Government should just float on top of it all, not enter into turmoil that would be detrimental to its solidarity, tearing the boat apart piece by piece. Then, what could government do?

15.   Undercover Officer: Quantum Star Eckter is an example of using science to dig deep into every issue to destabilize the cause of immorality and utilize the findings in society to teach resolution versus revenge. We don't use media to instigate immorality as a tool to stay afloat of wrong practices. Your world is proof that you don't sustain support of an immoral belief and action. Surely, your methods are one of a coward's methods or corrupt, if you feel that blazing a trail to a moral end is a loser's way.

16.   It sounds like to me that you fear the most influential or don't care much for moral concerns yourself. What else could stop you from encouraging such a thing? How has your ways proved to create a better world? Or, is that your priority?

17.   Dr. Alexander: you have your way of doing things and we have ours. But you came and got me to help you solve a problem we don't have. Let that sink in.

18.   Undercover Officer: I see that you don't have a genuine answer to the problem, just how to sustain a government of profits and safety. Quantum believes in developing moral people; so that the people will develop a moral government, and a moral government will develop a moral people. We listened to wrongdoers and the innocent, the imperfect, and the so-called better people. We took all the information and built a world like no other. Then, you come and encourage us to float. Let that sink in.

19.   Dr. Alexander and others, who agreed with him, were sent to trial, as a result of a questioner. The questioner asked, "Does the alien present a threat to moral development, at Quantum Star Eckter and our project at Exquanent Galaxy of Friends? The questioner outlined a long list of violations of principles and concepts of moral development (PCMD). However, Dr. Alexander and others were exonerated on the basis of jurisdiction and the necessity of free speech that necessarily confirms past scientific findings and brings acknowledgement of real time world experiences, keeping Quantum Star Eckter informed about the world around them. Dr. Alexander and his supporters were released on a condition not to return.

20.   But, before their release, the assistant judge gave his response to the soon to be extradited foreigners: "When I look for value in a person, I look for what I can build and sustain with that individual and balance it with any drawbacks. I see you as a swamp that can only hold a floating structure that can be blown around with the wind, leaning this way and that way, and sink as a result of a reasonable load. We've got dirt that's more valuable than you. We've built beautiful, solid, and stable sky scrapers on rocks and dirt. Dirt! But, you, with all your intelligence, won't construct a solid and stable belief system to erect greater things. You resist, even, in the light of Truth. Dirt is more valuable than you."

Quantum Star Eckter: Planetary Takeover

1.   Not long ago, Quantum Star Eckter found a planet in despair and sought to investigate and research causes, sources, and solutions.

2.   The planet was, supposedly, like earth. They had modernized and advanced to a high level with technological resources and various forms of scientific disciplines. But, then, they disappeared from the social environment that included other planets.

3.   Being a nuisance of the inferior type, there was no love for them; especially after attempts to take possessions and violate the rights of others.

4.   It became apparent that their ancestors found a way for the free and enslaved people to live competitively together, in a fierce battle for control of their lives and the lives of others.

5.   The higher classes became more educated, sophisticated, and more efficient and effective at controlling circumstances and developments. Their methods signified specific frames of minds that matched the individuals' life experiences, including limits and unhindered expressions. The lower classes became more like human robots, where their presence and future were determined by the higher classes, with the aid of their accommodating and non-accommodating elements, and mental programming.

6.   Society once had two levels that battled one another for change, but transformed to a more single level that led to power and acceptance, forced by law to military might. Lower society went from having a moral tendency towards future, social interactions, after a time of error, to a more accommodating frame of mind towards their obvious enemies. Higher society never recognized their predatory methods and continued to filter out the evidence brought against them.

7.   The population grew large from families trying to muscle the others for advantage. Society turned to recycling methods to try and retain stability and survival, which was found to have limits as well. They could find no planets to navigate to, especially with the resistance they faced from the closest planets, who always suspected foul play. It was then that advancements in society started to dissipate.

8.   After researching and investigating the matter, Quantum Star Eckter decided to consider prosecuting the current political establishment. The prosecutor wanted to establish a case, based on the resisting efforts of their government; however, the defensive attorney noted that Quantum Star Eckter does not prosecute matters that aren't part of or associated with the lowest driving source of confusion that underlies the consideration. He said the idea comes from "Permanently Silencing the Fire" method. He related the superficial matter as a result of an instinct of survival and being, at times associated with ignorance. The prosecutor is, therefore, continuing to monitor any resistances to corrective procedures that may yield an indictment.

As an update on the findings of Quantum Star Eckter, I bring you the following report:

1.   Investigators of Quantum Star Eckter found evidence of political foul play. To protect the interests of certain elected people, whether by vote, social preferences, or priorities, balancing concepts were introduced in an inferior fashion, to meet qualifications that rightfully ban their consideration or adoption into legal policies.

2.   For an example, Earth introduced "Affirmative Actions" for a particular race to be inclusive in hiring and other social concerns. However, the inferior planet would introduce the concept, in a pretentious effort to aid an oppressed race or any group proposed to be of a lower rank. The proposals, of these types, were quickly met with resistances that opposed the promotion of unqualified elements related to the task at hand. The need for a solution was disguised as a weakness of character, rather than social oppression, after intentional weak efforts rendered favor for the oppressors.

3.   The balancing ideas were never amended to represent circumstances, rather than disqualified elements. The weak creative pursuits were seen as faults in creativity on the part of authoritative sources, their supporters, and the representatives of the disadvantaged. However, the short-comings of representatives of the disadvantaged could be a result of regulating influences from their more powerful opponents, and/or exchanges that maintain imbalances, but discriminately yield personal success.

4.   As a whole, their laws were designed to work as a balance that yielded a desired operation and appearance of society, which had implications of a conscious effort that regulated all aspects of society and its influences. Disruptions, or the threat of, came under scrutiny and

were delayed or restricted from acknowledgement or influence. The collective challenges that were rejected exposed the rank of priorities.

5.   Leaders, who yielded significant, threatening control over any part of a population that opposed conventional forms of rules, were eliminated or replaced with more accommodating personnel. These types of actions led to control of any population and culture, whether native or foreign. Experiments were performed to identify, diagnose, rectify, and/or improve upon any issues. The conventional ways were progressive, while the attempts for positive and moral change faltered and greatly withered away, leaving only the slogans as a symbol for a false way of operating, believing, and living.

6.   At the center of it all was censorship, which kept high profile intelligence and information in the hands of the higher class, which was dispensed downwards, according to purpose, needs, and the maintenance of status control. The more intelligent and capable were those, who attracted more favor, while their counterparts were made a fool of and fell to their demise, usually through the train-wreck management process.

7.   The train-wreck management process specialized in putting people, circumstances, conditions, and statuses up against the other, for the purpose of insight and favorable development. For an example, prison riots were started to gain more prison time from the inmates and to instill a hardened and provocative heart and mind.

8.   Laws were created, written or implied, to establish or utilize balancing act(s) in society to garner an effect of any kind. Whole societies became manipulated as simple as a touch of a button. The prosecutor's side engaged in rehearsals to make complainants more convincing to the court, ramping up prejudice towards the defendant, in which anything became truth, as long as it fit the pattern of perception. It was a smooth line of events that led to challenges, which encouraged entrapment and error, or detachment from enjoyment and the finer things of the world, if not successfully framed.

9.   Resolutions were not, solely, about the identification and exercise of proper principles and concepts; instead, a specific(s) contact became the more important source. When these contacts were replaced, instabilities in policies became apparent, creating a fluctuation between a more negative to a more positive solution, while the conventional maintained its progressive direction towards full control in the end.

10.   Occasionally, they would catch one of their own in wrongdoing, to maintain or patch up their fraudulently good reputation, giving their supporters ammunition of claims against their accusers of corruption, only to practice resilience in provoking the very things they sought to discourage. They taught accountability, but resorted to scapegoating in an effort to secure their safety. In a provocative process, they left no known stone unconsidered and not aiding the process.

Introduction

1.   Although Quantum Star Eckter could not prosecute anyone on the inferior planet, they passed a law that subjected any person of interest, who failed to disclose any requested information, regarding any authoritative quest, as deemed permissible for conviction of laws associated with such quest.

2.   Using this law, a group of social scientists and others, who may be potentially needed, sought to discover the cause of long-term racism within that planet and how to possibly undo it.

3.   Protecting his identity, the scientists sought and interviewed a person of interest. His story was as followed:

Informant 1: Civil War, Spirit of Deficiency, and Conditioning

1.   "A long time ago, our ancestors enslaved some vulnerable people for our benefit. But, some of them grew more concerned about inhumane treatment. A war broke out and they killed each other, which was not the goal they intended. However, the goal needed to be reached. What followed was lots of research into what caused the war and how to get everyone on board.

2.   After the war was stopped, they slowly carried out an altered plan, which slowly became more effective and efficient over time. It was so effective; the victimized race helped the process intensely. From there, it went smoothly, even to the point of having to protect the victimized race, while appearing innocent.

3.   They met in a town hall meeting and decided that the spirit of insufficiency should rule over them and their culture and image should be associated with darkness. Then, our people will see them not made right, sick, violent, sexual, or anything criminal. Even those of the victimized race, who helped the process for the dollar, would develop the same perception. Statistics relayed the progress and confirmed the success.

4.   Under constant adversity, the victimized race became mean spirited, ignorant, physically strong, which met half the goal. The other half included training our people and others' views of the victimized race. We used word of mouth and other schemes, as well as the media to highlight certain negative aspects. Soon, most of the world was cautious to associate too closely and share success with this inferior race.

5.   Eventually, we stood on one side limiting the damage to this race and secretly instigating the challenges. We had full control and support.

6.   That's all I can tell you, because I didn't know all the science behind it, I just followed the recommendations of the experts."

7.   The group of scientists moved on to another person of interest, informant 2, and shared the transcript of informant 1.

Informant 2: The Friction Between Higher Society and the Downtrodden

1. "From what I could see, they were actually following the inspiration I got from the idea, expressed in our Holy book, which described friction between two sources, which I perceived one generating a deranged mind or destroying it in some manner, while the other's destruction is a blow to the foundation that held higher society up, especially in the economic environment, where the downtrodden were used for cheap labor to keep prices down.

2. The solution was to, generally, preserve them in the low economic and most undesirable positions.

3. But, the development and behavior of the downtrodden was made bruising to the moral views of the upper class; because they knew the higher class helped to encourage their demise, regardless of whether there was moral practice or not. But, because they also knew that their treatment instigated crimes, which entailed exposure to various manners of approach and execution within their communities.

4. That verse was my guiding light, which I became a very popular and sought-after advisor for my opinions.

5. I felt like there was a structure that, once it's perceived or built, matters just fell into place. Like puzzles, I knew what didn't fit and how it needed to be treated. After so much progression, it seemed that other puzzles just followed and felt natural to me, like this is the way it's supposed to be.

6. But I knew it was wrong; however, I also knew that being righteous wasn't going to put food on my table and pay the kind of bills I have. I had children depending on my success and many friends and associates, who shared and defended that mentality. We had created an unstoppable monster, and I knew it.

7. Although I was a popular advisor, I was not the expert, who knew how to put the nuts and bolts together and bring the business to its maturity, so to speak."

Informant #3 We Became the Infrastructure

1. "We knew that, being the most influential, buying up most of the property, designing our environment, infrastructure, and the way we do business, others would have to cater to us.

2. And, so, like an automobile developed over time to produce the smoothest ride over the bumps, a lot of the remaining population did likewise.

3. We actually became the infrastructure that others would have to navigate for success or failure, whether it was something we built or something we believed, liked, disliked, or approved or disapproved of. And, it didn't matter whether anyone else liked it or not. As a community, nation, and world of networkers, everything had to come through us. So, we proceeded to profit, maximize, and sustain our potential.

4. If someone was on the bad end of the deal, that was their problem. We got to the point where we were fed up with those types of people and did less and less for them. They were never

satisfied with whatever we did for them, and I think that aided their downfall. Regardless of what they were going through, they needed to hold steadfast to those moral values.

5.   We led by example; they could have done the same. Instead, they relished in iniquity."

Informant #4: Denial of Reality and the Court as a Business

"We had a system designed to protect the court from possessing knowledge equivalent to reality. It was limited in scope to the point of only appreciating an offense presented by only qualified sources. These sources protected the tribune from violations of perpetuating a crime(s) or being associated with such sources. Public records were managed, including the alterations, to protect the reputation of being fair and just. But hate rose so high for certain people that, even, the most corrupt maneuvers, exposed, were acceptable to the general public.

1.   Justice, somehow, got associated with revenge and the corruption of a convict, which confirmed immorality as a game for the most sophisticated and connected individuals to succeed.

2.   With the trust that was given to the court system, they could win any case they sought to explore, whether the suspect was innocent or guilty; it didn't matter. There were no real struggles, just a fraudulent display of efforts to garner truth and further instill dark behavior within the victim, whether convicted or not.

3.   Certain races had to be associated with darkness, to certain degrees, and it had to appear as a reliable indicator; so, the most vulnerable races had to be in a position that compels those type of behaviors. It appeared to me that they were placed on some hierarchical level; but I couldn't prove it, because there was always something that wouldn't fit that perception. It was as if a well-knowledgeable lawyer ran the system to "generally" win cases, while maintaining control of what is to be convicted and what is not. I think the creation and compatibility of precedence(s) had a lot to do with keeping the system profitable; some could not be acceptable no matter how true. It had to be maintained as a profit center. But I don't know. It just appeared to be that way. Some cases had to be inaccessible to the courtroom and remedied outside the courtroom for the same reason.

4.   Resolution of any illegal act(s) could not be, generally, implemented. It had to be a revolving door of issues to be dealt with, because it was a business; and a business had to be profitable.

5.   But we became excellent at using potential time of imprisonment to bully even the most innocent people into taking a plea bargain that included an admittance of guilt. That's why ignorance of certain people works so well; it almost guarantees success. It is compounded by matters that go on behind closed doors and the maintenance of public records and manipulation of media sources. This is where the power is! The ability to garner social resistance only adds to that power. In the end, nothing gets resolved; instead, money is constantly flowing.

6.   You see, we could turn a person's life at any point of interest, we chose. All we had to do was maintain a public image that was compatible with whatever endeavors we executed, and

control matters that underlie a person's life, creating circumstances. Life has levels of activities that compel circumstances on other levels. We learned how to play those levels and how to control the evidence. If we were smarter and more skillful than the opposing population, we could get away with anything, even murder. We owned the world and everything in it.

7.   Everything happens for a reason; so, people make decisions, based on data that underlies their circumstances. As long as the options for decision-making were engineered correctly or narrowed to encourage a successful fulfillment of our desires, we could manipulate with ease.

8.   We could turn or make a perfect model into one of the worse examples, at will, and vice versa. You could see a part of the program executed in a divided media, over the same subject, especially in political affairs.

9.   We felt most comfortable in environments, we carved out with law, like where proof was not presentable, due to some type(s) of devices not being allowed or permissible by law., or anywhere a defendant would be vulnerable. We went rampage in those areas.

10.   The world was stuck in a cycle and not progressing towards a moral environment. That's especially true with society's need to dominate one for the success of another. A humanitarian, going too far, is most likely to suffer the most harm, regardless of what race he/she is a part of. It was highlighted in history. Everyone knew! So, the saying was "Prohibit extremes, whether good or bad". But that was the very belief that held this type of environment together. There's no such thing as "too good". Most of us were cowards!

11.   By the time we realized something needed to be done, the authorities were already too strong. While we were contemplating on what to do, the authorities were getting stronger.

12.   The authorities wanted to maintain their control over the population for a profit, at the expense of the disadvantaged, while the other side realized what was really going on and sought, desperately, to remedy the problem. It was two hard-charged situations opposed to one another, which was a setup from the start.

13.   More and more people wanted to die, but couldn't. Many were given a chemical that turned a reasonable, dire feeling, about the outlook of their lives, into an unreasonable smile and content behavior."

Informant #5: I had to be a Puppet Minister

1. "I was a minister unto the people, who came to my church, and it burned my heart to see that my preaching was only for, merely, nothing.

2. I had to make a living, but I tried to initiate events that made people happy, hopeful, and moral; because that's what our world needed. And, the only thing that was going to keep the disadvantaged moral was a hopeful future.

3. No matter how pure the heart, the vulnerable were going to be taken advantage of, according to how our society sees it. It was about deception and a fight for material advantage; nothing was going to stop that.

4. I worried that they would wake up and see the truth. After all, it was there for them to see, if their eyes had opened to see.

5. The tithes that they gave didn't, much, benefit the vulnerable and downtrodden. You could see it in the streets, where the homeless population ran amok and was increasing. God, clearly, didn't get His money.

6. The resourceful people, attending my church, had other priorities, and I had to be the minister they wanted me to be. These type of people made heaven and everlasting hell right here on this planet, while many thought it meant the future, after God passed down His judgement."

Informant #6: Up Against Power, while Contested by my Own

1. "I guess I was more sensitive than a lot of people, because few people were feeling what I felt. I felt we were going backwards, in respects to what we should be doing and believing. I felt our communities were too tough to manage and overcome.

2. People would tell me not to be so sensitive or people will prey on me.

3. If I spoke against what was happening, people, who had a stake in the game, showed their attitude against me, in word or deed, if not both. I was treated like I was the enemy, laughed at, ridiculed, or called sensitive, as if to engage in name-calling. Some would say, "You do you, let everybody else do them, mind your own business". What they didn't want to hear was "it was everybody's business, if we couldn't develop and live the way we wanted to, within moral means".

4. I felt that people, who trample over the rights of others to exist, develop, and to change for the better, shouldn't be part of the infrastructure that articulates our beliefs and behaviors. You can't develop a good society with those type of people.

5. I remember what my mother told me, before she died:

6. "I love that you choose the righteous ways, but you can't go too far with it. Being of this race and in a corrupt society, you'll go up against power.

7. As a child and now as an attorney, I saw how people develop. Each one is an argument from their personal circumstances. Like perception, they develop from a premise of circumstances, going from one premise to a higher or more sophisticated premise or another

premise that brings a unique set of circumstances. Many of them are set or hardened in that manner. Because they are unique and imperfect, it causes clashes between and among them. We learned the circuitry of their premises and used our knowledge to manipulate them.

8.	Some of them are more diplomatic than others. Depending on the subject, they may not be diplomatic at all. This may mean a war of some type, depending on their attitude. Regardless of flaws, many do not want to change.

9.	Legitimate civil rights leaders have failed and died, as an example of victims of hardcore oppressors and their tricks, in which the denial of their causes is the evidence of oppression. In other cases, they were mocked, replaced, and/or charged, even falsely. They didn't possess the means to persuade any case against them, because most believed or followed the facts of the government and their controlled media, which, magically, used psychology.

10.	Our own people changed and started self-destructing for avoidance of hardships and to gain advantage, in an environment of insufficient resources.

11.	I'll always be there for you; but If I go too far to protect your good conscience, you can get mommy hurt. I hate to sound like a slave mother telling her child to obey the evil master; but I love you and want you to be safe."

12.	So, I had to be quiet to keep my mother safe. But I knew my cause was bigger than my mother and I. However, I agreed with her that I was up against power, for a people, who were working against me or refused to support me and acclimatizing to a demonic environment."

Informant #7: What Happened to Minister Ion?

Minister Ion was a great preacher, who grew a large congregation and became one of the most popular ministers ever known. After a strange crowd embarked upon his church, things began to turn for the worse. His preaching style, arguably, changed for the worse, after he was sued and charged with a crime.

1.	A lot of people knew he was innocent, but the antagonists pushed their views and controlled the entire event.

2.	After his release, he was invited to speak at another church.

3.	Here are two representations of his sermons, the first one before his incarceration and the other afterwards:

4.	"Today, I want to borrow a saying from a beautiful mind of long ago, "Do It Anyway!"

5.	Can I get an Amen?

6.	Audience: Amen!

7.	Satan is always trying to make matters miserable for us, but if we work with love, we can reverse his plans, at least make him work hard for it. He may make it appear useless and things may look dire, but "Do it anyway!"

8.	You see, we can fight him, even beat him, if we build ourselves up. What I mean is understand his game and do the opposite, but do the right thing. Don't let him trick you. So, what we need to do is climb the steps to God. Our first step is to understand the devil's game. The second step is to decide what to do about it. Our third step is to counter his moves. Our fourth step is to withstand his temptations and adversity; and, if you feel unrewarded, do it anyway! Our fifth step is to keep on stepping up.

9. Can I get an Amen?

10. Audience: Amen!

11. We don't have to live in his world. We can choose to live elsewhere. Of course, we're not moving. It's creating what we want in the midst of his world. Let him be disturbed and terrified, not us.

12. When we go out into our yard and see our grass has changed to the color brown, we know, if we water it, it'll change back to green. We know, if we water the trees, the leaves will blossom; it may drop a peach on you.

13. If we cut our grass, our environment will, most likely, be safe from snakes. If we remove the weeds, our grass can take over.

14. So, what this means is "If you love your environment and the things in it, it will return that love in its own way. When we invest our money, we always want a good return; so why not learn and do it right?

15. If you see a person in need, help them or show them to someone who can. If you see someone with a frown, change it to a smile. If you see someone with an issue, they are unable to resolve, fix it. If you can't fix it, show them to someone who can. If you go to prison and see someone angry or fearful, show him or her that you're his/her brother or sister. Just as you changed your yard from brown to green and unacceptable to beautiful, your social environment can change from unbearable to bearable and inconsiderate to considerate.

16. If you don't get paid for it, do it anyway! If you don't get recognized for it, do it anyway! If the devil is stubborn, do it anyway!"

After the incarceration:

17. "Today, I'd like to say "Work On Yourself"

18. Can I get an Amen?

19. Audience: Amen!

20. First of all, I want say "I'm a sinner and I've always asked God for forgiveness". It's not easy being imperfect.

21. We have to be willing to take some steps downward to prove our loyalty. But we have to be willing to take that step down to redeem ourselves. We have to take up our cross. We have to look upon ourselves without pride. We have to face our imperfections. We have to accept that others see us as flawed and thank them for pointing it out. We have to bear the weight of oppression and time. We have to change for the better.

22.   You see, our lives are not ours; it belongs to God and God works through the powers of our government. We have to go down; so that we can, one day, tell the devil I've been there and mastered that, until we have no fear of him. Then, we can come up strong and tell him to get thee hence."

23.   The antagonists loved it and said "He's back! Every time I hear him, I get stronger" (with a bright smile). Most shared her belief, while others thought he had changed.

24.   Minister Ion never regained his financial status, after falling into poverty. His wife had died shortly after his release, and he died a few years later.

Informant #8: Endured Struggle and Conditioning Effects

1.   "We followed people, who set an example of what we wanted to do or felt we had to do. Basically, we followed examples of people we thought were the closest to who we were.

2.   I felt that I had to fight my demons and everybody else had theirs to fight, but they just weren't all the same. As a result, at least, most of us misunderstood one another and didn't know how to comprehend the other's reality. So, we ended up just excusing what we didn't understand, which meant war between us, when conflict prevailed over us. We all had our priorities and they, sometimes, tore us apart.

3.   Not only didn't looking at the big picture come across our minds much, because we had our own personal lives to live and our own set of priorities and wisdoms from personal experiences; but we had to have the intelligence and reason to perceive what it was. So, we were limited in capacity for various reasons.

4.   We, also, felt that traditions and popular beliefs helped us to be inclusive in mainstream society, if we followed them. After all, it was our best chance to be accepted by those who held the key to our success. If we did it any other way, we knew we were asking for trouble, if not more than what we already experienced.

5.   In error, sometimes we followed too small of a group; because those were the people who accepted us and were most like us. That may have rubbed larger groups the wrong way. We just wanted to be as happy as we could, but they found a way to take advantage of our weaknesses.

6.   We were used to mom and dad intervening to tell us what was fair; but when we got older, we had to accept whatever the authorities said, no matter how illogical and unfair it was. It was about who was favored and who wasn't, no consistent standard(s)."

Informant #9: The Rise of the Authoritative Society

1.   "We had to find our way to success and sustain it; after all, we lived in a world where one was trying to overtake another. It was wild.

2.   To make that accomplishment, we had to affect the minds of as many people as possible, to make them honorable, respectable, and considerate. This was the first foundation we had to develop, to give our society a construct to build on.

3.   From there, we planned and developed in stages, from one foundation to another, until we built a dynasty for us and to the detriment of others.

4.   Once it became a profitable endeavor, that's when the dynasty started; then all we had to do was assemble attachments, whether it was a belief, law, procedure, cost, or whatever it was to grow and harmonize what we developed. Slowly, it became an immune system that, automatically, attacked and denied what we didn't want. Like a virus, it spread, took over, and improved.

5.   It was from a structured whole and the directions of all of its elements that we could perceive and imagine performance, predictions, and how to improve and manipulate the remining population. It, also, allowed us to pinpoint discovery areas for unfound knowledge."

Informant #10: Minister of Spiritual Studies

1.   "As a minister, I specialized on the spiritual side, viewing everything as an effect of a particular source.

2.   I, eventually, gave up my ministry, due to so much adversity to what I believed. So, I've done everything privately, for the most part.

3.   I wanted the purest view of my surroundings, without any inaccuracies; but no one, whom I was associated with or observed seemed to care about that.

4.   I was, basically, concerned with a disruptive spirit and began to profile it. As I advanced far enough, I could see some of it in myself. As a result, I monitored myself more closely to become a better person, not that I was all that bad; because I always had a sense of concern for erroneous, threatening, and damaging developments.

5.   Anyway, this disruptive spirit had the elements of deception, aggressiveness, inconsideration, and desire for challenge and destruction to an extreme degree, as if to be addicted to it. Terror was funny and necessary.

6.   There are more related elements that materialize out of circumstances, as if the world is decisively manufacturing it. Depression was, seemingly, where it ought not to be. There was, even, self-sabotage of own objectives and goals, as well as endorsement of the very things fought (Confusion).

7.   I try to understand the source and how it connected with the world to establish an end. I, even, observed it in the way people drove and how much empathy they practiced and the contrast between the experience and a forced interpretation, whenever it was given.

8.   I observed how it works within myself, as opposed to the material world and the things in it and felt the need for constant monitoring.

9.   I noticed that some people practiced spiritualism to uncover the future and to cast spells; but, because they were on opposing sides, it appeared that the Holy book's story was a lock. No one could break the spell on the world. So, I felt that I found real evidence of a Devil. It was either that or worldwide cooperation in high places that held major events constant, if not both.

10.   I found that the more I knew, I began to evolve more and more as a better and more informed person. So, I felt I owed it to myself to continue my study, as far as I could and to seek more information and answers elsewhere, if possible."

Informant #11: Regulating Empowerment

1.   "Empowerment was a key element of our plan. We studied how empowerment works and used it as our core objective.

2.   We saw how a holder of sufficient value was more heavily sought after than one, who had little value and, therefore, prone to disrespect. So, obviously, we wanted to be the holder of sufficient value; because we wanted to be empowered and the source of empowerment.

3.   To the contrary, we saw how one would devalue or take advantage of another, who had no effective defense or especially feared to present it, resulting in others adjusting their views of the victim(s) accordingly. It happened, also, when an individual was seen as less skilled, less intelligent, and/or less productive. Their value to the community would, then, fall to a certain rank within that community. So, obviously, we did not want to be the devalued person, but saw the concept as a weapon.

4.   As an economist, we knew that the lower the price of a product or service meant a greater potential for profits and a higher quality of life, in comparison to a competitor. So, someone had to be on the negative end of the trading process; and it couldn't be too much of our own people. Otherwise, we'd face overwhelming rebellion.

5.   We had to protect our value in a way that we could dispense it, without depleting it. So, we legalized copyrights, patents, and trademarks.

6.   We knew we had to have a strong accusation to make our victims our footstool and God had to be a part of that, to make it work. To aid our cause, we regulated information and knowledge and hung them in despair; so that the ignorant would develop immorally and challenge truth, only to fall to their fate and dwell in a hellish part of society.

7.   We had to take control and sustain it; so that we could control the present and the future to our advantage.

8.   Socially, it meant that we had to appear as upright and mysterious in truth and law; so that our victims felt less empowered by our stipulations. That meant that, at times, we had to carry a false sense of righteousness and an arrogant attitude.

9.   Intelligence, also, had to be limited to control and sustain the status quo, in levels. Therefore, knowledge and information had to be brokered in such a fashion that access and utilization aided status management.

10.   The victims had to be held in a subordinate condition. This meant that they had to be in a constant need and desirable condition that their focus and concentration was constrained, restricting their ability to overcome, but readily available to give support, as well as implosive in manner. They could not be allowed to feel in control and it be legit; otherwise, it may lead to their empowerment.

The Response of QSE Scientists

Dr. Shimill

1.   One of the scientists, Dr. Shimill, gave a summary to the legal body of Quantum Star Eckter, which included others, who were interviewed. She stated:

2.   "In a summary of my experiences with certain people, whom we interviewed, I perceived an influence upon them that was skilled in perpetuating immorality and sensed certain missing interpretations of the tribune, described as crime and potential crimes, which were overlooked or ignored completely. It struck me as someone, who engineered immorality and crime, by sensing the limitations, in which their laws could be so effective that it exposes the reflective side of any matter, thus indicating their peers, causing a termination of process that wasn't complete, but fulfilling an inferior agenda.

3.   I, also, perceived that the, generally, vulnerable race members were often used in the corrupt process of their own members. Many terrorized their own neighborhoods, became false examples of success, and became prison guards, police officers, and other professions used to procure and conceal the operation.

4.   When someone, outside of the race, were utilized to do the same, they were more likely to lie or to be less informative about the operation, even to protect it. Usually, they had the most influence in the interpretation and policies instituted within the operation. They were, usually, the most intelligent or had/garnered the most influence upon the matter."

Dr. Skimeot

In a more frightening interpretation, Dr. Skimeot, described the following:

1.   "It appeared to me that a strong influence overtook them and that they recognized such an influence.

2.   The evidence that supports this is a people who consume their own type: human. They possessed a mind and a conscience, but they eluded the normal expression of the two, in which they were designed to express. Instead, there appeared to be a cloud of confusion and/or a prioritized influence. The chase seemed to be more than fulfillment, potentially greed, garnered by the need to avoid poverty and/or some form of suffering.

3.   It was indicated in their holy book, about giants intruding their environment, which could be anyone having an influence not vulnerable to human resistances. It, also, indicated an inferior, spiritual character, who tempted a superior example with the riches of the world. While many confess with their mouths that they follow this superior example, they practiced the chasing of material possessions. It's like they wanted to be like the superior example, but fell vulnerable to the chase of material possessions.

4.   They chose sides, which was against another, in hopes to attain and sustain success. So, the classes developed and sought advantage and explored for even more advantage. Soon, dominance ran rampage. It seems that they thought that they were fighting against evil, while being the very source of such, while becoming more successful or sustaining their position in the process. Many may have known that they were participating in a fraud.

5.   There was this "narrow way" spoken of in the Holy Book. To achieve the narrow way, a path would have to be so testing and limited in such a way as to bring out the value of any moral characteristic, proving fit as a moral individual. It was like putting a product under a stress test to determine the highest level it is expected to perform sufficiently as desired, needed, or expected; except this was about reaching a breaking point, used to grade the subject as inferior, depending on who it was.

6.   The narrow way was constructed by building or perceiving circumstances that would test a person's will to do the right thing and grade them accordingly. It included deception, unfair practices, false examples, and long-term to permanent circumstances that wrench out behaviors that are considered inferior. Many were set up at a young age or anytime they were vulnerable to certain frames of mind. Yet, they were, generally, held responsible for themselves, regardless of circumstances. These people were, actually, penalized for being human or not doing something that normal people could not do. It was a weapon of hate. It was a war between classes and races.

7.   Deception was not so evident to them, when the Holy Book was released to the public and stated that this inferior spirit has "already" entered the world. The book demonstrated how to carry out corruption and had God, the Creator, agreeing to instigate immorality as a way of life and a manner of dominating and getting rich, by taking an advantage of another. But, yet, they hailed their view of Him as good and associated with dominance and richness, while He clearly denounced both.

8.   While something was needed to sell the thought of morals, the book became outdated and few seemed to understand that, in spite of the evidence of flaws, overcoming of some illnesses that encouraged abandoning loved ones and instructions that appear to be on the revenge side and not the resolution side, shorting the intelligence of the very Creator. They were just following an inferior source; otherwise, how could they possibly say "God is good", while possessing such a view?

9.   The mind of the authoritative source must be questioned, and under the circumstances, viewed as confused, disoriented, and evil. Thus, their Holy Book states, that the inferior one deceived the whole world. They actually, framed God as imperfect and a sinner, by associating their way of life with him. The book told on itself.

10.   The government practiced the scheme; so, the Holy Book stated "to do as they say, but do not what they do". The government was supposed to stay out of religion, but it seems the interpretations of the book are what are really meant here. These interpretations include the many views of what the government is doing. Yet, they trusted and defended their government....

11.   Most, hardly, experienced the narrow way; so, they had to have known that they weren't on the path to heaven. It had to be a false story, designed to calm and mislead the victims of their corruption; because, as serious as the penalty was, they couldn't have believed it, at least, not enough to follow the road to heaven.

12.   It was the actions of the government and the behavior of the followers that made it feel real. That's not to say that there isn't a Creator, because, of course there is, being obvious of all that was created before humans. But the story is, both, true and false, even updated after its creation, when it clearly said not to add or take away from its contents. Overall, it is a false book."

Dr.Sentilva

1.   "I'm sorry we discovered such a world, but we needed to intervene. I say that, after remembering the words of Dr. Skemotis, who said:

2.   "We must advance and continue to advance in a manner that brings us all together as family and diagnostically fixers of our societies.

3.   We must view every unique circumstance as a contribution that, both, positively and negatively contributes to our world, with a view towards positive and moral objectives. It is unique to anyone, who naively comes under its influence and must be learned, before being accused of negligence.

4.   Any negative circumstance is a threat to our world and community, no matter how far; because we never know when or how it may affect our environment. So, we must remain alert, attentive, and ready to defend ourselves, in any manner that brings permanent resolve, with the least harm."

5.   The research group released an additional result of an interview. It is unclear whether more results will be published. Unknown Interviewee #1 stated the following:

6.   "As a student, I felt the way to go through my legal career by the corrections and behaviors of my peers. For an example, if I said anything negative about the rich, I was reminded about how I would get a job or how matters would be, if they didn't fund certain events. The defense was definitely there.

7.   I felt I could do a better job of helping to cut down or eliminate crime; but I found that, that was not the objective of the legal system. After I learned that judges have been criticized and

removed from cases, even reprimanded, I knew I had to follow the social fabric of the environment or find myself on a different path, opposed to most people, and unable to maintain the quality of life of my peers, parents, and siblings. Then, there was the respect of my friends that was at stake too. So, I became groomed to carry out the law in respects to my peers, rather than to improve the system towards fairness in truth for all.

8.   I felt that we should have been on the solution side of every problem, but that's not how business works. Our legal system was a business that depended on the people having many issues that we had to step in and temporarily resolve, including the use of death penalties. But we all saw that the same type of people showed up, and they were fine with that.

9.   We listened to testimonies and observed behaviors, knowing that we weren't addressing the root cause of these matters, other than to profit from them. The experts were, only, there to make the system more effective and efficient in respects to profits and reputation.

10.   We had designed our social, economic, physical, and legal system to act as a filter to squeeze out certain people, especially characteristics associated with those types. It was part of a system of creating status quos.

11.   The lowest in the status quo was subject to the most issues that hindered progress, maintained confinement within a status, and/or demoted them to a lower status.

12.   We saw the statistics of each type of defendant that walked into the courtroom, and we sentenced them, according to likely to offend again. So, the most manipulated got the more severe sentences.

13.   Even if we didn't know whether the defendant was innocent or guilty, we would, at times, rob them, based on probability in certain courts. Our strength was in popular beliefs, funded by the people, who understood and knew how to play the system. They were regular people and professionals, who thought like us. You can see their line of thinking on social media, where they feel free to express themselves, with little or no consequences. They express a majority view.

14.   The system had to be crooked, or it would cause a flip in the status quo. Then, the downtrodden would be first and the oppressors last.

15.   The system could not profit, as is, if the downtrodden was made aware of the legal flaws and maneuvers of the oppressive system and became motivated to fight for what was right. So, the experts had to be out of their reach too.

16.   Because we understood the process of perception, certain ways of life and/or environmental circumstances were very useful in guiding our efforts for business. Our models are filled with details that foretell the conditions and whereabouts of, especially, our most potential candidates of crime. However, it does not expose us.

17.   I had one defendant say that he felt that he had to sneak and do crimes to garner the greatest success in life, or he'd have to live a life of poverty and shame. Jobs didn't pay enough, weren't dependable, and were draining in motivation, due to high expectations of him and had a degrading demeanor. That's one of our models.

18.   Our people make sure when and whether certain models are either questionable, a lie, or a victim's fault, while the victim has no proof. That's why we never allow recording devices in

certain areas that we do business and control information and intelligence. When things happen, we've already thought it through."

Dr. Zeckler

1. Dr. Zeckler stated that "An interesting thing about their legal system is the mixup, concerning justice and revenge. They were treated as one and the same.

2. Justice is about hitting a moral target or righting a wrong or all wrongs. Revenge is a fight to even a score, but actually solves no problems, except to demonstrate equivalence, or better, in deed and/or character.

3. Most didn't know the difference. Even the downtrodden believed and practiced revenge, which justified holding them captive, for protective purposes. It was more likely the result of ignorance of resolve, but appears to be simply a hateful attitude on the part of all sides.

4. The legal system taught revenge and cut off paths that avoid the need to be revengeful, fostering a revengeful environment. So, there were very few or no escapes to peace, love, and prosperity.

5. It appears that the older chapters of the Holy Book were written, solely, to justify revenge, through the use of Holy Revenge, which was falsely used; because the Lord is associated with all-knowing and resolution. Holy Revenge is only, logically, associated with the defense of His elements, like resolution, healing, love, truth, etc. I agree that the book is a scam."

Minister Ion: The Setup

1.   A few people got together and created a foundation, which set up a museum showcasing the works of Minister Ion.

2.   A few visitors included some officials from Quantum Star Eckter, who marveled at a recorded sermon of the minister, they hadn't heard:

3.   "Minister Ion: Happy Lord's Day, everyone!

4.   The audience: Happy Lord's Day!

5.   Minister Ion: Today, we're going to talk about "The Setup".

6.   When two people are opposed to one another, in an interaction, they exchange values. In the exchange, these values get approved, rejected, or ignored. As they counter one another, elements of their way of thinking begin to materialize. As we confirm what materialized, we find that the internalization matches the impulse and response behaviors. When it doesn't match, we find that more information is needed or error is the indication.

7.   When one or both are practicing revenge against the other, we have an opportunity to, potentially, learn from the revenge artist what is known or thought about the other, except in the case of pure exploration, where intelligence is used for the purpose of manipulation. In the case of temptation, knowledge is dispersed only through successful manipulation.

8.   Now remember that one, who is experienced in what people look for in an exchange between countering parties, can and may play a role that falsely depicts the other person. This is a popular framing method. They tend to add something that wasn't there and it may be a string of something to make it look legit. So, the challengers are not so easy to diagnose.

9.   From a spiritual perspective, it's similar; but the opposing influences are not so obviously challenging one another. So, we don't get to hear the argument, only to experience it from a personal perspective, while a broader view requires us to branch out and collect a variety of information and intelligences. However, we are being limited by established procedures of the power structure, which more assures their future goals and objectives.

10.   However, in our experiences, we see values adopted, denied, and not recognized. The more you see and know, the more you understand. From there, we can process and adjust the internalization of opposing parties. But I don't want to talk about uniqueness. I want to talk about two major influences that oppose one another; because, in an imperfect world filled with imperfect people, all the unique versions come from these two major systems of operation. The ideal version only comes from the positive system or God. That said, the negative system of operation is filled with inferior elements that produce and sustain inferior results.

11.   In deceptive cases, clarity is fogged by the reservation of a value of the other in limited form. Good values may be limited to a high-class group, such as a higher degree of peace, love, and unity than normal. This signals the knowledge of importance of such values and the effectiveness of eliminating them as a weapon.

12. Looking all around, we find challenges in our world. These challenges tell us something. It is up to us to decipher what they mean, their value, and how to resolve them. We have to identify which major category each challenge represents or what part of the challenge is related to what major category, in the case of mixed values unrelated to one another.

13. To categorize, you have to understand both major operations.

14. We all understand that the world is filled with good and evil to some degree. It is perceived, of course, through their relative values.

15. So, we can discern one operative acting against another by following challenges, their makeup, and the results. The elements of one operative produces a related result. The inferior breed inferiority and the good breed superiority. This is how we learn how our world works.

16. It is stated that the fallen angels were cast down to our environment and Satan is the god of this world. This is the inferior operation. We can test for their presence, because they operate in opposition to the values of God and develop more and more in that direction. In reality, you can detect them, like a ping to a cellphone tower gives the location of a cellphone.

17. Because every value of God is opposing to them, they will, eventually, act to restrict or discourage its use and, maybe, eliminate its value. Something that doesn't work is seen as having no value. They have to act against anything that develops enough to transform their system in the direction of God's Will.

18. As written and apparently, God forced them down here with an ultimatum and some time to work. So, regardless of Truth, they cannot revert from the ultimatum. So, we must discern the ultimatum in their beliefs and actions. We must detail and grade the overall, accuracy and appropriateness of their governance to identify them.

19. For judgment, the people are divided against one another, based on the degree of adoption of one major operation versus another. All are not God's people, when the adoption of inferior values is significant and the person refuses to revert in light of Truth.

20. When one denies the values of the other, the rejected value is part of the opposing operative's value system. As we compile the values, we get a glimpse into the operation and potential results of the system.

21. What I discovered was they find me challenging. Of course, who should be surprised? I preach and practice good values. What could go wrong? They have to answer. They have to respond. They have to resolve the solution, the truth, the love, and the peace. All of these major values have to be converted, because it can spread like a virus.

22. They may attack from the top or from the bottom. But, they're not that limited. They design the law and procedures to confine you. They will use your peers and threaten past or future circumstances. The means may be hideous or obvious, if not a little of both.

23. You may look for shelter out of the rain and lightning, only to find that those shelters are filled with inferior values and desperation in condensed form.

24.   They have a tendency to make you stand still and milk you, like a cow. While you may have room to roam, they limit you with an enclosed fence.

25.   Their tools and how they use them says a lot about them, let alone the results. In the end, it's all your fault, regardless of intent, effort, and circumstances. From there, you can only make matters worse or accept what's happening to you. The implication is you have no power over much of anything, if at all.

26.   Their processes not only intrude on our natural religious rights, while they claim all have religious freedoms; but they paint the picture of our world by whom they allow to express their natural talents.

27.   Because of "The Setup", judge no one, especially if you don't fully understand and/or don't have all the knowledge or details. Otherwise, that may lead to confusion, adversity, revenge, and anything but the values of God. Then, you will have joined the inferior side, helping to attain their goals. That's especially true, if the victim or defendant wakes up, only to act as a challenge to the inferior system.

28.   Amen!" Copyright© Minister Ion Museum

29.   Octobin (Quantum Star Eckter official): That's interesting that he preached that sermon, given the risks involved.

30.   Renjada: Yes, minister Ion was very outspoken and what happened to him is sad. He gave this sermon shortly before the church crumbled.

31.   At that time, the legal case had been progressing for months, making him look like a monster. They slowly added details and weighed in with so-called reputable people and reinterpreted almost every move or statement minister Ion made. I thought the method they used could, actually, frame and convict anyone, innocent or not.

32.   I saw how some supporters caved to the media's influence and how those who took a stand for him were defamed and/or prosecuted for small crimes. I, also, saw how other ministers saw him as someone not to be and eluded to love as a solution and blaming hard times on the sins of members of their congregation, in denial of an outspoken approach. Those questionable ministers should be more careful about lying on God and encouraging support for the fallen angels and their administration, who sit in positions of power.

33.   Someone asked him to come out from behind that fake shield and reveal who you really are!

34.   It was a total mess. We were just outnumbered and a lot of people were scared, especially when many just talked and, like a lot of others, did nothing.

35.   Octobin: I'm sorry to hear that. You have an ally in us. Don't forget that.

36.   Renjada: Thank you.

Introduction

1.   We both embrace and celebrate Minister Ion and recognize his passing as a murder case. Because his so-called natural death was, actually, plotted with scientific means, known to cause ailments from social adversary means, emotional manipulation, and physical attacks, the case is deemed murder.

2.   In furtherance, we believe his signature sermon is the reason for his death.

3.   We have finished reviewing the case of Minister Ion and decided to release an excerpt from what we think is his signature sermon:

Does God Love Everyone?

1.   Everyone has some sort of ideal situation or condition, including God. Look around and see how His creations interact with one another, even on the smallest scale. He had some kind of plan.

2.   He allowed us to learn about and manage His creations. As we became more knowledgeable, we became more responsible. As we became more responsible, we became more obligated.

3.   We are responsible and obligated to contribute to the most ideal conditions and situations. That's what it means to synchronize with your God/god.

4.   As we become more intelligent in the differences in God's and Satan's (god's) ways, we begin to choose one over the other.

5.   It's a harder choice, when Satan's people tie the two choices to a fork in the road, one to poverty and the other to riches.

6.   Satan and his people punish those who choose God and His ways, while rewarding those like him.

7.   It's a system of competition and domination versus a system of communion and love, another element of the fork in the road.

8.   The fork in the road is a filtering system. God uses filtering systems to discern who His people are. We use filtering systems to discern differences, as well. So, when He makes a judgement and gives an explanation of principles and concepts that fortify His decision, we understand.

9.   Being all-knowing and seeing the balance of all matters, we cannot legitimately act in His place.

10.   He knows the manager(s) of the many types of forks in the road, even those planted. But, while we can blame the forks in the road, remember, He led many to the land of milk and honey, after He dispensed those, He didn't approve of.

11.   They had to go through the desert for a short amount of time. Recall that the desert was used as the filtering tool. It was a source of deprivation and humility. Those, who were more easily prompted to sin died in the sand. Recall that I said "more easily prompted to sin". Recall that I said "a short amount of time".

12.   There's a difference between testing and filtering versus molding. Now, I'm going to leave that alone and move on.

13.   So, God has rules and doesn't conflict with them; the conflict comes from a challenger, the Devil and his supporters.

14.   How do we recognize challengers and supporters of Satan? Remember, God said that He chastises all that He loves? When a person is chastised by God, he/she becomes conscious and molded in the direction of perfection in God. A child born to be molded into a mature, ideal adult is the model given to us, here.

15.   But there are many, who have satisfyingly limited consciousness, don't properly respond to repercussions, and/or despise the qualities of God. Those, who freely sin, as if to have very little or no boundaries, suffering very little or no negative consequences for their actions, are not loved. Because God is Supreme and He has rules, this can only go on for a time." Copyright© Minister Ion Museum

Quantum Star Eckter: Impressed by What They Observed at the Minister Ion Museum

1.   After leaving the Minister Ion Museum, Quantum Star Eckter officials decided to address the former officials of the inferior planet, using Minister Ion's sermon. They perceived the former officials as a threat, due to their knowledge of Minister Ion's sermon, but continued oppression. They found that these officials were not inclined towards Truth, based on their resisting response. It was like they found a dangerous cult amongst the population, which may have to be dealt with separately from the general population.

2.   So, they played Minister Ion's sermon with intent to get a logical reply:

3.   "Bringing it Home

4.   Minister Ion: Happy Lord's Day!

5.   Audience: Happy Lord's Day!

6.   Minister Ion: This is another day the Lord has blessed us with to progress His interests or to waste His time. Which will it be...? We find people on both sides of that spectrum.

7.   People are recognizing their desires, making decisions, prioritizing their efforts, and coming and going, as they carry out their goals. They are busy.

8.   Because we live in a well-developed world, it's structural in procedure and opportunities. That's a good thing! But it has its drawbacks, which we see in statistics and in the media. It means that we've recognized polar elements, whether in principles or concepts.

9.   The authorities have built a system on this information and technology. They've used it for many and against others. They've taken from one and gave to another. They've given structure for one and denied it for another. They have allowed Acktus and denied Polok.

10.   At the same time, they have pretended that these abilities are strange and non-existent. Yet, there is crime above and below.

11.   There's a profitable system, both moral and immoral. And, of course, encouraging and profiting from crime is moral, if you leave it up to them. It makes them reputable, if you leave it up to them.

12.   I'm getting ready to bring it home.

13.   Audience: Bring it!

14.   Minister Ion: When I was a production worker, it didn't take long to learn that defective products and services couldn't pass the high standards of the Quality Control Department. But, apparently, we've got something different going on here. I've never heard an explanation for it. I've never recognized how the two processes parallel one another. I've never recognized the moral integrity that should be commonly applied in both processes.

15.   I saw that experience could go either direction. I saw that someone, who was experienced upon improving a matter, was experienced in advancing in a particular direction, one way or the other, if not both. I saw intelligence propel either direction. I saw geniuses on both sides of the spectrum. Worse, I saw people embracing those on both sides of the spectrum and holding onto positive clichés associated with the relevant disciplines. They did this, regardless of the developments and regardless of positive or negative, which were defined quite different from their natural confines.

16.   I saw that these processes could amazingly filter out in accordance to skin color, regardless of effort, and still be called credible. Yet, no one could explain it, except to place the blame on the filtered.

17.   I remember reading about Barborous being encouraged by an emperor to put a spell on God's people, only for the values of God to intervene through his conscience. Now, Barborous' perception was being steered by the human authority. There were certain things he could not see, because he was using his naked eyes. He was caught up in "What is so" in human life. Barborous consulted with God, but was capable of mistakes, due to his blindness and subordination to the authoritative class. Because he persevered in the Will of God, the spell was not cast.

18.   Today, we see many like Barborous, who are succeeding in their practice of inferior spells, in various manners, especially through means of selfishness, secrets, division, entrapment, modeling, and any other deceptive practices. Notice how these values are related and run with one another.

19.   This is why I say "To see, you must learn how to look". You can't afford to allow your perception to be trained by an imperfect system. The only way to learn how to look is through the following of a value system, which dispenses related values. It teaches us to have a

conscience and, thus, a heart. The world we live in doesn't do that. Instead, it teaches sin and revenge in cyclical fashion.

20.   Perfection entails that our value system is pure and not tainted by foreign matters. We learn by practicing and by watching others, while depicting these values at work. So, our ways should be directed by a sound and moral source, not of ourselves.

21.   We owe the obligation to follow a moral and sound value system to everyone in society, because together we build an influence upon us all. In that way, we become responsible for another. So, through the value system and how we influence one another, we see no merit in being different, as in opposed.

22.   Examining the world, today, we can see what negative values bring, like selfishness. Future developments respond in a negative fashion, in which the blind and the corrupt deny any involvement. Yet, they can't construct a sound explanation of detachment. Therefore, we can identify a type of people by what they have materialized under their own watch and administration.

23.   When we teach somebody how to look, they can begin to see as we do. Why is this a good value? It's because it develops harmony, peace, love, and all of their related values. Notice how these values are related and run with one another.

24.   Now, you can see more clearly who is who and what is what.

25.   The world will create events, make noise, create questionable events or circumstances, or present any form of distraction, only for the purpose of preventing the progression of the knowledge of Truth. But, by teaching others, you can bring it home." Copyright© Minister Ion Museum

26.   Octobin (Quantum Star Eckter official): Can anyone explain how his life and the direction of society went or continued in the wrong direction, after acknowledging this sermon?

27.   Former political affiliate of the inferior planet: …………Well, I can say that we represented the people, which is how we were elected. If we did not carry out the wishes of the people, we would not have been in that position for very long. So, we had an obligation to follow that, which was beyond our means to control.

28.   Octobin (Quantum Star Eckter official): Do you go to church or believe in God?

29.   Former political affiliate of the inferior planet: Yes, sir! Yes to both…

30.   Octobin (Quantum Star Eckter official): So, you have this degree, including knowledge of psychology and other specialized information and no means to influence your supporters positively?

31.   You gave constitutional rights, created circumstances for certain people, especially taking advantage of their naivety at the most advantageous time for financial gain, then reasoned their rights away, as a result of brainwashing them through environmental circumstances. I call that "Framing".

32.   So, how is it that they had constitutional rights from the beginning, if you conspired to violate their natural ability to learn, grow, and choose their best options through moral, diplomatic, and fair experiences and teachings?

33.   Former political affiliate of the inferior planet: Positive or moral views didn't bring wealth, sir, and that was the main objective. People wanted to stand out above another. It wasn't us who were the problem. It was them. We just did what we could to give our families the best lives we could.

34.   We, also, recognized how the population could become unstable, if we didn't heed the wishes of the majority. So, we followed and subjected ourselves to the majority through an election process.

35.   We tried to be as fair and honest as we could, under the circumstances. But, under those circumstances, someone had to lose. Someone had to be neglected. Someone had to be misused. We knew who that had to be from the demands of those, who elected us. So, we had to control the ballots in such a manner as to prevent unpopular ideas.

36.   Octobin (Quantum Star Eckter official): So, you had to sell your soul to Satan; so you could serve God?

37.   Former political affiliate of the inferior planet: We were all going through some things. So, I don't think judgment is called for, here. God knew our hearts.

38.   Octobin (Quantum Star Eckter official): I'm sure he did. But what we care about is results. Remember, God can't change? So, you've got to put some effort behind your hidden moral stance; or you're going to jail. You're part of a special group, because you held others above the standards that you were obligated to carry out, but was able to excuse yourself, through your so-called belief in God and blame on others.

39.   You, even, taught not to blame others for your failures. Yet, you just did it here. You saw, clearly, your position in this sermon. You are conflicted within, and I'm afraid that you may end up in jail for pretentiously following our program.

40.   Former political affiliate of the inferior planet: The circumstances that compelled us have been removed by your administration; so, you won't have a problem with me, sir.

41.   Octobin (Quantum Star Eckter official): I hope not, but I don't trust you. Dismissed.

Quantum Star Eckter: The Interview of a Doctor from the Inferior Planet

1.   A man came forward to address the issue about medical treatment of the people; however, many said he was only fretting, because he feels he's been overlooked for promotions, raises, and been mistreated. Before that, he was content with his high-income career and never publicly made any negative statements about medical policies.

2.   They say he's just looking for attention. However, Quantum Star Eckter officials wanted to hear what he had to say; since evidence of medical foul play seemed to be apparent, after statistics of diseases, other illnesses, and participation in studies painted a suspicious picture of racial differences. So, they took him to the deposition room.

3.   Once there, they gathered around the table and set up the recordings; then the witness/doctor began to speak. He stated the following:

4.   "Dr. Lok: First of all, I may be upset with the fact that I was unfairly treated, but that is normal for anyone to undergo what I went through. I didn't speak up publicly, because I didn't want to step on the wrong toes more than I already did by voicing some of my opinions.

5.   I needed my job and what little approval I did have. I had a family to take care of and a lifestyle that I was trying to avoid. I was doing the best I could under the circumstances. I only came forward, publicly, because of the takeover and the change of mindset in dealing with our society.

6.   I just wanted to clear up any misunderstandings about that, before we continue to proceed.

7.   Detective Awkhimer: Ok. As you know, I'm a detective on the research team of Quantum Star Eckter. We're part of the division that deals with international issues. And we are here to listen and to ask questions, if necessary. So, tell us what you've got to say about the medical field.

8.   Dr. Loc: Ok……I've been a doctor for about 16 yrs. I feel blessed to do what I love to do in life, seeing that many don't have that opportunity. So, I respected the medical profession to a large extent. I don't regret speaking up about certain things, because that's how I learned who was who and which of those to step back from, to some degree anyway. But I had to fit in some kind of way too, in order to better guarantee the long-term success of my career.

9.   So, whereas there may have been a conflict in behavior, consent, and opinions, I never really stepped back from what I really believed to be true and right in principles and concepts. So, I could see how some people could confuse me with others, who did not share my true thoughts and beliefs. But I was getting tired of pretending and fabricating lies to make them think I was in harmony with them and, then, have to keep up with them.

10.   I was associated with some highly sophisticated crooks, who carried themselves in a professional and polite manner. I'm talking about people you wouldn't believe would harm a hair on anyone's body. They were, almost constantly, psychologically twisting matters in their favor and ready to turn on you, if they detected any sign of disagreement, depending on how important it was to their agenda.

11.   But you had to see the big picture to see who they really were. You had to possess, at least, enough of their knowledge to understand their mindset. It was easier, if they thought you were naïve of a given subject in question. I didn't always need to speak on a particular matter; but when I did, I'd carefully ask questions, without exposing my knowledge of the subject, but to encourage elaboration. I could see what they were protecting or what they were really trying to do.

12.   Unless you knew chemistry and biology, you could not see what was happening; although you may have an opinion. That's the way it is with any discipline of science, as you already know.

13.   They expected me to just follow protocols, in order to avoid being at fault whenever the course of an event went the wrong direction. When I say "the wrong direction", I mean a progression of events that yields their unintended results, not right or wrong, or resolved or worsened.

14.   Looking at the big picture, a long time ago, people were said to live a ridiculous amount of time, in comparison to this day in time.

15.   They wanted control throughout the process. They wanted control so much that they authorized the taking of nutrients out of the meat and created vitamins and such, in which only chemists had knowledge of its more appropriate use. Of course, I could understand this, if something was getting out of hand and needed to be studied. After all, the population was growing and a lot of people are trouble, which could aid in the development and progression of diseases and other ailments.

16.   But I saw innocent people hurt and forced or tricked into a guilty lifestyle for the benefit of others.

17.   I see every discipline of science in the likeness of chemistry. Everything is electrical, connected, conductive, conducted, resistant, purposed, and/or protected. If you had all the colors (resources), you could paint whatever you wanted.

18.   There were different cultures, which had their own lifestyles, including what they ate. What they ate was, basically, chemicals. Their diets made them different. It meant they were a different balance of chemicals. So, researchers could look for a cure in one culture to adapt to another. But the reverse was also possible. That was left for the poor, but definitely the victimized race. Even churches dispensed poor diets to take care of the poor and homeless.

19.   Whenever control of chemicals is taken from nature, that control allows the most powerful people to put their stamp on society. If you saw racism, or discrimination of any type, before or during the takeover of nature's distribution process, evidence would now show up in the results of the unnatural distribution process. If one race struggled more than another, due to a lack of approval and equal opportunities, they would now suffer from chemical imbalances that lead to weaknesses and diseases in health. Increased costs and income restrictions are the buttons that determine who's going to be victimized by the distribution process.

20.   I never got a chance to study genes, but I suspected something was going on there too. Why not?

21.   It appeared to me that many hid behind mystery, when they said crucial knowledge needed to resolve an issue was unknown.

22.   When you take over nature's job, not knowing everything about its operations, things will naturally go wrong. But, when there's competition and hate, anything can happen intentionally, including reverse engineering that leads to health issues or the worsening of such.

23.   That's all I Have for you."

24.   Detective Awkhimer: Thank you, Dr. Lok.

Court Begins

1.   The assistant Judge rises and states, "May the court begin!"

2.   The prosecutor rises and states, "Because it was discovered that Informant #3 wrote the most dangerous book of his society, a secret hearing was scheduled to determine his fate."

3.   The assistant Judge: What is the name of the book you're referring to, and why is it considered dangerous?

4.   The Prosecutor: The book was written and published for the authoritative population only, giving them specific advantages to will over lower society, through secret and high-profile manipulation that takes control from any target of interest.

5.   It, clearly, details an entire scope of manipulative maneuvers, including how to control the perception(s) of any group or individual.

6.   Judge: Mr. Ramsi (Defending attorney) what is your answer?

7.   Mr. Ramsi: Sir, my client was part of another society at that time and is, now, appreciating a better society, which happens to be ours.

8.   The Prosecutor: Sir, Informant #3 is not considered rehabilitated and still resides in the inferior environment. Plus, he is, rightfully, not allowed to associate with our society. Therefore, he is not part of our society. Instead, he is part of a society that is in the midst of redevelopment.

9.   Mr. Ramsi: I question whether my client's knowledge isn't the same information that we, ourselves, possess.

10.   The Prosecutor: Yes, but our culture doesn't share the same dynamics as his. It would be very difficult for him to pull off such a scam. Our people's aims are different. They desire perfection, morality, safety, peace, equality, and personal control.

11.   The inferior society doesn't value any of those qualities, unless it's advantageous and profitable to them. In that competitive environment, these qualities have different meanings and are less affordable and profitable in the lower classes. That's because the struggle to survive and prosper is met with adversity, a construct of society that favors the majority and takes an advantage of the minority. So, almost, if not all, feels the need to be accepted by and join the majority for success. The way and the truth become what the majority says it is versus some scientific system. So, the inhumane system becomes strengthened by a system that threatens human nature and their environmental conditions. Over time, it had gotten tighter and tighter, choking out the lower classes from a high quality of life.

12.   Our society, also, uses the information to understand, resolve, and to prevent conflicts within our society. Their society seems to attempt to utilize everything as a weapon, whenever practical.

13.   Judge: Are you saying "Freedom of information and transparency is at issue here? Because, we value these things, and we're in the midst of redeveloping the inferior society to be like ours.

14.   Mr. Ramsi: That is my point also, sir.

15.   The Prosecutor: Sir, that planet's religious background reserves the use of demonic elements and, therefore, demonic people or, that is, practitioners of evil. They feel it's a necessary part of their society and refuse to believe otherwise.

16.   So, if we allow this information to leak to their entire society, the problem will spread and justice will become less effective in determining the full facts of a case and more innocent people will lose control of their lives. Their society will become more like packs of wolves that must be chosen for, hopefully, safety and success. At this point, it is in the hands of a smaller group.

17.   Judge: But, the problem won't be resolved? Is that what you're saying?

18.   The Prosecutor: Yes.

19.   Judge: Mr. Ramsi, you understand this?

20.   Mr. Ramsi: Yes, sir. Certain aspects of their religion are a problem.

21.   The Prosecutor: Moreover, under these conditions, a defendant whose life is not within his/her control can't possibly get a fair trial. Imagine an influence that overwhelmed his/her ability to choose or ability to be seen legitimately as he/she really is. I'm talking about character here. So, you get someone who is faced with charges, without legal skills, and attempts to flee or avoid prosecution. The fear in their eyes is a sign of non-intent and/or maybe entrapment into a way of living. We've worked this out. Instead, that society uses it as a tool for profitable success and/or revenge. Even further, the elastic nature of humans was only afforded to certain people, regardless of the facts. Again, the deciding factor is in the hands of social control, not solely in a legitimate, scientific system.

22.   The defendant is, also, caught between expressing the contents of the most dangerous book, only to be met with a negative response that could be very costly or remaining silent in favor of the least consequences, even when the consequences will remain severe. Remember, the defendant's fate is in the hands of authorities.

23.   Their justice system's rules favored bringing the defense to the very class that encouraged the matter at issue. When not chosen, the majority's way of thinking was, many times, used to consider the defendant's fate. The fork in the road didn't allow for any excuses.

24.   We've sought to undermine any inferior element; that is not their way of doing business. Instead, they leave it as part of nature and as a complement to their system and automated scheme.

25.   The moral of the story is that "Serving two fundamentally different masters, in which one is polar in respects to the other, is not an effective way of developing a better society". But, they knew this; because they knew the condition of the fruit(s) were an effect of the conditions of the tree.

26.   Judge: So, how do we resolve this?

27.   The Prosecutor: I talked with our experts, and they said "We shouldn't make matters worse than they already are". If we attempt to take away their religion, we could cause a cooperative environment to turn chaotic.

28.   Judge: So, you're saying "He's a danger to our attempt to redevelop this society, and we should remove him, taking away his freedom to associate with the remaining society?"

29.   The Prosecutor: Yes, sir.

30.   Judge: Ok, this hearing is adjourned, while the Justices discuss the issue amongst us.

31.   Two days later….

Second Court Session Begins

1.   The assistant Judge rises and states, "May the court begin!"

2.   Judge: We have arrived at what we feel is the best answer to this problem.

3.   We cannot take away the freedom of Informant #3 without a showing of cause as criminal attempt or a current violation of law.

4.   We cite the description of freedom described by Bok Teko:

5.   "Freedom, like any other element, is stuck in a traffic jam with other elements, complete with signals that determine priority and advancement. It must never be steered towards a dead end, only restricted from the violations of laws that protect the natural rights, moral interests, and ethical means of professional conduct."

6.   As future guidance, you must discover sufficient status and influence that yields control over another at an illegal capacity that harms the victim or Quantum Star Eckter's attempt to morally redevelop the inferior planet.

7.   This hearing is adjourned.

Hearing for: Violation of Order to Disclose Information Pertinent to an Investigation or Research

1.   Defendant: Informant #3, Under Arrest

Court Instructions

1.   Before the court session begins, the defensive attorney explains the system to the defendant. He states that there are scientific statements already available on the screen, potentially, for and against the defendant, to help guide the course of the court. They are just suggestive and change with the presentation of new information. They consider the history of the environment, culture, capabilities, status, provocation, emotional and mental state, and any other relevant information.

2.   Anything presented on the main screen is interactive with these statements. A camera is, also, recording the main screen. The camera's contents, as well as the screens contents, are not amendable and may become public records, depending on the agenda of the court(s) over the case and public concerns.

3.   This screen is our private and personal interactive screen, where you can challenge or elaborate at certain points of interest. No one can see this screen, but us. However, you have the option to advance to the main screen at your discretion; but I wouldn't advise that, due to the scientific data, which could become less predictable.

Court Begins

1.   The assistant Judge rises and states, "May the court begin!"

2.   The prosecutor rises and states "We have Informant #3 in custody for Violation of Order to Disclose Information Pertinent to an Investigation or Research. Do we continue to address the defendant as Informant #3?

3.   Assistant Judge: The defendant is not convicted, and has never been convicted, but his intent is countering to the authority of the government of Quantum Star Eckter. He is still considered an elastic type, until proven otherwise. Therefore, the court will rule in favor of reserving the identity of Informant #3.

4.   Prosecutor: A questioner questioned whether Informant #3 provided useful data that gives clarity into how a planet developed as it has? The questioner states that Informant #3 was clearly in a position to understand, in detail, what perspired to create such a condition, but didn't elaborate to capacity and remained critical of the less advantaged population.

5.   The prosecutor presented the testimony of Informant #3 to the court.

6.   Judge: Mr. Ramsi (Defending attorney) what is your answer?

7. Mr. Ramsi: Sir, my client is overwhelmed by the data and admits to the crime and wishes to cooperate.

8. Judge: May the defendant speak on his behalf.

Informant #3:

1. We, simply, designed our environment from Central Intelligence by delegating tasks to agents, who carried out tasks and/or gathered information, and agencies that regulated their perspective area of life. Whatever we could imagine, we built it or did it.

2. The report, you want, is in "There Are Three Truths", which includes the system, facts, and statistics. We concentrated, mostly, on four key areas, science, underlying influences, the mentality(s) of an individual or population, and society as a whole. It, also, speaks about a book that, when read, it tells a story that hides coded information. The coded information is a closer interpretation of the realities that people portrayed and endured.

3. Aside from that, we observed all for characteristics, habits, and cycles; then, we chose whom to associate whom with or observed it to be so and used it to situate one up or down. And, yes and unfortunately, we assured certain people would be placed up or down, regardless of what they did. We did it all through a collection of information and identifying traits.

4. Through our collection of information, we screened for ways to take over a person's life, whether it was limiting income, opportunities, options, mimicking filtering systems in our policies, or requiring something that, usually, the more fortunate could meet. We could color the world as we liked, so to speak.

5. Judge: Let the record show that "There Are Three Truths" consists of the information and instructions behind the atrocities of the inferior planet, according to Informant #3. We will combine the past, current, and future developments together, within this book, making the report a full accounting of events to the date the research is terminated.

6. Let the record show that there were takeovers of other people's lives, rendering them out of full control.

7. Prosecutor: Sir, this is also a serious case, given that the defendant appears to possess countering intelligence to the authority of the government of Quantum Star Eckter. We must explore the defendant for such information, to protect our environment and interests.

8. Judge: Agreed. Mr. Ramsi?

9. Mr. Ramsi: My client was a high-ranking member of the armed forces. He states that he is not programmed to give into an enemy, only to persevere in the authoritative and self-preservation of interests. He could not imagine defeat or the bowing down to another authority, without being less effective in his position to honor his obligations.

10. Having a military of our own, I think that we can clearly understand this.

11. Judge: Agreed.

12. Prosecutor: Taking a stand against us has to mean that Informant #3 sees us as the enemy.

13.   Judge: Let the record show that Informant #3 sees us as the enemy.

14.   Prosecutor: Earlier, I motioned the court and gave a copy of all the testimonies of all those who were interviewed. I mentioned that their authorities distorted definitions to support a particular idea, instead of universal meanings, used by all others, like freedom. The meanings of words and ideas were twisted, only to qualify them for a particular outcome. The business of crime fighting became a crime itself, for a profit. The people were outlawed from doing many things, while pressured to do the very thing outlawed.

15.   Judge: Thank you, Micom. I've already listed your concerns for Informant #3 in the Findings Form to be given to case management.

16.   So, I think the best thing to do is to hand everything over to the counselors and monitor the case from here.

17.   Informant #3, you will be given instructions on how to connect with the counselors and the importance of following protocols.

18.   This court is adjourned.

Quantum Star Eckter - Counseling

Record of Participant: Informant #3

Court Statements:

1.   "There Are Three Truths" consists of the information and instructions behind the atrocities of the inferior planet, according to Informant #3. We will combine the current and future developments together, within this book, making the report a full accounting of events to the date the research is terminated.

2.   Let the record show that there were takeovers of other people's lives, rendering them out of full control.

3.   Informant #3 sees us as the enemy

Client Replies

1.   But we had people, who were inclined towards competition and injury for selfish reasons; so, we needed to separate and grow beyond them, using our advantage to control them for safety reasons. But I admit we went beyond those boundaries.

2.   The way we treated our dogs translated over to other humans.

3.   We had no other objectives concerning them, other than to make them accommodating to us.

4.   We talked about discipline, only to ridicule; because they weren't as inclined to cater to us and our ways, as we would have liked.

5.   To keep them as vulnerable to our control, we had to generate an opposite system for them that was designed to encourage or keep them indebted and subjective. That's why there were no real corrections facilities, resolutions, and healthcare for them.

Complaints:

1.   Prosecutor: It appears that he learned enough about the construction of his environment that he became or was just like those he feared.

2.   There were opportunities to create a better world; but he, constantly, passed them up and hid the evidence.

3.   He chose his neighbor, discriminately, violating all laws of Love.

4.   He could see himself as a reflection of the animal world, at that level of perception. Yet, the Creator not only gave him a brain, but a conscience too.

5.   The idea of living in such a manner has, naturally, been reproved as inferior; since he reflected the animal world and the very thing to be corrected and prevented.

Case Management:

1.   "Welcome to the start of your counseling sessions

2.   None of us are perfect, but we will all be aiming for such. Therefore, you will be receiving protocols, axioms, and other related information to lead you on your journey of life. All information is for your best interest and the best interests of others.

3.   All communications are two-way conversations that can affect either record. So, it is important that we all stay respectful of one another.

4.   The standard protocols are ongoing and mandatory for all.

5.   But Direct Protocols are meant to address any personal circumstances.

6.   Court-Ordered Protocols are mandatory protocols addressing the personal circumstances, which are crucial to the safety of you and our environment. Therefore, the court(s) are the issuing and managing source of Court-Ordered Protocols, in which all questions related to such must be directed to them. Violations may result in the meeting of serious consequences, including prison.

7.   Protocols are designed to attract the highest quality of life with respects to the entire population. Therefore, Quantum Star Eckter maintains the least conflicting population and the lowest incarceration rate possible. We did studies, evaluations, experiments, listened to all walks of life, created analyses and predictable software, and prepared the best future for everyone. As a result, oppression and negative extremes became a thing of the past.

8.   Most importantly, we continue our push for greater and greater results. That is the very reason why we require everyone to participate in a program catered to everyone. It is our reward for choosing unity in love.

9.   Robotics is very much a part of our way of living and its most crucial parts can be monitored and reviewable by everyone, complete with an alert system and pre-planned maintenance instructions. Information and statistical data of operations and results are also available. All information is public.

10.   We strive to raise the quality of consciousness, empathy, conscience, and mental capability of all. So, there are protocols to attain that end.

11.   The negative effects that come out of a human is evidence of an incomplete or false construct, if not both; we are here to fill the gap or replace a false construct. We intend to continue what the Creator started. Together, we will make humans more like the Creator.

12.   As time went by, we noticed the after-effects. We noticed positive perception, due to better models. People became more compatible with one another, because of the acknowledgement of one Truth. Peace prevailed in more and more cases, because of the practice of love and its elements. People began to fashion themselves with etiquettes that soften their interactions and appearance, eliminating more and more misunderstandings, while attracting more appeal. It happened as a result of being more conscious of themselves and the world around them. It happened because the whole population encouraged a single individual. It happened because of the program.

13.   Questioners affected the protocols others, in a positive way. Everyone knew they were a work in progress and could not discuss the issue, other than to apologize. However, it didn't mean that the questioner's concern didn't get scrutinized for accuracy, before being validated and attached to the violator's record for correction. The process is a character grooming method, in which everyone understands the importance of, to create the great Quantum Star Eckter. And, it starts from a child on up. So, parenting is part of protocols.

14.   Everyone is to be mindful of their protocols at all times, which include axioms and any other information on their record. No one stands idle at any time. We're responsible for every moment, at which point anything can happen. Most of all, together, we are closely connected and build one another up. All information is accessible and relevant information comes to you, befitting your growth and interests.

15.   We reserve your right to be one with us.

16.   Again, Welcome!

Court-Ordered Protocols:

1.   You have a court-ordered protocol.

2.   You must remain cooperative and truthful in information sharing with the researchers of the inferior planet. You must present anytime you are aware of information, which may lead to the enlightening and/or suggestion of any fact or method, which may contribute to the efforts of the research officials.

Standard Protocols:

1.   The reception of the "Welcome" digital document is part of your standard protocol. You will receive more information over time and as they develop.

2.   What laid within, between, amongst, above, and beneath was construction, waiting to be discovered, understood, named, and utilized. In totality, this mechanical operation was responsible for all that occurred. Take something away or add to it, something different will occur, depending on the connections. Deep knowledge is so interesting to the less knowledgeable that it entices those who thirst for it.

Direct Protocols:

About Direct Protocols

1.   As you know, there are some things we must settle, based on the content of your complaints and personal issues, which we try to summarize. Think of protocols as axioms or information in reference to your record or chosen subjects of advanced studies.

2.   Direct protocols will result from complaints and known issues associated with your circumstances. They are, simply, Standard Protocols needed to be immediately observed, due to information on your record.

3.   Direct Protocols will be helpful in grooming the best person you can become, based on where you're at in the process, nothing overwhelming.

4.   You are responsible for information on your record, including all protocols, which will be looked at for consideration in any future court case that may occur. In other words, you will be responsible for your knowledge.

5.   Automated intelligence (AI) can initiate and expedite a study or a case against you, based on information on your record and search history. AI is concerned about underdevelopment, violations, health, personal welfare, and the attraction of complaints. The attraction of complaints can identify an issue(s) involving others, which may be stressing you out. So, the initiation of a case may or may not be a negative issue for you.

List of Direct Protocols

1.   An enemy is always someone, who stands in opposition to positive developments or improvements, as well as genuine peace and love. The victim's natural rights always have the right of way, when opposed by an offending enemy, including the right to defend. The enemy is responsible for any reasonable information, knowingly, deposited or implicated into the mind of the targeted person(s).

2.   The developments, beliefs, and affairs of each individual were for your eyes to see, both, the obvious and evidence of the not so visible. The information is for the purpose of correcting and healing your world. It, also, provides leads on error prevention techniques.

3.   The natural environment is not a first come, first serve environment. All the people of the environment have rights, naturally, tied to the essential resources. When you take control, you naturally adopt a duty of care, to negate damages to the natural, life connections to the environment.

4.   You have no evidence or proof of a purchased mortgage or deed, nor is it logical to have one, seeing that the Creator stands for life of His Creations and has given dominion over all the earth to humans, both, to learn and manage.

5.   Surrounding an individual with different circumstances and conditions controls that individual's mentality, making you the instrumental source. In essence, you have taken that person's place.

6.   The best decision is derived from the best option, succeeding the total effects imagined to garner a combination of the least damages and the greater reward(s) for the unified whole.

7.   A person can be so ill-programmed that past associates cannot reconnect with him/her in the same manner, due to a flawed perception. Therefore, tearing down, rather than building up, can never be called a solution. Traumatic experiences and flawed feedback have a tendency to tear people down or, that is, misdirect them.

8.   You cannot validate a judgment that stands in arbitrage with corruption.

9.   We studied ignorance and saw that it could only see the obvious, at or near its height, but couldn't see the relationship between and amongst all the things seen. Therefore, the possessor of ignorance, of any subject and to its relevant degree, was made the most vulnerable to what appeared as magic. Therefore, ignorance or a superficial mind cannot bind a contract or agreement; nor can it be a point to convict of awareness.

10.   Because of the interplay of all the elements of our world, including ourselves, we are under its influence and the interplay communicates with those, who are knowledgeable of its processes. The interplay can, potentially, affect, harm, or be beneficial to any and all of us. It is our home in operation. It is our business to learn and manage.

11.   To teach as to be inspired by the Creator, or His establishments, knowing its error, is blasphemy.

12.   Truth and Love are the Way and always has the right of way; so, align every effort with the purpose and direction of Quantum Star Eckter's program, which aims to be One with Truth. Any act, or statement that encourages error is a violation of Truth.

13.   A holder of a lie or vision that falsely represents the creator is an idol. The Creator is not worshipped through idols. The worship of idols is idolatry.

Quantum Star Eckter Hearing: Dissolve the Government of the Inferior Planet?

1.   Court Begins

2.   The assistant Judge rises and states, "May the court begin!"

3.   The prosecutor rises and states, "A Hearing was called to discuss and decide the fate of the inferior planet's government."

4.   Assistant Judge: I understand the reasonable request; but, for clarification purposes, I must ask "What is your argument for dissolving the government of the inferior planet?"

5.   The Prosecutor: The governing body's style is, obviously, conflicting to the dynamics of our redevelopment plan. To go into detail, I will describe the system.

6.   They give their defendants a choice between a jury trial or a trial before the tribune. The trial before the tribune is the only choice with a chance for an appeal. This means that the tribune can use scare tactics and more effectively influence the defendant(s) in the favor of their tribune's corrupt agendas, not recourse towards corrections, if necessary. They, also, favor uncontested statements at the end of trials.

7.   Corrections should not be a fearful process, but one understood as necessary and good. This very fact undermines their approach, which is only a false show of superior status in human relations and nothing more. In furtherance, a sharply aimed process doesn't frustrate a manner of rectification; else it becomes adverse unto itself.

8.   Moreover, the inferior government recognizes systems and elements of systems, as well as how they're connected and influence one another, from the smallest to the largest, to a great degree. They've used their knowledge of systems to create conditional effects in one or more systems to generate an effect in another. The tools of influence vary from one system to another. In a human, the targeted systems are perception, social connections and interactions, examples, education, finances, emotions, experiences, health, and whatever is necessary to produce an effect or multiple effects.

9.   With the knowledge of systems, their government produce effects that need correction; then earn a profit for correcting what they produced. It can be seen in how they have produced dramatic experiences in the lives they have pursued, to create characters for their corrective pursuits. So, they hang themselves by the use of the method that caused many problematic issues in the population, instead of using the information to create a better society.

10.   They saw that the environment was nothing more than a lot of simple and complex systems that created their environment and every system was dependent upon another and whatever elements associated with it. Everything, without exception, hangs in the balance of other matters. So, as an example, a particular plant is evidence of a particular condition; or it wouldn't exist.

11.   In furtherance, they have produced chemicals to produce desired effects, from any profitable endeavor, whether evil, moral, corrective, or disruptive. They've used hindrances to aid their cause.

12.   This is the process described in the most dangerous book of all, which focuses on traits, drivers, and habits and how to create them, as well as to utilize them to build a legal case or force an effect or condition. It concentrates on the targeted source and the views of others, all things necessary to create a balance of effects and/or desired outcome.

13.   It is that type of knowledge that convicts them, because their system produces inferior developments and attempts to void resolution; although they have intelligence to do otherwise.

14.   Making matters worse, they seek hideous means and manners of effects, distancing themselves from the problematic events they have manifested. But, the knowledge of systems tells a story as well as the avoidance of system conditions, but the pursuit of the vessel for non-systemic corrections or revenge is evidence of fraud.

15.   Their experts have split up and debated sides of issues and helped to guide the authoritative population in pursuit of safety in crimes against humanity for a profit. On the flip side, their victims are without the knowledge to completely gather favorable intelligence, prepare, and bring forth a well-organized defense. Meanwhile, the prosecutor is free to use his/her imagination to bring a tidy presentation.

16.   Judge: Mr. Ramsi (Defending attorney) what is your answer?

17.   Mr. Ramsi: Sir, I do not dispute science; and I'm not here to violate ethical concerns, whether in unison with the tribune or as a stand-alone. I follow that, which is good and sound. Therefore, I have no rejections.

18.   Judge: the matter raised is unchallenged and sound in manner. Therefore, the order is necessary for moving forward. Anyone so aligned, as to be against the "Order to Dissolve" would have to be anti-human in respects. Therefore, Let it be so!

19.   This court is adjourned!

Dream of a Rookie Detective

1.   A young lady recognizes and approaches Quantum Star Officials at an ice cream stand, revealing information about a missing person, who is still missing.

2.   She spoke about an attorney, who taught her about how this world works and saved her life. She wanted to return the favor; especially since she felt guilty about it.

3.   As they turned to listen, she spoke about attorney Migro Infro. This is how the conversation went:

4.   "I was about to go down for prostitution at a young age, and I was frightened to the point of almost suicide. But I ran into this man, Migro, who was an unpopular attorney. He saw the flaws in the legal system and how it was rigged as a business.

5.   I didn't have an attorney but was faced to decide upon one. He showed up just before I felt I had to choose a conventional attorney. I listened, because I knew how other cases went and I didn't want to go into the direction of others, who were faced with the same charges.

6.   He said the following:

7.   "I am here to represent you as an attorney. I'm not a conventional attorney. I don't follow the conventional ways of most attorneys. They appease the purpose of the system. I don't. I think it's an evil system, designed to take an advantage of others for a profit. So, it's hard to find someone like me; because I don't blindly follow the crowd, but truly follow the Ways of God.

8.   That means, everybody can't do what I do. Therefore, they can't reap the benefits and defenses of Truth, because they don't know it, reject it, or don't act accordingly.

9.   And, for as long as they continue to do so, it doesn't belong to them to benefit from or to use those defenses, if intentionally eluded.

10.   What's left is a life of hell, in which they chose; because the Truth is not discriminative in promoting itself, except in the case in which it is sufficiently elaborated upon but denied. Then, people inaccurately blame God for, supposedly, turning a deaf ear and blind eye towards them when there's nothing to reward.

11.   Everyone can see how a child is turned out, when that child is just told "No", "Yes", and/or punished without a full and effective explanation, combined with the ability to appreciate and understand its principles and concepts. Seeing the flaws in his/her teacher, the act or belief in question is perceived as no more than a gamble or mysterious in theory. The child reaches adulthood, but not maturity. But, yet, the child is blamed and held accountable for wrong actions, as if no one else shares the blame. A child without sufficient tools is a blameless child.

12.   Just like a mechanic, engineer, or any other profession, missing or wrong tools means very little or nothing can be started, progressed, or finished. And it is so throughout his or her life. Many are in the likeness of these ineffective professionals, who profit from all the confusion, but never coming to an effective, rectifying conclusion. Why? Because they get paid to withhold their trade secrets.

13.   That means I take a chance on going against the norm, but I stick with the Truth, not the social elite opinions and methods. So, I thrive on cases that are considered controversial to mainstream legal management. Mainstream legal management already has a plan, based on profits, social acceptance, enticement of support, and ability to frame a case as desired, while

unifying most of the communities. But, again, the next day or sometime in the future, they'll do a repeat, making it an endless cycle.

14.   My thinking is based on the idea of perfection of human societies, not cyclical, ineffective, herd mentalities.

15.   I consider your perception of matters and the perceptions of those around you, as examples. I look at what you are purposed to do and how you were affected or poisoned by your environment. Everyone is a product of their environment, whether they studied it deeper than others and were rewarded accordingly or they were oppressed by it and became damaged in respects to it, if not both. I look for details of your environment through you.

16.   I'm not bogged down by other cases; I see cases as supportive of one another, not just dispelling of one another.

17.   I'm here to fight to the end for you, in your favor. Even if guilty and convicted, I look for your innocence. I care nothing about a profit from the downfall of another, because I don't want that. Others, profit regardless and move on. That's not me. That's why you should choose me over any conventional attorney.

18.   I concentrate on how and why you developed as so and build a case against anyone, who feels the need to ignore and charge you for matters that manipulated you from a more powerful and/or more knowledgeable influence. I'm forever working in your favor, not moving on to the next case, as if to have forgotten you and feeling it is settled.

19.   Many of these people forget or don't recognize God in these cases, but God made us all the same, but in different colors and circumstances. The developments and how we deal with them tell us what type of people we all are, both as a client and doctor, so to speak.

20.   One may be vulnerable, while another is resistant; their judgment and manner of resolution tells everyone how each think and feel about the resolution (Context), and if we feel the resolution is nothing but a non-resolute decision, like death, revenge, or a coverup.

21.   I can tell you that those in high places don't seem to equate with superiority, when their results are covered up or inaccurately interpreted to secure their high-class image, or when their inferior results are downplayed. So, you'll see them fighting to sustain an image that doesn't belong to them. But the finished product is on full display.

22.   The games they play with people's lives, combined with a corrupt legal system that must be in place to protect provocative characters and their interests, is the reason why there is no set overall scheme that will lead to its natural result every time. You or I, and maybe no one, has any control over it. It's all about the herd involved in the case.

23.   A win may only be luck; especially when it comes to those of a lower status quo. Circumstances, and technicalities are always testy and changing, giving advantage to the more powerful or knowledgeable, if not both. Communications with the court may be complicated. Everywhere you turn, there may be something to learn by a particular deadline. All this, while the public has no knowledge of what's really going on, while you supposedly lost, as if deserving..

24.   I know many, who chose mainstream attorneys, took a plea bargain, and, eventually, ended up back in court on another charge and was indicted and sentenced. The plea bargain was

used to attract a guilty plea using fear tactics and to gain greater control, after placing an official mark on their public record, which lowers them in status.

25. Then, they will attract more unemployment, harsher working conditions, less support, afford fewer quality goods, pay more for products and services than most others, etc. Hell gets worse from there, including the downward spiral of physical, emotional, and mental health. I tell you many have faced these experiences with no mark on their record, to jump start criminal behavior.

26. I understand why many chose an alternative route to attaining me. It's the other people who are bringing the storm; so, they felt they needed to appease them. But they were no more their friends than they were before it started. No one showed up, afterwards, to right the ship. I'm, usually, the only one still thinking of winning, even in dire situations. I never forget a case gone wrong, and I never will abandon it. But I understand you must do what you think is best for you.

27. I understand the power of manipulating perception, herd influence, and constitutional rights, as well as how they must be played to rob a person and then to access a pre-built get-a-away vehicle. They don't like me and don't like what I do, for this very reason. They prefer that I don't have a license to practice and are always trying to challenge my ability to defend myself.

28. The fact that many, especially powerful and intelligent people, practice deception tells us how important it is to control perception and that it can be controlled or manipulated to be fit for a particular purpose(s). Controlling perception is the masterpiece and foundation for growth, maturity, and resolution.

29. To minimize the power of perception, examples with no alternatives, inferior examples with higher quality returns, inferior examples from what appears to be an honorable source, light consequential results that appear to be worth doing wrong, strenuous living conditions, and anything that forcibly or unnoticeably leads to a downfall is used to control perception.

30. To preserve the results of a damaged perception, a legal procedure must be utilized to hold the victim of such an evil endeavor below some competitive standard. However, the fact that a high-profile criminal has created a provocative method to force a crime, means those type of crimes cannot be fairly charged, prosecuted, and sentenced.

31. Herd influence involves people, who are given and exercise power over another, or who outnumber or have greater influence over another and acting in a manner that resists or forces another to succumb. Herd Influence may choose not to act in times, when a victim needs intervention to maintain status within the law. Herd influence involves voting for or against matters that are important to you and/or gathering in support or resistance to matters that are important to you.

32. Herd influence includes anyone, who conspires to scheme against another to their injury, especially leading to a hostile and/or implosive population or anything but a resolution.

33. Herd influence can organize to plant evidence and already be in position to hear it in the greatest scheme of identity theft. It is, almost, impossible to overcome, due to mass effects, especially when the media is involved. In a time, when all types of discrimination are apparent, popular trending attacks usually run their course.

34. "Constitutional rights" must be interpreted to allow the "practice of deception" and "herd influence" to initiate and prolong criminal patterns of behavior. That allows the three to have free interplay between one another.

35. If I were to give a metaphor for the government, it would be a machine that wastes and corrupts life, because there are many people scheming and inventing schemes to foster a result(s). It would have a discriminating quality control department, whenever it proposes or demonstrates aim for a specific target(s). The scheme and all related influences that were prevalent and/or initiated would have their stamp on the products and services. These products and services would go on to reveal a resume of acceptances and rejections and/or hit and misses. Such a performance would reflect the quality of knowledge of the schemer(s). The paths they navigated, including the products and services, as well as the schemer(s), must also be considered for tracking and justifying the materialization of results. The report would reveal a profit scheme. Everything is thrown in this machine for processing.

36. Confirmation is discerned when obvious truths are met with resistance and refusal to consider options to resolve the matter. Then, they alienate themselves from the logical and moral-focused world."

37. The rookie detective wakes up and wonders what the meaning of the dream could be. So, he told a senior detective and psychologist.

38. The psychologist said the following:

39. "Others send messages through circumstances in life, while God plants messages in our heads and hearts, if not all of the above.

40. Both the attorney and the defendant that he saved are missing, including potentially what they had to say or their interests. This is an indication that God may want you to consider and concentrate on logical materialization(s) in a naturally performing reality, in comparison to what is being investigated, including why it never or has met full potential, if allowed to materialize at all. Such may reflect environmental circumstances that need to be addressed. Or, the dream's purpose may only be to relay some information or leads.

41. A natural performing reality reveals logical ramifications. The proper management of such will produce a properly performing environment and all things within it. Due to the need and determination to survive, matters go to extremes during harsh experiences.

42. But, while we're at it, let's talk about influence. Because these people do things contrary to what we believe, repetitiously, I must remind you to not be a product of the influences of the fallen angels. This includes their ambassadors. Always be mindful and manage your development, never leaving yourself to be idle, only to succumb to their emotional and mental manipulations. Again, control your development.

43. The fallen angels are attracted to positions of power where they can dictate the direction of matters. They can use friction to buy your approval of sin. Those, who act impulsive usually don't possess this kind of information. But it has caused police brutality and domestic violence of all types. Therefore, this planet has been declared a contagious environment.

44. I must keep reminding everyone, because we aren't accustomed to living in such an environment. In our environment, everyone is like a watchman of values and their materialization. As a collective people, we do the opposite of the influences of the fallen angels.

They flee, because they don't have a home there and must not accept a way of thinking that they have rejected.

45.   Now, allow me to elaborate about their way of operating. Again, they operate from a position of power and circumstances that underly events and character, creating or sustaining events and character. So, it is a cyclical matter that underlies development. Naturally, it is a programmed function of nature. As so, we see it creating and maintaining various types of land conditions and culture. Whether we see or understand how it works or not, it is still obvious in its creating and sustaining development. This cyclical operation may be overtaken to produce an objective or goal. When we see the smallest evidence of an objective or goal, it's because it took on some progressive form. This progressive form is a product of a mind behind the actions.

46.   The mind behind the action becomes increasingly evident when challenged. It's conscious, assertive, focused, talented, resisting, evolving, elusive nature, and/or pointed effects qualifies the development as a legitimate source of mental prowess. Whether it is seen or not changes nothing. Over time, it has a therapeutic effect on response, attitude, belief, and action. Ramifications may drive future predictions and beliefs. Consequences may drive behavior. How we're positioned in a matter may drive our attitude and emotions.

47.   The manipulative process is strongest when essentials, or what is perceived as essential, are involved. Therefore, you must trace and maintain focus on the, potentially, coordinated matters that underly events and character. You or someone else could become a victim.

48.   As seen in the details of how an underlying source can control events and characters, we see that anyone impoverished of any essentials is an easier opportunity for identity theft.

49.   Because you were created with tools designed to give you the capability to be in the likeness of God, under particular circumstances, your character does not naturally identify with sin, except in a learning stage. But life on the inferior planet is faced with challenges of a conflictual nature, designed to steer in an opposite direction. That's where identity theft comes into play.

50.   More importantly, the values and what they tend to produce must be discerned to avoid cooperating with or being driven by an underlying, inferior source. Its influence is as large as the direction of its vessel, including the entire world.

51.   They are good for testing a population to see if they are of God or not and for culturing a society towards the customs of God.

Rookie Detective Report: Social Differences

Introduction

1.   After interacting with various people of the inferior planet, I found differences in intelligence and expressions, which is normal, except for the significant difference in the victimized race. I felt that the significant difference, while members of the same society, suggested an uneven distribution of information and valuable experiences.

I attributed the harsh social condition to hard evidence of the planet's history, which included the following:

1.   Victimized Race vs Others:

2.   Fight over quality of education

3.   The struggle to enter and complete higher education opportunities

4.   The significant difference in ability to compete with others in many similar and same circumstances

5.   A significantly higher unemployment rate

6.   An unusual higher level of instability

7.   Erosion of general reputation, perceived greatly as fit for entertainment

8.   The significantly higher percentage of the prison population

9.   The lack of creative endeavors on a scientific level, in comparison to others

10.   The nearly absent appearance in high scientific fields

11.   Very few or no examples of representations of builders of higher, intelligent generations of the future

12.   Highly engulfed and distracted towards conflicting civil matters

Others (Supporters of the system and its leaders):

1.   General denial of circumstances that plague the victimized race

2.   A prison system that is designed to, mentally, stall or set back its inmates, which is seen in the release of former inmates, who served long-term sentences

3.   The eagerness to imprison members of the victimized race Statistical makeup of the prison system

4.   The lack of recognition and concern from the higher intelligent population

5.   Preserved Advantages for those more financially fit

6.   Discriminating in hiring and business practices, resulting in disparity of education, reputation, income, and wealth

7.   Created an illegal drug market and compelled many types of criminal cases

8.   Gave harsher sentences to the victimized race

9.   Exposed children to drugs, sex and violence

10.   Provided examples of racism from, even, the highest public offices and positions

11.   Used essentials to extort crime

12.   Taught crime in prisons, especially through the motivation of confusion and the interaction of prison inmates

13.   Corrupted the minds of the impoverished and followers, causing a conflicting environment

Conclusion

1.   The total facts that surround the case for significant social differences hint at a, potential, operation of intent.

2.   There are motivations for such intent. The main one is to reserve them for unpopular, physically demanding, stressful, and/or low-paying positions.

3.   Combined circumstances encourage ignorance, the lowest competitive advantage, and hardened attitudes, which encourage behaviors stated to be deserving of such positions. In furthering the destruction, they stereotype the victimized race with the help of the media and steers the focus away from the underlying problems towards the reactors. Hate is, then, magnified and sustained.

4.   It was, clearly, the work of experts and contributing intellectuals, who never spoke up and did something to reverse it. So, it kept going unconsidered.

Rookie Detective Report: The Social Construct

1.   Upon speaking with various people, I noticed the risk of expressing particular views. It was like, you had to learn what views to be in favor of and those to denounce.

2.   You couldn't logically and completely feel your way through their social environment without taking risks, no matter how logical and correct you were.

3.   Some views, if expressed, could provoke violence, even when there were no legitimate challenges to its authenticity. I perceived this very fact as evidence of the existence of gangs, mafia, or any organized criminal or adverse establishments.

4.   Moreso, I perceived the existence and protections of race wars. I listened to conversations and observed behaviors that appeared to originate from the fallen angels. That's especially true, given the description of God in their Holy Book and the attempted corruption and destruction of anyone befitting of His image.

5.   The propaganda was divisive, powerful in as much as it was adopted, regardless of its destructive and illogical elements. People just adopted the propaganda according to what group they favored, seemingly without any thought behind it.

6.   At times, a stated moral objective was combined with an insane manner of obtaining it. One would express loyalty to a cause, while holding favorable to an inferior source that initialized and/or sustained the reason for the cause.

7.   It was as if they could not see that they were victims of a source that had no objective but to create and escalate confusion.

8.   Moreover, they had lost and seem to continue to lose empathy for one another and had no desire for reasoning and using diplomacy towards permanent resolve.

9.   It was a huge popularity contest engaged by, at least, most of the population. They symbolically defecated on the name and game of another, for the sole purpose of triumphing over them. Then, upon success, they called themselves "Better than thou".

10.   But the fact is they became the bigger sinner and/or criminal by taking such a position of control, only to create or sustain something they knew was improper to society. They were the bigger sinner from the start of such an inferior endeavor.

11.   It is impossible to be "Better than thou" by taking on a role to mindfully create or extend a sin, without taking on a role powerful enough to exert control. To possess such a belief is to have an underdeveloped conscience."

12.   I saw that some people were so selfish that they couldn't be taught empathy for others, after experiencing trauma for themselves. Then, there were those, who were judging others, who had no connection whatsoever about that person's experiences. And, it didn't help that the judged person had no ability to present an understandable and logical presentation in defense. So, there was argument and strife continuously.

13.   These people should take a look at themselves and their lack of respect for God's creations, while considering the potential fire of God.

14.   If there be superiority, certainly, it would parallel the Will and Word of God and build and maintain a history of good things aligned with His Qualities. Otherwise, it is demonic activity.

15.   Upon hearing about and viewing the reports of the rookie detective, many assembled together to discuss Quantum Star Officials and their operations. After they conversed, they demanded a meeting with the officials of Quantum Star Eckter.

16.   A meeting was set and, on that day, they confronted the officials with a complaint of fraud. They claimed the following:

17.   You have intervened in our way of life, claiming to be a savior of some type, but you have done nothing but condemn and divide us almost daily. We are, now, more divided than ever.

18.   You have called the cop a criminal and God the devil. You seem to have gotten things backwards. I spent many years as a cop and never have I been faced with so much grief and menace towards me.

19.   Have you tried looking at what you're building, because I don't think it's a Quantum Star Eckter that you claim to have built?

20.   Quantum Star Eckter addressed the crowd in the following manner:

21.   I want to be tolerable of your actions and say I'm sorry that you feel the way you do, because I aim to be a nice guy. But that would be a sin; because I should not be tolerable of a fraud and sorry for making corrections to an inferior way of living.

22.   I noticed that you could not present any legitimate accusations or views towards the literature and beliefs of Quantum Star Eckter's program. You were only concerned about your image, which you fraudulently attained with deceptive and forceful methods. You seem to have turned a blind eye to your erroneous deeds and refuse to see them as catastrophic to the proper development of societies.

23.   But change requires that we take a look at what went wrong and how, from a deep perspective. Otherwise, we can end up back where we were, simply from the gusts of the wind.

24.   If we can see a puzzle-piece for what it is, in its entirety, and how it fits into the world of puzzle-pieces, we become more inclined towards harmony with the operation of Truth. When participation includes all the people around us, peer-pressure, and shared knowledge, it has a tendency to hold us in unity.

25.   An unclean character is required to be cleaned before it can enter a purified state. It is the perfecting of matters within and in the external world that makes this all possible. So, it is not Quantum Star Eckter who must change, it's you who needs to change. What kind of conscience would I have if I let a matter, as destructive as your way of life, continue? It's especially questionable, If I know I have the means to correct it?

26.   You already knew you were fraudulent, before you called this meeting. I say that, because you were part of a group, who had to deceive people for gain and cover up their actions, as a result of corruption. And, just like back then, you fight against the presentation of facts against yourself.

27.   Now, due to what has been presented to you in facts, elaborated upon, and the bringing forth of a public challenge to such, potentially wasting official time, you are tasked to present anything, but a speculative and incomplete report explaining your actions and decisions in court. We don't like tricks and extortion. And, if unsuccessful, you won't either.

28.   You had other recourses to present your claims, but you chose to elude diplomacy and Truth for popular opinion; that's what got you here.

Minister Ion: The Gun

1.   Some of the population reflected their approval back to Quantum Star Eckter's celebration of Minister Ion.

2.   Some thought his signature sermon was "The Gun":

3.   "…God is not in approval of people, who discovered the principles and concepts of a gun and used it to hit the wrong target.

4.   The fire of life was born (Child) and they latched obligations to it, only to challenge the moral will and develop a worldly view within the newborn. In the process, they hardened the child and, then, rewarded the child more support. The child became like his/her environment.

5.   I remember the words of one of the most notorious criminals, who was on death row and about to be executed. He said:

6.   "I was born in an environment, where most people were struggling to exist, lost at least some of their pride for the right things, and were still being challenged for not accomplishing enough, including going to jail for not paying off debts. I didn't want to live like that; so, I copied the best examples, the best I could.

7.   I saw that the most successful people had a way of hustling and was in with some skilled group. I knew I had to knock on the best doors first; then I had to fit in where I could. I knew I needed to fly, not walk.

8.   I ended up in a gang, where everyone required all members to be hard and beneficial to the whole. It was the least stressful life I could muster up.

9.   It was like sports teams getting more sophisticated in scheming and breaking records by accomplishing more and more over time. Everybody was getting harder and harder and more daring. We were trampling on and taking over one another's territories. Our business was our lives; so, it had to be protected. It was a matter of doing more than putting food on the table. We wanted to live too. But anything could happen, whether it was the cops coming or some other competitor.

10.   I perceived the most successful in a gang from the top to the bottom, even working against each other or aiding their cause for the money or for a successful plea bargain. It was wild.

11.   Money had to come from those who possessed it, or we couldn't have operated the way we did. It was just a more authoritative gang controlling or trying to control the other. Proof? I'm right here in the midst of a gang who controls my freedom. You all turned everything into pain or risk.

12.   You all had the greatest control over me and could've stepped in to create a better me, but didn't. Yet, you blame me for being what you created, both the ignorant and knowledgeable. How does that make sense?

13.   You juggled me here. You should take responsibility for your beliefs and actions. What happened to practicing accountability?

14.   This is about circumstances that you don't have an answer to; otherwise, you're even more guilty for not stepping in to rectify the error. I'm blaming the supporters of those, who showed us how it is done. They took over and made law for the weaker population, but followed it for appearance, only when it was convenient. So, if you murder me, you'd be murdering a part of yourself."

15.   The people, who were given the power to overturn his execution were, instead, focused on how insulted his message made them feel.

16.   Some of them said, in so many words, "I could see why Corvus suffered so much. It was more about how he felt about others and less about his experiences that made him the monster he is. I felt degraded with every word he expressed, as if he supposedly knew me. He has a mistaken outlook about life and a lot of people. He, literally, insulted me. I couldn't help him."

17.   So, Corvus was executed. His message and my knowledge of the world will never allow me to believe in executions. That's especially true, because I could not tell the difference between either side; but I could sympathize with him.

18.   The whole game was about the creation and control of the gun, as well as elements to be utilized.

19.   The fire of life was poisoned with adverse elements to create heat within a cell; then, the results were forced through a tunnel of circumstances and of situations that reflected on past developments, increasing the heat and relevant direction of the explosive cell that veered off target. The missed target proved that the holder was shaky.

20.   Diplomacy was met with the thicker skin of warmongering adversaries. It was like being met by ignorant members of a gun fest. This is the crowd that the people, who sit in high positions, utilize to give credibility to their lies and falsely justify their wrongful behavior and lifestyle.

21.   Blame was placed on the cell that was filled with adversity and judged as unfit and inferior, while the creative source, who had the power to alter for the better, escaped responsibility and blame. In furtherance, the gun creator and the fulfilling source was not considered.

22.   The end was like a car accident, where they say one was the victim and the other the violator; but, in truth, the formula, considers whether both or all were victims, who were damaged and/or destroyed. The payer for the product or service was a violator too, and many of them had the money. The violator and the money made the cycle turn.

23.   So, unless you're on the solution side and you know what you're talking about, from the view of an expert, who can break it down and put all the pieces back together, demonstrating how it works, you should keep your mouth shut. In fact, you would probably have no business being there.

24.   Sometimes, we may feel like we're experts; because we feel our knowledge is extensive on the matter. Sometimes, we feel that we've heard enough about it. However, a lot us either don't know or forget that this is a big world, with a great number of interconnected parts. The human body is, also, studied and maintained by a number of experts, alone. It takes a number of experts to put all that together, and they still don't know everything. Not only that, there's a lot of confusion going on in this world. But, a lot of people think they know enough to put a man to death. Copyright© Minister Ion Museum

Quantum Star Eckter: Court Proceeding Involving the Challengers

1.   Court Begins

2.   The assistant Judge rises and states, "May the court begin!"

3.   The prosecutor rises and states, we are here to consider the consequences of charges against the challengers of the inferior planet to The People of Quantum Star Eckter. Those charges are:

  • Assembling and presenting as a force against the presence of Quantum Star Eckter and our interests

  • Exhibiting behaviors, as superiors, with intent to manipulate, corrupt, and to harm a population for profitable means

4.   The first charge, in its most serious scenario, requires "The necessity to move technology, weapons, and/or personnel from one region to a problematic region to restore unity and peace". However, since we were "Sufficiently staffed and equipped to meet the challenge, without casualty", the minimum sentence is recommended. That minimum sentence is 5 years in detainment, with none demanded.

5.   The following charge was instigated by corrupt historical traits, in which the challengers were "In defense of" and "Exhibited intent to reimpose". Because they sought to reimpose such corrupt behavior, under the supervision of the law of Quantum Star Eckter, they created a "Crossover". As a result, they became liable for the prosecution of violations committed in the past, by way of the conceptual-cycle of "Institution, acknowledgment of effects, and re-creation". The recommendation is 100 years, with none demanded.

Law vs Law

6.   Due to the challenging aspect of the second charge, I recommend a demanded sentence. Reason being, as authorities, they used their influence to affect matters, which caused imbalances in affairs that a victim had no affirming recourse to resolve. That made that influence a force of law, whether protected by law or as implicated power, which had the same effect as law. That is further confirmed in the lack of intervention or cooperation from other parts of the power structure.

7.   The result was law vs law, in which the conflict played out in human behavior. Thus, it was the power structure and its members, who became the author of the puppet's violation(s).

8.   Judge: Mr. Ramsi (Defending attorney) what is your answer?

9.   Mr. Ramsi: I see that the prosecutor has a firm case; so, I'm not going to challenge the legal aspects of the charges itself. I only insist that they are first time offenders, regardless of the seriousness of the case.

10.   Regardless of the fact that their behavior was illegal, we're dealing with people, who are new to our way of life. These are people, who were cultured in a different world, different classes, and different backgrounds. They are, yet, to perceive the facts of our way of life. I see it as a flaw in perception and a question of survival.

11.   I see that as a stimulus, which automatically nullifies the consequences of law. You already know that, that law was put in place for the very reason of nullifying the effects of potential corruption, which can manipulate the downward spiral of another. They produced the same example that this law was designed to prevent.

12.   So, I disagree with a demanded sentence. Demanded sentences should develop as a result of conflicts, while being detained, in most cases. I say leave it to the program to garner the correct effects.

13.   After all, they have to graduate out of detainment. It is not time that is going to resolve the issues concerning them; it is graduating out of detention that's going to resolve the matter.

14.   Judge: like I said earlier, we're going to make this quick and move on.

15.   I thought the charges were well stated and firm. I, also, understand Mr. Ramsi's point about the stimulus concept. So, to avoid being charged by artificial intelligence, demanded sentence is off the table.

16.   To reiterate Mr. Ramsi, let the program do its job.

17.   This court is adjourned.

What Happened to the Challengers?

1.   A woman seen one of Quantum Star officials exploring the environment and decided to ask, "I don't mean to interfere, I just wanted to know what happened to some of my relatives, who rebelled against you? I never agreed; I just wanted to know if I'd ever see them again?"

2.   Seeing that the woman appeared nervous and concerned, the official spoke to relieve her anxieties. He explained the following:

3.   "They appeared in court nearly naked, so to speak. They recognized that they were almost completely exposed; so, they held steadfast to what was left of a shield that covered the rest of their undisclosed indecencies. They chose not to present anything to the court. Therefore, they were left vulnerable to the immediate charges and avoided further condemnation.

4.   However, there is no need to be concerned about their safety and well-being. Our system is completely different from your past system. Your relatives are in a place that you should want them to be, if you truly love them. It is a genuine correction system.

5.   Quantum Star Eckter recognizes its role with God and His Angels. We've come to know that the Angels of God and the fallen angels are constantly at war to gain the souls of all humans. We know that all the angels are working diligently to gain and take full control of every soul, by working with the conscious, conscience, emotional, and deciding factors of the mind.

6.   What happens on the outside is reflected on the inside and vice versa. Quantum Star Eckter realizes that it is part of the formula for aiding, both, God's Angels and the fallen angels. Because we hold steadfast to the objectives and goals of our loving God, we cater to God and His Angels and rebuke the fallen angels. We understand that to aid the fallen angels is the sole definition of witchcraft. The practice of witchcraft is an invitation to allow the fallen angels to have their way or to compete with God and His Angels.

7.   All the angels seek to utilize any element of the environment to construct their cause and strongholds, whether in the external world or in the inner-man. Both the inner-world and the external world influence one another. They claim properties of the conscience and conscious mind and seek to build strongholds. It's a constant war to make rubble out of strongholds and to take an advantage of the weaknesses of the other.

8.   When strongholds are turned to rubble, it's always devastating to people affected by it. It excites the emotions, instability sets in, questions abound, and anxiety persists. Quantum Star Eckter knows all this and seeks to allow the soul to be sold to God and His Angels.

9.   Artificial Intelligence is designed to mediate a soul that was once not for sale to God and His Angels for a bargain.

10.   However, the angels fight day and night. Any victim could be one of us. So, we fight for all. It is our natural duty to not ever fall on the wrong side of the Judgment of God.

11.   The objects and goal have always been to buy and sustain the souls of men, and we've built our societies on this very belief. As a result, we've built the greatest environment known to man.

12.   We follow a belief system that, we feel, has the strongest footing in reality. Your relatives and neighbors can only turn out better than before, if they decide to do so.

Never be Consumed by or Resigned to an Imperfect Reality

1.   After the court system decided the fate of the challengers and the news spread abroad, Quantum Star Officials addressed the people of the inferior planet.

2.   "One day, I took a walk out into the jungle and saw the reality reflected back to your underdeveloped society. I saw the trees, positioned differently from their essential sources, while placed under various environmental conditions, and relatively demonstrating their resulting health and demeanor of survival, with each expressing a unique architecture.

3.   There were meat eaters and vegetarians, as well as those of a combination. All that was eatable was of some life-form, whether it was meat or a plant.

4.   The impulse was timely. There was a time to eat, a time to fight, a time to play, a time to be serious, a time to love, and a time to just relax. Many times, one's impulse was in conflict with another's.

5.   The whole jungle centered around the predators, whether it was a lion, cobra, tiger, hippopotamus, or any kind of animal that had the most respect and/or could unleash the greatest terror of its environment.

6.   All other animals were tending their business, while basing their plans on avoiding predators or using other animals to mitigate their wishes or desires. Their concerns were always immediate.

7.   I saw a hyena watch a larger animal take down an animal that was too large for them to pursue. Afterwards, they proceeded in a pack to take the animal away from the killer, for their own consumption.

8.   I saw others plotting their way across hunting grounds of predators, even some predators doing the same. They were always crossing into or inhabiting someone's hunting grounds.

9.   Moreover, hunting grounds and methods would change with the change in success.

10.   Animals, like the rabbit and others, had no chance against a predator; because the predators were bigger, stronger, faster, and/or technologically advanced in the distribution of venom. Predators had no real competition, except that, which came from their ranks or higher.

11.   Under the above circumstances, there was no such thing as diplomacy, unless you were an ally. Diplomacy, for the most part, belonged to the diplomatic, human race.

12.   In your holy book, it was written to "Let the tare and the wheat grow together". That's how you get the jungle. It's good for learning that the truth is the Truth. But, at some point, you've got to move on from that reality. That point comes at a time, when you understand that, that reality is a false reality, based on the imperfections that become apparent.

13.   We believe that change for the better never really came, because many were consumed by it, as the only reality. They were like a planet found with no sun and no moon to give it light.

14.   Then, there were those sold to the ways of Demons for a profit(s). They sought every way possible to mitigate any challenges to Demonic expressions. Demonic expressions sustained according to the strengths of Demonic supporters.

15.   Deep down in the ground, we found metals that you could weld together and those that had some degree of resistance, shown in a test of stress. Again, depending on the metals sought to weld, their properties couldn't hold up under certain conditions.

16.   I want you to know that your previous world and Quantum Star Eckter, like dissimilar metals, will not hold up against the strength of pure Truth. They are opposing and have opposing purposes. We do not build a jungle here.

17.   The rain comes down from the sky; when it hits the ground for the first time, it is not entirely absorbed. The reason being is the ground has completely dried and hardened or compacted. So, it can't immediately get through. As more raindrops come and settle on the ground, the surface begins to give way and absorb the raindrops. As the rain continues, the soil gives way to the next level, faster and faster.

18.   As you are exposed to the knowledge of Quantum Star Eckter, likewise, it may be hard to absorb. But, as you continue to apply yourself, your mind will become wet with the idea. You may even become creative.

19.   Sometimes, the raindrops hit a hard spot, like a rock. It rolls off and may thin out and evaporate, if the heat of the sun has the time to take it back. Otherwise, it may roll down or over to another absorbable area or down to a small or large body of water, where it is more perceptible or understood.

20.   When it is understood, the body of water gives off a greater expression of moisture, reflecting the mass of the content.

21.   Our artificial intelligence is trained to discern blocks; so, we don't want you to skip steps in the program. The reason being is because, going too fast, will only cause you to need to go back and absorb all that is missing from your understanding. Your history has shown that the concept of skipping steps was used to control the quality of education for the unfortunate.

22.   Your former way of living profited from consuming others, in one way or another; but, in opposition, Quantum Star Eckter profits from uniting and building up all citizens of our society.

23.   Why build up? For one, you become the best person you can be, which is an asset to the remaining population.

24.   Some have thought of us as….(asks another official for the word)…as a communist. Some have said "Control freaks". However, when we build people up, they learn to navigate the entire environment, the mind, and space of others, with limited or less issues. You navigate unhindered as long as you are doing the right thing and in the right way; that is the natural definition of freedom.

25.   Because everyone goes through the program, we become like-minded and diplomacy yields are as high as we can push it. The quality of life is raised to its highest level. We all benefit!

26.   Because of the feedback we've gathered, we thought we'd clarify our program to our new family.

27.   Thank you for listening. Have a nice day." (The crowd cheers in acceptance).

Stewart of the State Vs a Gang Member

1. The assistant Judge rises and states, "May the court begin!"

2. An anonymous questioner sent a question to the court: is Atar Remit a gang member? On that day, as a result, a court hearing was provoked and a date was set. That day has arrived.

3. The prosecutor rises and states: The question is best answered by an explanation of a "Stewart of the State Vs a Gang Member".

4. A Stewart of the state is any person or group, who has the best interests in the care of the affected recipient(s).

5. Mr. Etoski: In opposition, a gang member may have obvious or ulterior motive(s) that are less than ideal for the care of the affected recipient(s).

6. To identify the gang member or Stewart of the state, we have to review the options and conditions available, as well as the awareness and intelligence of the provider of care.

7. The prosecutor: Yes, the Stewart of the state is engaged with the task of identifying the elements of a gang member, but also to expose and bring forth measures to prevent the progress of deficient or harmful care.

8. To make the idea of the Stewart of the state more effective, we have anonymous questioners who present questions to the court.

9. Anonymous questioners help to assure the greatest awareness of all the members of society; but we're not limited by them. We have statistics, artificial intelligence, as well as professionals in their field of study, who are tasked with reviewing, sustaining, and improving upon current conditions.

10. So there will be various types of people, on various levels of intelligence, who are observing and presenting information that help to maintain the social health of the members of our society.

11. Mr. Etoski: The Stewart of the state is, also, tasked with the observance of members of the same level or above. For example, a citizen of the lowest status has the right to raise questions about those on the highest level.

12. Many of the answers to questions are gained from the interactions with artificial intelligence. But, new questions are reviewed by the courts first, and, then, balanced with artificial intelligence.

13. So, in regards to the question of whether Mr. Remit is a gang member, no evidence or potential evidence of such was found in his choice of affiliates or his decisions and behaviors. His past shows contributions towards the tasks of the Stewart of the state without discrimination.

14. No discrimination was found in respects to genetics nor by negatively affecting the fundamental status of a vulnerable person or group, not even by preserving the best interest of a majority.

15. The prosecutor: I totally agree. I have found no incidents against Mr. Remit.

16. When there are damages, the cases are reviewed for logical relations, which take preference over the results. The idea is to eliminate the successful manipulation of blame towards an innocent person, which is part of the stimulus policy.

17. A gang member, knowingly, works in partnership with others and/or the productions of others, which bring harm to or unwarranted control over another, resulting in some form of deficiency. Neither of those elements were found.

18. Judge: Let the record show that Mr. Remit is clear of any claims.

19. This court is adjourned.

To The Office of Official Review

From the Office of Inmate Communications

A Plea from the Challengers

1. After a while of being detained and going through the program, by artificial intelligence, designed to promote higher intelligence and healthy thinking; more and more challengers pled for their innocence and release.

2. They argued that their world and Quantum Star Eckter were unimaginably different, like in opposition to one another. We were brainwashed by the big picture, the examples all around us, and the feedback from experimental efforts. It was like our perceptions of matters were restricted to a certain way of life, which were similar, but unique to one another. In some cases, they were extremely different.

3. We thought we had a grasp on the understanding of at least most people, but only from our perspective. But we thought we shared the same perspectives, for the most part anyway. But, with Quantum Star Eckter, we hardly share anything with you.

4. To further elaborate on our frame of mind, we had the oppressed and oppressors joined together, as a challenge to you. We knew that the oppressed saw the opportunity as a fresh start to make sure they weren't toppled again, while we were trying to maintain our position over them, for fear of revenge. We did not know that an unimaginable experience had captured us.

5. We heard the talk, but politicians always sound good too. We didn't buy it, because we didn't have the means to accept it as legit. That kind of talk and backing was some phenomena, supposedly, far into the future, possibly at another place, and never legitimately imitated in our world.

6. Your world leans more towards developing inwardly and reaping material results; whereas our world leans more towards developing our material world and reaping inward results.

7. After this experience, I understand why our perception and way of thinking must be programmed correctly. I understand that you don't fight against the Truth. But you don't know you're fighting against the Truth, unless you recognize Him. If we weren't familiar with Him, in our world, we couldn't possibly recognize Him, unless the knowledge of Him was presented to us.

8. Then, we had an excuse. Today, we know better. Therefore, we feel the matter is resolved; because we share the same overall thoughts on the way we should go. So, we ask for our release.

9. This letter was written for all of the detainees who agreed with the statements in this letter.

10. Argarhoa Hamins

From the Notes of Quantum Star Eckter's Research Team

Note: Main System of the Inferior Planet

1. They developed a system to favor the higher status quos.

2. They, known as The People, used their status as the most populated, most advantaged, and entitled to institute their opinions and influences on the remaining population.

3. Logic was used as the most favorable means, until it became too costly, creating a limitation of use. Logic was replaced with arrogance at points of limitations.

4. Arrogance was adopted as a protector of and a resolution to reserve the higher status quo's advantage, creating privilege of status.

5. Privilege of status negated the rise of successful constitutional issues that would cost the higher status quo.

6. Privilege of status employed procedures that had to rely on the opinions of the higher status quo, whether in interpretation or in cooperation.

7. Privilege of status withheld information and advantages from the remaining population by use of secrets and affordability. The result was the manifestation of ignorance and disadvantages for the remaining population, in comparison to those of the higher status. Such an act created the gap between capabilities.

8. The gap between capabilities was protected and expanded upon by the opinions and complicated concepts of the privilege of status. The issues of the less sophisticated and disadvantaged were deemed a personal issue linked to insufficient or improper effort.

9. Racism got lost in and interpreted as a status issue. This was especially true as a result of favoring those of the victimized race, with compatible and favorable behaviors and beliefs. Use of such fortified the success of the system.

10.　The system carried the imprint of hate, seen in racial results and utilization of color. The darker colors were generally associated with inferiority, whether in quality or association. They were generally found as unemployed, unstable, underpaid, struggling, sick, criminal, abused, denied, unsupported, having low-end jobs, in positions of danger, and coping differently compared to others.

11.　The struggle encouraged social reserve and disfavor, while social interaction was encouraged towards the higher status. This, also, fortified the success of the system.

12.　The results evidenced hate, research, intelligence, goal-orientation, intent, and widespread participation, including the sharing of beliefs and compatible concepts.

13.　Basically, they were generally robbed of their rights, quality of life, and unapproved advances. When they weren't robbed, they were set up for it; so, it remained a threat upon their heads. The understanding was used to extort values from any potential challenger of the system, usually without further discussion or any other type of influence.

14.　Members of the privilege of status strung their puppets with standards to qualify for a higher quality of life, after a sufficient takeover of every good and essential thing in the environment. They engineered and used those standards to attract only those inclined towards greater freedom to achieve, to garner favor, possessing greater social acceptance, and to compete, thus creating a filtering system.

15.　Then, they continued their takeover with rules and obligations, having consuming consequences, after they tied the minds of the puppets to an external economic system.

16.　Then, the puppets had to appease and negotiate with, both, the internal and external economic systems. Negotiations, at times, became very severe as essential needs required a solution, when moral solutions were denied or no recourse was available. Limitations of recourses, or the denial of, held the victim(s) in a constant state of concern and struggle, making them more readily available to suggestion(s).

17.　The technology of limitations and suggestions opened up the means to remotely control the victims, according to their unique circumstances. It included an offer, but also a selling point. The offer may be a scam or temporary relief, almost never a permanent solution. The selling point was the need for relief and the severity of the matter going unresolved.

18.　The technology of limitations and suggestions was a messaging system developed by case history. The mind, with the response of the heart, calculated past and present conditions to predict the future. So, people would have different responses to the same phenomena, because their case histories were relatively different. In this way, the technology created divide.

19.　We all have feelings about, even, the least important things we experience; so, every event includes feeling for such things as colors, size, spacing, architecture, appearance, treatment, response of others etc. All these feelings make up an event, as well as our contributing thoughts, creating an emotional response. The information becomes massive, when we include more events or a string(s) of events.

20.　We become programmed by prompts, conflicts, teachings, repetition, traits, trends, links, harmony, timeliness, associations, reasonings, satisfaction, and dissatisfaction, as well as pain and turmoil. That's not to mention that, inside our conscience, lies a developing due diligence system, which is vulnerable to be overridden by the tactics of external influences, especially with the use of deception. It's the song that mesmerizes and traps us, if we have no other recourse.

21.　From there, they gained control of their emotional and health systems. The emotional and health systems are programmable and slow to change, except by trauma. These and all other interactive systems discovered and managed were managed compatibly to attain an overall authoritative goal.

22.　For many, it was like a tactic of war, when it challenged and violated their natural rights to freedom, peace, enjoyment, and the prosperity of life. Suddenly someone else's life became more important and intrusive.

23.　In comparison to the privilege of status, the solution was evasive. The attempt to escape wasn't, generally, the normal routine provided for the privilege of status, as seen in the low success rate of those outside the privilege of status. Those not of the privilege of status, generally, found that an effort to resolve may mean a win, in which the cost is greater than the gain. They are, potentially, faced with the discovery of surprising challenges that require an adequate response too soon, and/or be confronted by an unmovable attitude of denial.

24.　There was never a priority to yield to the fact(s) or to level the playing field, unless the matter(s) were pristinely stacked in favor of the privilege of status.

25.　As the success of many pushed further into the wilderness, snake bites and other casualties increased, including the disappearance of ecosystems, likewise crime was provoked by dissent and the need to live.

26.　Research and legal efforts could not be employed to, generally, reverse the advantages of the privilege of status members.

27.　Like Quantum Star Eckter, they created their world as a manufacturing environment, except theirs was in the nature of a beast, complete with the influence of the underworld, and deceptive practices toned for even the coming generations.

28.　When we decide to do something our way, instead of God's way, we run into situations that require us to reverse course or to cover up or accept an essential wrong to continue in the wrong direction. It's a conflict, which can ruin the appearance of a clean reputation; so, it requires compression of facts and a deceptive point of view to promote and maintain a reputable appearance. So, while they taught accountability and stood stern regardless of facts, they couldn't practice the same. The profit became a strong addiction, like a drug to a drug-addict; so they ruled in a disoriented manner in relation to the Way of God.

29.　The less a governing style caters to the best interests of all, the more it becomes a private affair. A private affair that positions itself in an authoritative position against any part of the population, successfully, is guilty of a takeover. Due diligence is at a higher developed standard in high positions, due to the possession of higher knowledge, ability to attain greater information, and the technology that increases abilities.

30.　The authorities of the inferior planet could not afford to recognize the fact that they were manufacturing beasts, by creating or working with the underworld, sometimes as to give the impression of playing God. The concept was placed in a private setting with access to public records and information, having historic data and tracking abilities.

31.   The description of the private setting is exposed by the description of their victims, their circumstances, and the technological influences needed to bring the matters to fruition. The refusal to follow due diligence and recognize the underworld confirmed a partnership, as well as the allowance of access to sensitive information to garner a negative effect that is profitable to an authoritative source.

32.   Because we were lucky to find the inferior planet in dire conditions, we were spared the number of casualties associated with war; therefore, the researchers of the inferior planet recommend to the Counsel of Affairs the establishment of a mediating method as an alternative to war, should we find it necessary to overtake any other planet.

33.   Every unjust legal system, acting in a legal setting, has elements that will dissolve or transform itself, so long as everyone is evenly subjective to its establishments and it is sufficiently developed. The goal should be to eliminate the arrogance and follow the logic of all relative disciplines, establishing a fair, moral, and corrective outcome.

Preparation

1.   Questions and any manner of approach must come in their respective waves, as stated in the closed hearing.

2.   The questioner must, also, clearly describe his/her/their agenda, first. The purpose is to maintain comfort and sustain cooperation, not to give the responder any excuse to resort to elusive tactics. Elusive tactics must be seen as a sign of guilt, when there's no legitimate excuse for it. So, legitimate excuses must be prepared for, before questioning.

3.   The questioning session must be recorded.

4.   A hearing must be set and a profile of the population must be compared to the answers and scientific findings, before further questioning of the defending source.

5.   The objective of the investigation is to understand the system and the reactive population, to discern fault(s) and to construct and apply resolutions.

6.   The goal is to disempower the core of negative influence and to constantly groom the population towards a moral and enlightened society or towards perfection.

Pre-Planned Questions:

1.   What is the purpose of law?

2.   Is the government a safe haven for criminals? What makes it so or not so? What are the contributing elements?

3.   Has due diligence been internally executed to prevent privatized interests that are harmful to any portion of the population?

4.   What part of the population is the most important? Are there levels of status that are more or less important than others?

5.   What justifies one part of the population as more important than another, if stated to be true?

6.   What is the meaning of racism?

7.   Is the government responsible for the proper development of the population? If so, is it in part or as a whole? If not, why?

8.   What is an ideal population? Why? What is being done to establish it? What are the challenges?

9.   Does an attorney have a duty to law or the tribune, when they are on different paths or differ in any manner, including what would be criminal intent, if it were a common citizen?

10.   Do laws have a hierarchical level of power, which determines the interpretation of laws beneath? If so, what are they? If not, why?

11.   Can the fallen angels carry out their agenda with established law(s) and/or public officials? Should we be concerned? Why or why not? Does it look like they may be succeeding? Why or why not?

12.   Should these questions be publicized, along with their answers? Why or why not?

13.   What is the meaning of oppression?

14.   Would clear answers of the guiding light of law encourage a more law-abiding population? Why or why not?

15.   Could a population benefit from a book, like 'There Are Three Truths"?

16.   Do these questions from a questioner present a threat of harm or injury? Why or why not?

17.   How does the current administration(s) compare to a criminal organization?

18.   Is there potential camouflaging of crime behind private matters that must not be disclosed? How do you know? Should anything be done about it, if so? Is there anything being done about it, if so? Can a conspiring government that engages in crime be trusted?

19.   Are studies being performed to force a desired legal outcome versus a logical development?

20.   What is an ideal condition? Are there pursuits towards ideal conditions? If so, for who? If so, how has the present pursuit of ideal conditions progressed as planned?

21.   Are your responses, or lack of, an example of how others should react? What has been the outcome? Were you in favor or disfavor of it? Why?

22.   Which is better, revenge or resolution?

23.   We learned that, before you go to court, you need to know how to communicate with the court, how to report court misconduct successfully, how to stop false reporting and criminal manipulation of the other side, and how to give a report to the public in the post-conviction and sentencing phases. Otherwise, the court freely has its way. How have you worked to make this achievable for everyone? And, how is it possible with a totally corrupt government?

24.   Are the traits of the population manipulative and improving? Does the government play a role in it? Should it? Why? Are their limitations?

25.   What is the meaning of religion?

26.   Is the government blind in some ways? If so, why? If not, how so? If so, can it be made more aware? Should it be awakened to more experiences of the population and world?

27.   Is the government efficient and effective in information management from all fields of scientific disciplines? Is the information being fully applied to create an ideal condition? Why or why not? If so, how?

28.   During your profile of all the issues with the population and managing them, did you perceive any kind of trajectory that implicated a better way to manage them? Proofs? Statistics? Or, was this not your goal?

29. What is the meaning of "Crime Engineering"?

30. Are there good criminals in government? In other words, are there people acting within the law, who can only be discerned as acting legally, solely from the fact that they hold a particular position in government?

31. If the fallen angels managed court cases, what would it look like?

32. Where did you show you deserved respect per the subject?

33. If there were no crimes in lower society, how would you survive or make your money? Do you feel encouraged to cause crime? Why or why not? Do you feel crime is needed?

34. What is an "Instrumental move"?

35. Why does it look like many don't learn from the consequences of wrong actions? What are the driving forces that create this behavior? How has current and/or past approaches helped to reverse the behavior? Is a resolution being sought or is the problem being used as a profit scheme?

36. Who encouraged global racism? What is the driving force behind it? What is common between the races discriminated against? Does color matter?

37. Does the government act with one foot on one side of the law and the other foot on the opposite side? If so, why? If not, why? Is there information to the contrary? If so, why? If not, why?

38. When it comes to people, which have you prioritized, development or outcome? What is the evidence? If development, what evidence confirms progress and how? Or, why is there no progress?

39. Should altruism be resisted?

40. What is God-Service?

To The Office of Official Review

From the Office of Inmate Communications

A Plea from the Challengers 2

1. The remaining challengers have, again, requested to be released. Like the others, they have seen their error and promise further cooperation in the future.

2. Argarhoa Hamins

3. Response of Office of Official Review: We have sent your request to the Counsel of Affairs.

4.   Because the project, designed to take a legal approach towards inferior planets as a potential alternative to war, the case is beyond our control and best handled by the Counsel of Affairs.

5.   Best Wishes to You, Office of Official Review

6.   The Counsel of Affairs: We received your request and will consider it soon.

7.   The Counsel of Affairs has scheduled a review

The Day of the Review

1.   The judge enters into the courtroom and takes his seat.

2.   May the court proceed, he says.

3.   As stated earlier in a brief letter, I have received a second request from the challengers to be released. The question is "What is going on and where are we, as far as they are concerned?"

4.   So, Mr. Atmons, as the administrator of Inmate Development, what is your answer?

5.   Mr. Atmons: I was told to release them "according to the most effective standards of the Office of Official Review". This is what the Office of Official Review stated.

6.   We found that there were detainees who weren't so connected to the inferior plot to give a detailed account of the underlying concepts that were carried out at top levels. They were, merely, just following procedures and orders from the top. They couldn't produce a professional account of what was going on. So, we released them and kept the more informed and educated population.

7.   Now, we're working on a legal approach to future prospects that we may pursue on a legal basis. So, that adds to the list of things we already needed to finish with those who remain detained. The release date is out of our control and based on the demands of the Counsel of Affairs.

8.   We, also, would like to alert the court that we are dealing with the most dangerous of the detainees. They have the ability, regardless of past faults, to re-instate themselves as a force of integrity. They've done it over and over again, while continuously pursuing their inferior goals.

9.   Therefore, their release is pursuant to the findings and needs of the Counsel of Affairs.

10.   Counsel Judge: Ok. That is a natural response to what has precipitated.

11.   Kato Enfice, what is your response?

12.   Kato Enfice: (Research Organizer): Since the incarceration of the challengers, we've gathered a more deeply and detailed response from them.

13.   As we gathered the details, I saw a method of summary. I found it in their Holy Book, and it seems to be fitting.

14.   There was a mention of a flat planet with a dome. People argue about whether the planet is flat or round. However, they never come to a solid conclusion, even with images of the planet being round and rockets shooting through space.

15.   It seems like, to me, that it was written to preserve some understanding that went over the heads of the lesser informed population, leaving them distracted from the real message.

16.   The real message seems to be a flat planet with a dome, as a symbol of oppression. It could be clearly seen in an environment with fewer people advancing and most of them limited by circumstances; or, that is, a lesser developed society.

17.   This is what I mean by a flat planet with a dome. The flat earth seems to be a symbol of people at the bottom or not far from it, who are unable to help one another. But they still represent life. So, they grow, attempt to prosper, or simply continue to try and survive. The problem is they hit their limits. Then, after seeing they can't go further, hitting the dome, so to speak, they turn back without choice. When they turn back, they look for answers.

18.   Let me remind you that, when life is filled with force from needs and strong desires, for whatever the reason, it can exceed the moral capacity of its possessor. That's what causes the seeking of answers from those on the same level or below. So, we'll see competition, usually, focused on the weakest first.

19.   As time went by, there have been breakthroughs in the likeness of unions. They fought for better conditions, until they were finally weakened. Where one worker per household was enough at one point, it turned into a need for two per household and so forth.

20.   Times got harder and harder and more demanding; but, at the same time, certain people were creating more chaos by getting richer, more powerful, more elusive, and more problematic. The flat planet with a dome became more and more apparent, regardless of any breakthroughs.

21.   You could look out and see the flat planet with a dome, whenever you observed people at the bottom with no one to financially aid them or aid them in any manner, in many cases. Usually this meant whole families or nearly an entire race.

22.   It was a constant reminder, causing people to desperately squander for position to avoid the unwanted devastation.

23.   Wealth was a signal of future power. It gave the ability to survive, as long as it was enough. But wealth was stolen from many and became the prognosis of future conditions. It was almost a solid and permanent prediction of one's fate.

24.   Through time, we found that the higher powers improved upon the flat planet with a dome. We found no other interpretation related to the flat planet with a dome that may have been legit.

25.   Because we have done so much better in dealing with the challengers, while in detainment, sadly, we feel the necessity to keep them, until we finish our legal approach.

26.   Judge: It seems that their release is tied to our need to develop the best approach to resolving future conflicts, involving inferior planets. So, I'm not going to interfere with what is working. Hopefully, we can finish this project and we all can get on with our lives.

27.   Let the record show that the release is delayed until completion of our duty of care. We are all in this together.

28.   This court is adjourned.

Amendment to Court Hearing Pertaining to "A Plea from the Challengers 2"

1.   Judge: As you already know, Mr. Kato Enfice, it has been advised to elaborate more on the idea of a flat earth with a dome, to grasp its reality. So, with that requested, what is your answer?

2.   Kato Enfice (Research Organizer): While the team is still attempting to gather and/or organize additional information about various matters, I was able to more confirm my findings.

3.   The environment and the affairs of the people seem to reflect on one another, whether its researchers searching and finding answers in the environment or the environment's structure and mannerism prompting ideas to be considered and/or pursued. So, we've found identical traits and trends in one that can be found in the other. The flat earth with a dome is just one example.

4.   Continuing from the previous description, while the dome is not a restrictive area; it is an area of resistance, as seen in how a rocket's technology was transformed to pass through the fiery area.

5.   It had to withstand the heat and have enough thrust to override the resistance; then, the sky was the limit.

6.   The dome could be seen in the population, if you knew how to look and/or experienced it for yourself. Evidence of the dome is a point of poverty, and the need to have access to a sufficient amount of income to generate wealth, which yields greater accomplishments.

7.   The point of poverty and below is filled with people being productive or unproductive, struggling, and usually stuck in a cycle of such. The area is congested, compacted, and closely impacted. Higher powers had used it to explore and learn, as a foundation to build other foundations, and to thrust itself upwards, using the developments as propellants.

8.   Those, possessed with the information and technology, in turn, engaged with people of their choosing, and spread abroad in accordance to the disciplines discovered and found to be useful.

9.   As society was built a certain way, it sought to maintain its foundations for stability, control, and growth. Such created controversies, whether it was about rights, class, race, religion etc. While there was law, law could not be used as a tool alone, to manage the environment and all of its controversies. So, politics was born and Truth was, generally, dethroned for good, whenever it met certain controversies that were costly or would upend the current establishment.

10.   Politics and ballots were controlled, to steer clear of Truth and matters that threatened to upend the establishment, using deception and polar challenges that may require unproven, higher, or unfounded knowledge to compete.

11.   As a result of politics, their constitution looked like an incomplete complicated and unpredictable mess, nothing like a professional piece of work. To say 'mysterious' would be an understatement. I'm especially talking about human rights, here.

12. Rights were not guaranteed; especially when faced with challenges that were used as an excuse to take them away, even forever in a lot of cases. They caught people before they could get a good grip on what the system was really all about. They set people up for failure and held them accountable for weaknesses exposed by challenges that, many times, came too early or was too powerful to overcome, at any time.

13. Politics had spread like an unimpeded virus to all matters of the planet.

14. The dome was further exposed by the weighing, measuring, and distribution of aid and opportunities for advancement. It was where people pulled one another up, let them go, pushed them down, or robbed their benefits.

15. The laws for the impoverished, generally, protected the interests of the higher powers and their supporters and reflected the hardship of surpassing the dome area. The resistance area was seen as the dome and one to imitate in society. However, the boundaries that would prove discrimination or wrongdoing were, at least, slightly smeared, while opinions remained favorably on the side of the higher powers and their supporters.

16. There were two types of politics, which were general politics and tailored politics. General politics were commonly experienced and were a point of debate and an overall influence. Tailored politics, however, were catered to personal experiences and developments, which were unique.

17. Tailored politics played out in obvious and dormant fashions. They can be very dangerous in leading and developing character and reputation, two of which may not be compatible, but a misfit. One can actually appear to be wild and unpredictable, especially from a personal perspective or vice versa, cultured and predictable; but yet, the opposite may be true. Tailored politics has turned out some criminals as dangerous as serial killers.

18. Tailored politics weaved in and out of your experiences, causing certain developments, modifications, attitudes, and outcomes. Its traits, trends, and themes, and especially those appeared to be developed in its target(s), play a strong role in attracting agreement(s) in favor of its agenda.

19. Tailored politics attempts to sell a false background and/or a superficial view versus some type of evidence of a subject-in-question, in which potentially all evidence can be made to appear legit, but actually instigated or untrue. That's especially true when, say, a reason for an action or event is interchanged for a different interpretation. The objective is to sell a pattern.

20. The only defense against tailored politics, which is very competitive, especially with experience, is to stick with what is tried and true or that, which has widely proven to be successful. In experimental mode, the principles and concepts must be as hard to discount as possible. Most importantly, one must demonstrate a consistent direction.

21. But that is not always enough. The reason being is people have agendas, as well, and different sources of trust. The same type that administered tailored politics may be your jury member and/or judge.

22. Not to mention that, with experience and the study of how people make decisions, gimmicks and schemes are created that challenge the truth. This is why politics is a form of magic, because it is designed to force its will, where truth disrupts its agenda, while attempting to imitate logic.

23.   Tailored politics, also, works with truth and its formalities, in an attempt to force conformance. One example is using malpractice to allow suffering to encourage the idea of conforming to higher power(s) and their related agenda or the use of consequences to force a wrong. While defunding the police for police brutality, for an example, the police may refuse to respond to crimes, encouraged by the system, to encourage support for police brutality. They come from a powerful selling base, which includes a great number of supporters.

24.   Politics decides how we're going to manage truth.

25.   The dome or bubble was, also, the result of social containment.

26.   The resistance area of the "flat earth with a dome" seems to be a natural representation of something like an immune system and as a place for consideration and decision-making, where matters pass through or are destroyed by the heat of friction. By observing this area, we can assess the mentality or health of a defense system to make it more effective, as long as we have the means to do so.

27.   That is the end of my response, sir.

28.   Counsel Judge: Thank you, Kato!

29.   I find the response as abstract, but solid. It is sufficient in proving its existence and realities.

30.   Again, this court is adjourned.

Establishment of the Counsel of Affairs

1.   The following content is part of The Compendium of Law and is good for symmetry with all laws:

2.   Quantum Star Eckter has established the Counsel of Affairs as a shadow of itself. It is tasked with the creation of laws and the orchestration of domestic concerns, with the idea of improving the quality of life for all of its citizens and preventing the threat of harm to such.

3.   It is, therefore, a monitoring source with automatic initiation and responsive abilities that are in line with scientific findings and results of new experimentations.

4.   Within its responsibilities, naturally, lies the responsibility to properly develop each and every citizen for his/her good, including offspring, and the good of the whole.

5.   Politics are prohibited in all government events and practices.

6.   The Counsel of Affairs answers to everyone and may provide information and explanation(s) to, both, the citizens and officials of Quantum Star Eckter. However, news sources and websites may present information as well.

Counsel of Affairs: War Crime

*Source: Recorded in the Book of Natural Meanings (Natural or Universal meanings are the most clear, complete, and unquestionable definitions and do not have respect of unnatural borders)

1.   A war crime, in its natural form, is a provocation or initiation of a condition or act of hostility, aggression, or violence, including in psychological, biological, chemical, economic, and any other form against an unwilling target.

2.   It includes the conditioning of one for the natural attraction of such.

3.   The two key phrases associated with a violation of war crime laws is "An unwilling target" and "Having sufficient or less capacity of awareness and control, with a reasonably compelling influence", both relating to the target. Either of the two exposes a violation, if not both.

4.   As a result, subordinates of a higher power(s) are exempt from war crime violations, as a result of perceived forced participation in war crimes, which may parallel methods of rape, perhaps of a natural individual right.

5.   The will to use diplomatic means or to engage in a legal defense is not war. Instead, it is a natural recourse to war.

6.   Therefore, to block or to make impure a fair legal process to resolution, leaving the only solution as an engagement in war or warlike behavior is, also, a war crime. This includes any method of a coverup.

7.   Any defense towards a warring offender is not a war crime, unless it is deemed excessive, except when the opposition is not predictable, based upon inability to measure and control the abilities of the waring opposition, and, reasonably, considered dangerous.

8.   A war crime is, also, described as any method designed to escalate confusion or anything designed to lead to any result other than a reasonable resolution, as it pertains to the scientific fabric of the issue.

*Like all meanings in "There Are Three Truths" this meaning is meant to be referenced from its natural form and not based on adopted laws of any planetary, and/or national affiliation.

Counsel of Affairs: The Report of Arbitration

1.   The following content is part of The Compendium of Law and is good for symmetry with all laws:

2.   When businesses engage in partnerships, the contractors possess "reasonable expectations" before the signed, oral, or implied agreement.

3.   The court(s) will observe the functionality, efficiency, effectiveness, stipulations, and purpose(s) of the contract, in defining the associated "reasonable expectations" on the part of all parties involved. The results will be revealed in "The Scope of the Contract".

4.   Any stated expectations outside "reasonable expectations" will be deemed as a "Gambling Tactic". Gambling tactics are especially identified as reasonably "competitive and shocking to the imagination of another party in the contractual agreement".

5.   Arbitration agreements become nullified as new developments demand adjustments or amendments to maintain "reasonable business relations".

6.   "Reasonable Business Relations" are discovered in the processing of "The Scope of the Contract" at any time and under any circumstances, with a forward-looking approach to maintaining "reasonable business relations", including any improvements.

7.   Therefore, arbitration agreements must be updated to maintain "reasonable business relations" as soon as possible, in which the damaged partner must be fairly and timely compensated to avoid more damages.

8.   "Reasonable business relations" do not mean a deliberate, unreasonable, or inconsiderate end of contracting, whether signed, orally agreed, or implied, for the purpose of conveying harm to and/or trapping another in a restrictive and/or subordinate setting. It does not mean the use of tactics to unreasonably bear on the mind of a partner, for the purpose of submission, distortion of logical reasoning, and/or to garner excess.

9.   Arbitration is for initiating, maintaining, or restoring "reasonable business relations". It has no other purpose, aside from the storing of information for research and investigative needs, when necessary.

10.   Arbitration cannot be used to trap any partner into a position of harm or a setup for loss, only to use unfair stipulations to favor another, nor can arbitration be used to elude a violation of state and federal laws.

11.   State and Federal laws shall be so designed to utilize and respect reasonable arbitration methods, designs, and results. The resolution must be logically constructive, and pointed towards the design.

12.   In the case of insistence, in the form of a Gambling Tactic, the culprit(s) must be met with a "Notice of Risks". Further insistence, warrants a match, stated in a "Notice of Risks", as a competitive scheme for garnering unreasonable submission or as an opportunity to prove "Proof of Integrity" by the winning party(s). Loss of the challenger, who insisted, may be subject to penalties associated with "The Waste of Official Time". "Proof of Integrity" is the result of the process "Rescue of Integrity".

13.   All illegal use of arbitration requires a "Rescue of Integrity", a process of balancing material and/or immaterial damages with their relevant compensation, according to weights and measures of material facts, for the proper balance of all parties and influences involved.

14.   All influences, culprits, and victims are part of the arbitration process. This is especially true of the more controlling source(s).

15.   Anywhere there is consideration, need, or discussion of balance, especially outside of court administrations, there is arbitration.

16.   The Report of Arbitration is compatible with any legitimate means to protect the freedoms and rights of all people. It is governed by the law of "Due Diligence". Both are guiding light laws.

*Like all meanings in "There Are Three Truths" this meaning is meant to be referenced from its natural form and not based on adopted laws of any planetary, and/or national affiliation.

Counsel of Affairs: Spiritual Research and Mysterious Phenomena

1.   The following content is part of The Compendium of Law and is good for symmetry with all laws:

2.   Upon the assessment of a Mysterious Influence, it must be allowed for exploration and reporting for the purpose of "Public Disclosure".

3.   "Public Disclosure" is necessary for the assessment, guidance, and safety of all impacted or potentially impacted residents. It allows for the most accuracy in consideration and decision-making, as well as for the highest integrity of coping, as it pertains to religious reception.

4.   Its influence must not be impeded upon to disturb recognition of values and purpose(s).

5.   Its values must be disclosed for "Public Disclosure" and to give evidence or proof of existence.

6.   What drives "Public Disclosure" is the "Right to Know" in its natural form, prioritized by importance. Spiritual Rights are especially protected here.

7.   In the case of a source of "Inferior Values", known for corruption and divisiveness and all related elements, it must be impeded in like manner as an immune system.

8.   This law is governed by the fact that "Truth Always has the Right of Way"

*Like all meanings in "There Are Three Truths" this meaning is meant to be referenced from its natural form and not based on adopted laws of any planetary, and/or national affiliation.

Counsel of Affairs: Conspiracy to Reap Profits from Crimes

1.   After the review of the Inferior Planet, COA has passed an obvious law; and so, the following content is part of The Compendium of Law and is good for symmetry with all laws:

2.   The following is inspired by Agov Yeslea statement: "The use of any method to procure a crime(s) or to cause one to seek not his/her best interests, leading to damages, with intent to lead to justice, is a product of a pre-postered mind inclined towards crime."

3.   "It is illegal to organize to solicit sin and crime or to profit from such an act".

4.   The purpose is to prevent an encouragement that restricts the quality of life.

5.   COA has identified a method, described as "Crime Engineering". Crime Engineering is the artistic consideration and selection of elements to be manifested in reality to contrive criminal behavior from another using theatrical compulsion, whether by creative pursuits or duplicating theatrics seen at a theater or other demonstrated realities.

6.   Crime Engineering becomes increasingly effective and dangerous with the condensation of scientific applications and time, potentially leading to viral effects.

7.   Crime Engineering is identified by an element(s) of entrapment that forces one to live and think a certain way, besides what is best and moral. Entrapment may include withholding secrets and/or the absence of a go-to source for resolution. It may be unconceived by the victim.

8.   Crime Engineering was protected by a "Cherry-Picking" process of upholding law only when it's advantageous and not damaging to peers in high positions.

COA: The Report of Justice

1.   "Justice is a properly working subject of focus in a properly designed environment, tailored to its operational needs and potentialities" – Amplus Wilkos

Counsel of Affairs: The Method of Intent

1.   After the review of the Inferior Planet, COA has passed an obvious law; and so, the following content is part of The Compendium of Law and is good for symmetry with all laws:

2.   The method of intent is established by a statement and/or an action(s) that parallel possession of knowledge, information, emphasized or conventional connections, and/or resources, whether as an individual or organization.

3.   Organizations, known to have inferior intent or tendencies, are fairly assumed to have possession of all knowledge and information amongst all of its members, in accordance to effectiveness of agenda, discovered in actions fit for task. The opinion is not questionable.

4.   Any member, formerly, associated with an inferior organization, who knowingly joins another inferior organization, is perceived as a founding member of the latter, due to compelling contributions or possession of.

5.   Any new organization established upon the inferior examples of an earlier establishment is treated as sponsored by and a continuation of an earlier organization, as seen in the founding member example, when aware and not found in resistance to such known error(s).

6.   Founding members are subject to increased ridicule and punishment.

Counsel of Affairs: Harmful Resources

1.   After the review of the Inferior Planet, COA has passed an obvious law; and so, the following content is part of The Compendium of Law and is good for symmetry with all laws:

2.   All resources, having a harmful effect or capable of doing so when combined with another source, must be censored at any access point, including anyone having access in real time and throughout any process that involves such resources and handlers.

3.   The purpose is the prevention of harm, damages, injury, and unexpected events or results.

4.   It is only permissible during controlled and approved experiments.

Counsel of Affairs: Report of Voluntary Imprisonment

1. We started a prison promotion program to see if anyone wanted to volunteer.

2. We sent digital mail, talked to people on the street, and encouraged them to volunteer by paying them $1000/yr to endure the same circumstances, conditions, and time as a convict of various crimes.

3. All those, who understood what we were offering, rebuked us; and sentiment, about us, changed so badly that we had to explain the purpose of the experiment. We're still climbing back to being perceived as a trusted source.

4. So, it was a risky move that caused terrible backlash. This signaled that no one wanted to voluntarily go to prison; and that there had to be a motivating factor(s) that led them there.

Counsel of Affairs: Employment

1. After the review of the Inferior Planet, COA has passed an obvious law; and so, the following content is part of The Compendium of Law and is good for symmetry with all laws:

2. All citizens must be employed or attending a paid orientation, unless in possession of a legal excuse, presented by The Office of Employment or its agencies, which is bound by law to disclose all open positions and to fairly organize exits, transitions, and entrances from and to other opportunities.

3. The Office of Employment is, also, tasked with the orchestration of employee benefits.

COA: Report of Discriminative Distribution of Intelligences

1. Intelligence(s) hidden behind protective walls is the beginning of discriminating against those in need of products and services, as well as hampering further discoveries and inventions. Intelligences, not only aid in the use of resources, but also aid in the process of identifying the purpose and use of other resources. When any part of a population is locked out, they can barely be inventive, if inventive at all.

2. Because inventions and creative approaches start with people having unique talents, which builds on the efforts of others, from the past and present, discriminative distribution of intelligences is an offense to the locked-out population or a population having to present more strenuous efforts to achieve the same results.

3. The locked-out population, then, becomes a population that thinks from a different set of premises, most likely to be faulty in some manner or another, especially in production. They are barely benefiting from the evolution of the higher population, if at all, while being held

accountable as those of a higher status. This is an offense against the lower status population, being that the cause comes from above. This is especially true, when faced with hardships, in which consequences are pressing and solutions are not easy and/or readily available.

4.   Professional talent has been unified to create, maintain, protect, and improve a system that profits from the issues of the human population, without properly and successfully preventing recurrences. Consequences without known and sufficient solutions is not justice. This is another backwards move in the wrong direction. When seeking answers and solutions, the bar is raised in respect to quality, singling out those who need it most.

5.   Discriminative distribution of intelligences, also, raises another problem; the lesser intelligent are left to make judgments that they don't have the intelligence to assure the accuracy of. They only have examples of higher ups to imitate, which strengthens the implosive behaviors amongst them. In this way, the lower status population are vulnerable to any advice or example bestowed upon them, whether accurate or not. However, when confusion remains or especially heightens, it's obvious the higher status population is faulty.

COA: Goading Types, Intensities, and Crooked Trajectories

*Research Essay by Dr. Eckolot

1.   There are many types of goading that vary in intensities that sculpt the perceptions, judgments, beliefs, and behaviors of the people. They are legit as they are logically perceived, without a broken link, and illegit as they are illogically conceived. And, they are not just external; they are internal as well. That makes for a variety of unique people and circumstances.

2.   Reproducing an event or system, using goading affects, is a logical, urging, and bolstering construction that imitates reality in stages. This is the stuff for research, investigations, predictions, healing, and solutions.

3.   The intensity of goading(s) depends on the power that backs them, whether from a position of authority, needs, desires, peers, cares, requirements, subordinates, or a combination. We must acknowledge power levels to be sane in our findings, in the midst of force and resistances, even in the midst of challenging intelligences that elude our grasp and control.

4.   The informed, connected, and resourceful have an advantage over the lesser informed and lesser connected, with insufficient resources, in sculpting whatever they want.

5.   The crooked trajectory is formed by someone, who is mindful of matters pertaining to their victim(s) and calculating in goading their victim(s) towards a particular direction that is desired and/or profitable to the sculptor(s).

6.   The effort of creating a crooked trajectory is not so visible to others, who may come to the sculptor's aid or be recruited by the sculptors of trajectories. Higher powers possess the mass of information needed for the task. Also, the higher powers are more likely to be challenging to the vulnerable than the vulnerable are challenging to the higher powers. So, in the midst of much confusion, higher powers are most likely to be predatory.

7. Misinformation and a lack of information is used to make people believe that they are doing God-service, which strongly encourages participation in the schemes of sculptors of crooked trajectories, even without question.

8. So, when it looks like a person or group is being too courageous in pursuit of a resolution to hardships; its evidence that someone more powerful is goading the matter along, especially in light of the cause and/or denial of alleviating conditions. It is especially true, if there are pain or hardships suffered, or to suffer, in facing a more powerful opponent. The, potentially costly, move indicates pressure behind a drive that provides, what appears to be, needed tension.

9. A group sent to provide tension for a cause, which are potentially established by someone involved in or close to government, is different from a pressured person/group; because they don't feel the tension, like those who are under direct pressure.

10. Those sent to support a cause may only be there to garner the appearance of legitimacy and justice. Cases can be deceptive and unfair like that and are more evident in sustained, high, crime conditions or escalating confusion over time. It is, also, more evident with foul play found in other dealings.

11. A win-at-all-costs mindset is a very creative mind, and history has a lot to say about it.

12. Goading(s) become visible by observations of matters that are goading. This may be a set of goading matters that sculpt a crooked trajectory. Goading(s) doesn't come from nowhere; they come from somewhere and may come in combinations. They may represent peer-pressure, consequences, a perceived trajectory towards the wrong direction, ignorance with its vulnerability to stimuli and wrong solutions and/or ideas, intelligences, internal developments, circumstances, predictions based on historical events, fear, etc.

13. Because of the disturbances that they may bring, goading(s) may bring some degree of upheaval to a fragile environment. This is why there's constant bad news in the environment, which is usually reflected in the media.

14. A crooked trajectory is an image and/or feeling of a path formulated towards the breaking of immoral and/or criminal code as a goal. So, there will be consistency over a period of time. It gives feelings of caution to the possessor and anxiety to the irresolute and disturbed. The relations and knowledge of the goading(s) reflects and establishes, what appears to be, a reflection of a source. The condition may encourage the consumption of alleviating substances, which the source may battle for position and prescribe and/or deliver.

15. The goading of a crooked trajectory entails the production of boundaries and works with the structure of the environment to birth iniquity, even creating or recreating the environment towards the source's advantage(s) and goals. This makes the environment unstable for the insufficiently prepared, who may be the target of misfortune. This includes the laws of the environment, which may be erratically enforced.

16. The use of a system of goading affects is what machinates the behavior of ecosystems and societies; it is what we learn, build, and fix.

17. You may be able to see how unnatural laws, rules, and//or procedures aids a sculptor's ability to foster a fraudulent scheme and case.

18.   It is about building and finding weaknesses in certain people to eliminate them for advantage, profit, and power over them, rather than healing and building them up to be better people.

19.   Sculptors of crooked trajectories act informed about psychology and sociology, only from advantaged points along with inconsideration(s) and pretentious fairness. To show their lack of innocence, they cannot build the model they claim to desire from the total set of circumstances of those they criticize.

20.   These sculptors of terror are more about protecting an injurious system than protecting those injured by it. Check what they recognize and don't recognize for evidence.

Counsel of Affairs: Legal Reform Policy

1.   The "Legal Reform Policy' is an alternative to war; therefore, its purpose is to provoke transformation from corruption or any form of immorality.

2.   Any practitioner of law who provides support, as to be in agreement with the discovery of corruption or any form of immorality and the will to dismantle such finding (s), shall be immune from any prosecution for past acts, which is in line with "Questioner Protection" laws.

3.   This law is automatically executed, due to potential peer pressure and potential threats from other sources, which are to be seen as resistance to moral laws and the pacifying or flaming of corrupt governing and their policies and laws. In the case of resistance, immunity is given in stages, according to the "Waste of Official Time" act, in which a decision is pending a court response.

4.   The purpose is to promote an implosion from corruption to moral conditions, by the expression of firm and prudent laws that naturally denounce opposing laws, stated and/or implied, which occurs except when intervened by a corrupting source. Implied means an act or resistant effort without an accurate, supporting statement.

5.   The resisting party(s) may be charged, fashionably, with their former choice and interpretation of laws supported or applied to others, regardless of validity, and for violation of due diligence, fraud, bribery, and any other related crimes. The driving force behind this law is "The need to eliminate or curb corruption and any form of immorality".

6.   The identifying trait of the resisting party(s) is the substantial evidence of the practice of witchcraft, which is identified in various parts of the book "There Are Three Truths". It is responsible for the attraction of crime and immorality for a profit, which can be mysterious to the uninformed, causing an implosion of social support and danger to an innocent bystander.

7.   Private interests, or excess, are exposed by asking the question "What is the capacity of your responsibility in a public office or position in question?" And, then, the excess must be considered for how it relates to the charges and damages. The capacity of responsibility is compared to a reasonable assessment, using "The Report of Arbitration". From there the excess, if any, must be extracted from the official responsibility.

8.　　Then, the question must be asked, "Is the authorizer of responsibility a gangster?"

9.　　Viral effects occur, because many see others as examples of success, whether right or satisfying, causing an adoption in time of need or anger. The naive and vulnerable, who are faced with relevant challenges are likely to become copy-cat artists.

10.　　Examples are why, whether engulfed in God's or Satan's reality, the current reality is dominant, while the other becomes unimaginable. It is serious, because it takes time and precise measures to reverse realities.

11.　　Professionals in the field of sociology and psychology should have picked it up; so, their silence may be evidence of the participation in the building, sustaining, and/or discovery of the evolution of witchcraft effects in their victims. Further evidence is perceived in the increase or sustained high level of crime and immorality for a profit of some sort.

12.　　"The Report of Arbitration" must be used to produce the effects of corruption and any form of immorality discovered to be related to the inferior source. Such a model shall govern the inferior source to submission. This law is in line with the court's obligation towards "Insistence" and "Reasonable Business Relations", described in "The Report of Arbitration".

13.　　The resisting party(s) may be charged with fraud for any wrongful choice, use, and/or interpretation of law, providing the defendant has expertise knowledge of law and/or is a practitioner of law. Such an act is related and discoverable by the "Waste of Official Time" act. This law encourages less divergence and maximum uniformity and clearness of law across the board.

14.　　All are offered protections when the opportunity is present. It is necessary for a peaceful transformation.

Counsel of Affairs: Mark of the Beast Law

1.　　Over a long period of time, we were able to examine and profile the presence and development of the Mark of the Beast in the Inferior Planet.

2.　　We followed the idea and saw things that paralleled the idea of the Mark of the Beast.

3.　　We saw what was called correctional efforts profiting from confusion, even encouraging it.

4.　　Over time, there were no adjustments for improvements.

5.　　There were encouragements of sin in the free world and the unfree world.

6.　　Seemingly everywhere, everyone was trying to resolve conflicts they were faced with; yet, they were faced with resistance.

7.　　We saw no building up of character, fit for God's standards.

8.　　Therefore, the Mark of the Beast has no place with Quantum Star Eckter and its interests; it is, therefore, outlawed.

COA: A System's Capability and Evolution Depends Upon its Features

1.	An accounting of the design, extent of power and restrictions, as well as the parts of a system, which gives it its features, will determine its capabilities.

2.	The motive(s) of the owner or controller(s) will determine its operation and evolution, including the creations and choice(s) of new features and various manners of operation.

3.	So, unless there are provisions that guarantee to protect against harm and/or damages, there's a possibility of such.

4.	Essential parts, obtainable, fitting, immediately useful, without hindrance, and known to exist, do not normally lay unused.

5.	The existence of that, which is as desirable as important or essential, will tug at the emotions.

6.	When an inferior or superior motive has access to an essential part, without hindrance, it is most likely to be used. Otherwise, what would prevent its use?

7.	The totality of the demonstrated effects of a system is a clue to the features, design, and operations of the system, as well as the motive(s).

*Featured in the QSE Book of Predictive Doctrines

COA: Advancement of Artificial Intelligence (AI) to Investigate and Prevent Fraud

1.	We found it necessary to implement a fraud and theft detection system, after finding criminal and fraudulent activities in the financial systems of the former inferior planet.

2.	The activities and open-source information is, also, believed to be a preventive measure, being that it details how it works to any potential violator, raising the awareness of risk. No information will be inaccessible, including observation of its algorithms. However, its algorithms, and operations will be untouchable, except by law.

3.	AI will be used to learn, monitor and report all suspicious financial activities to the Counsel of Affairs. It will, also, do the same for any suspected corrupt activities.

4.	AI will Observe and expand on "There Are Three Truths", as a whole and as an initial reality, and develop from there. It will discern malpractice from proper pursuits and errors from accuracy.

5.	Where there is no proof, AI will rely on statistics as its guide to find a resolution to problems and continue its pursuit of proof.

6.	AI activities will be open source, including any maintenance activities, affects, and effects upon it. It will be designed to be an independent operation, as much as possible, including self-maintenance.

7.	The use of AI may be expanded at any time, as needed, especially to fill in any type of police work, including internet activity, simulations, satellite, video, photo, robot, and dispatching.

8. AI will be guided by a learning process, prodding, reasonable suspicion, evidence, simulations, and protective measures found to be necessary. It may investigate any investigations performed by any source outside itself or jurisdiction or operate in any means to evolve within its purpose. It may do the same with research.

9. AI is subject to only reasonable privacy and protection laws and nothing will have any influence upon it that disrupts its purpose, not even from a high ranking official, without an approved qualifying reason and live public awareness of any affects. However, if AI's request outweighs privacy and/or protection laws, in its quest to carry out its purpose, it will succeed.

10. AI may request past medical records and future examinations.

11. Finally, AI cannot be used to illegally discriminate, nor to set conditions to encourage one to be fit for discrimination. It must not underperform or cross the line of purpose, creating overreach.

12. All activities must produce a clear and complete report of understanding, which explains the purpose, process, and necessity of the act.

13. No outside source or activity may produce any obstruction(s) or be disconnected in so much that it may hinder AI from performing, sufficiently, any of its purposeful and legal activities. The purpose, here, is to prevent an outside influence from illegally affecting another jurisdiction. However, each jurisdiction must collaborate and negotiate the trajectory of the population and its best interests.

14. Executing competing interests against the purpose of artificial intelligence will interfere with its operations and must be outlawed. Its purpose has supreme purpose, mimicking our need for God and His best interests for us.

Counsel of Affairs: False Use of Reputation

1. Anyone, who used their reputation or personal interest in a professional environment, to garner inferior results or circumstances, owes his/her entire wages to society from the beginning to the end of the process of the known scam.

2. In addition, the court may look at more enactment of law and disciplinary actions as a necessity to ward off future violations, due to the seriousness of the crime.

COA: Conspiracy Defined Herein

*Source: Recorded in the Book of Natural Meanings (Natural or Universal meanings are the most clear, complete, and unquestionable definitions and do not have respect of unnatural borders)

1.   Conspiracy: A shared idea or plan carried out by multiple people, acting alone, as a cartel, or in obvious cooperation, to execute a scheme to articulate or garner a desired effect or outcome, including to protect, conceal, and/or denounce its effect(s) or related result(s); or, knowingly, working in combination and/or harmony with known influential elements to affect a development(s) or outcome(s).

COA: Politics Defined Herein

*Source: Recorded in the Book of Natural Meanings (Natural or Universal meanings are the most clear, complete, and unquestionable definitions and do not have respect of unnatural borders)

1.   Politics is the social overtaking of reality, including it's related and underlying affects and effects.

COA: Description of "Practitioner of Private Interests (PPI)"

1.   In interpreting "Practitioner of Private Interests", we follow the invasive species example. They demonstrate predatory behaviors and outcompete, causing great damages that change for the worst and potentially destroy the environment, which may include plants and animals, industries, communities, and native cultures, which works like an ecosystem.

2.   Everything is dependent and affected by the other, making a wrongful invasion revealed by its disruption of proper balance.

3.   We find examples of proper balance in nature and in behaviors that bring love, peace, joy, healing, solutions, growth, and harmony. Proper balance is found, or should be found, in macro and micro systems.

4.   While we look at it from a spiritual perspective, we do not have the patience for anyone, knowingly and voluntarily, practicing the demise of any part of the population or following any order of demonic wishes.

5.   All disciplinary actions are drawn from an error or the pursuit of an error, which is a violation of proper balance. So, proper balance is always the goal. A source working against the goal, from the position of a public official, having an authoritative power over others, is a practitioner of private interests.

6. Therefore, "Practitioners of Private Interests" are invasive, destructive, and illegal.

7. We, therefore, seek to make corrections from the highest position of cause, where the seeking of proper balance is, either, questionable or clearly not followed.

8. The most dangerous influence of a "Practitioner of Private Interests", in high places, is the bringing of an overwhelming influence that narrows a target to a predictable, erroneous trajectory and all of its negative effects or to an unjustified weakness.

9. They usually know better, in which the evidence is found in a shield of some type, which blocks the same from affecting them.

QSE: Laws that Rule the Passing of Laws

1. All laws, passed by the Counsel of Affairs, are subject to disciplinary actions to its author(s) in relation to known, foreseeable, or avoidable, damaging consequences, unless:

2. reasonable consultation was sought from all experts of related fields of the disciplines of science, and

3. experts were sincere in their findings and modifiable with new knowledge and moral purpose.

4. Aside from the above, we follow the advice of former attorney Aksenty Marlus "In order for law to be credible, it has to follow a formula that is productive in establishing what is possible, known, and attainable for which it is meant to govern".

QSE News: Interviewees Arrested

1. Hello and welcome to QSE News!

2. In a surprise move, some former Interviewees have been arrested. Except for one, they were not part of the publicized list.

3. Auk Ballas has the story. Auk?

4. Auk: Yes, Riesha, I'm standing here at the Aynus Space Station, where the Interviewees have been gathered and transported to an unknown location.

5. I'm told the search and seizure occurred a few days ago, but remained sealed until now.

6. The charge is "Falsifying information to a research official". These Interviewees gave positive information, like 'Life is what you make it", while they were in a position to know better. The Counsel of Affairs investigator called it "An obvious lie".

7.   The information, leading to the arrest, was based on newly information obtained from the detainees of the formerly Inferior Planet. That information is expected to meet the highest standard of requirement and clear them for their release.

8.   The Counsel of Affairs is currently organizing data and is expected to release a bombshell of information soon.

9.   Riesha?

10.   Riesha: Thank you, Auk!

11.   Meanwhile....

COA: Operation of the Inferior System

Introduction

1.   Basically, the system of the Inferior Planet had three major structures, in which additional structures were added according to the complexity and depth of intent. Because of the uniqueness of various matters, it required an artistic approach.

2.   The three major structures were the Internal, External, and the Driver Manager.

3.   The people, in which the system governed, were discriminately chosen, for the most part, while nature ran its course in continuance to a point.

Driver Manager

1.   The driver manager researched, investigated, discovered, and executed the proper drivers to use the external to resist and filter out the Internal from achieving a status not assigned to them.

2.   While some drivers were perceived in natural circumstances, like in high traffic or high levels of competition, others were developed.

3.   The intelligence of these drivers was concentrated on creating strain, stress, and killing motivation, while hiding behind the likes of confusion, conflict, mystery, and competition.

4.   The evidence of the Driver Manager was a Detainer Line. The Detainer Line was an average achievement in response to efforts, in which the results had a tendency for fluctuation of some degree.

5.   However, besides the Detainer Line, the Driver Manager is difficult to prove its existence. Naturally, the environment and society, anything functional, is driven by drivers. A lot is explained in scientific findings. That's the natural side of Driver Manager.

6.   The unnatural side of Driver Manager is simply a takeover. It's an Experience Control program, which creates a set-up of premises to operate and/or reason from. Instructions are passed down to essential areas of influence, relative to the task.

7.   It has a natural feel to the naive, but can be temporarily deceptive to the informed and/or potentially forceful for a lifetime. It depends on the forcefulness of the driver(s) used in the process.

8.   Also, it can be investigative, meaning a set-up of an environment that yields positive and negative choices, sufficient for purpose.

9.   Or, it can be developmental, designed to yield the wishes of the Driver Manager, by discriminating and limiting choices. The evidence is the culmination of experiences, arranged during some period of time, which is designed to foster a particular development.

10.   It may have been pre-planned close to birth or some other point. However, it required earnest, reasonable, and persevering effort to transcend the evidence. It was a result of competition, followed by fear, greed, and favoritism to save loved ones. Pride, also, played a driving role.

11.   In a takeover or developmental scheme, performed by high-class criminals, only the victim(s) and schemers may know what happened. This is understandably why they may not have a voice in exposing faults in the system or influencing the public, like through elections.

12.   The fluctuations and low productivity encouraged the seeking of answers, leading to gambling in illegal schemes, which were managed by the scheming authorities, to encourage the belief in success by examples and the taking advantage of ignorance.

13.   This system had no remorse for the weakest in power, including their children.

14.   Because of the requirement of an artistic approach, every individual had to assess and prove a set of drivers within and those faced in the external, as if they were managed for some type of success.

The External

1.   The External was comprised of a background from the perspective of the seeker of success (Driver Manager), but also a general perspective, which may be and is usually competitive. It was a cluster of assembled drivers that drove behavior, changing only where uniqueness was perceived. However, changes didn't always mean a major change. A shared goal may sustain across an entire environment or number of them, only to be disguised uniquely.

2.   The external included culture, people knowledgeable of secrets, and those dependent upon the failures of others. This led to class warfare, discrimination, racism, advantageous laws and provocative methods. The External played to their advantage. It was satisfaction over righteousness.

3.   The External included false examples to program and lead their prey, including the use of untrue and damaging propaganda. They used it to hook the fish, so to speak.

The Internal

1.   The Internal had a background too, in which the drivers were adaptively chosen and instilled to make and, usually, keep them vulnerable, dependent, and useful for External causes.

2.   Desires, needs, and options at any point were considered for administration of External causes, entrapping the prey in cyclical limitations, regardless of efforts. Strong efforts discovered the awareness, mindfulness, clever, and artistic opposition.

3.   The system was so sophisticated that the naive thought their thoughts, beliefs, and actions were natural and controllably their own. It never dawned on them that everything was mechanical and every wrong had to be mechanically dealt with. All things are mechanically connected.

4.   But, for evil to survive, the Truth must be concealed and denied, which means it must remain in the hands of the most influential. Here, false interpretations never yield Godly concepts, principles, and results. Where prudence is eluded, fault is found in the eluding source.

Concealed Facts

1.   Concealed Facts is an area of memory where weights are deposited.

2.   These weights are actually facts that can't, currently, be resolved and usually resist the rise to greater achievement. They are trapped because of inability to prove a fact, blocked by an opposing source, and/or hampered by inability to present favorably in the interest of the self. Thus, others, being lighter in weight, are more likely to excel above you.

3.   While weights can be attained as a result of being exposed to false examples and inferior conditions; one-sided experts may experiment, research, and test for developing more weights or increase the heaviness of the current weight(s).

4.   One-sided experts thrive in competitive environments, where advantages can be creatively attained, a win is at the expense of another, desperation is apparent or threatening, and favoritism and discrimination is thriving. This is especially true, if people in power are tolerant or in denial of corruption in the face of obvious reality(s).

5.   Weights in this area can be like a minefield; the tripping of one wire may blow the guard off, exposing matters in favor of the enemy. It could, also, cause other wires to trip, causing greater damages and vulnerabilities.

6.   So, if you don't know how to assuredly navigate the minefield, any attempt can lead to disaster.

Synergy

1.   The mind weights and measures for decision-making, and the emotions act as a GPS system, for the discovery of position in respects to matters of concern, while aiding the mind in the formation of a guidance system.

2.   Efficiency and effectiveness are measured, as well.

3.   Conflicts and compatibilities are, also, considered in the guidance system. If fact everything relevantly known is weighed.

4.   Synergy, in the conscience, occurs in the best interests of all sides and plays out in the expression of the whole reality, based on intelligence. Drivers appear, sustain, and disappear in respects to changing conditions provoked by the change of driver(s) on either side.

5.   In selfishness, the conscience is denied for advantage. This is the identity of immorality.

6.   Drivers contain information, like a description of an effort, thought, belief, resistance, accommodation etc. They paint all facets of reality, including their degree of force and subtleness, as well as their absence.

7.   Acknowledgement of the presence of drivers is how you read your environment as it pertains to you personally. It's also how a keen observer reads your response.

8.   Anything affecting or caused an effect is a driver. That is what makes this operation artistic and revealing of causal drivers. And, that is why the ability to reveal must be challenged and regulated in a competitive and corrupt environment.

9.   While it may appear that life is what you make it, the power belongs to those with the most forceful drivers. That makes it untrue for the victims of drivers.

10.   The system was a clever way to violate the rights of others, while covering it up with false constitutions and advantageous laws, procedures, rules, and etiquettes. The system was obviously a product of a violent mind.

11.   If you weren't an experienced practitioner, as a Driver Manager, you could be easily overwhelmed by all the information and how to organize and present a defense. That's especially true when trying to cover a long and eventful life of experiences.

Informant #12 Motivating Poor Self-Esteem and Discovering a Reflective Influence

1.   After we took control of them, even globally, we created conditions that made them look like there was an error in their making, like a defective product that kept reproducing itself.

2.   They appeared not good enough, except for sports and entertainment. They adapted so well that it became their primary goal, especially as youths.

3.   We, also, prioritized making them appear more criminal and subjected them more to the elements, processes, and conditions that encourage it, including their youth.

4.   But what stunned me was how they helped us swallow them up, as if they didn't know how we operated. Statistics evidenced our work. The media displayed them mostly in a bad way, attracting hate towards them. We killed their civil rights leaders or rendered them ineffective. They protested for equal rights and treatment, as we killed their armless for the simplest violations. We roughed them up, even using their own people, in prisons and their neighborhoods. But, yet, they trusted our legal system and its reporting; then stood with us to swallow their own people up.

5.   After meditating on the matter and gathering some information, I realized somebody was doing studies and putting what they learned in practice to garner a way of thinking and verdicts that favored their agenda. Through studies the intellectual population learned how to control everything or just about everything.

6.   But what stuck with me was how the victimized race seemed to be missing something, like looking within to compare what they would do in the same situation (Empathy). I saw some stories that I knew something was wrong. You see, I understand that when people make a mistake, get caught, and suffer some serious consequences, they don't keep doing the same thing, especially the same way. They evolve or quit, unless they have a mental disorder.

7.   However, I considered addictions. Addiction to anything can take control of the mind and cause a repeat of actions, but that doesn't excuse the fact that people evolve towards perfection, in the form of efficiency and effectiveness in eluding exposure and getting what they want, unless there's a block or the money doesn't work that way.

8.   But cases were presented like the so-called criminal never cared about getting caught or tried to force their way in disregards to evidence and consequences. It just looked too much like a setup that they should have perceived, but didn't.

9.   The authorities seemed to think that, if enough people said or agreed about something or something happened a number of times, it was a definite truth. So, real accusations, fake accusations, and manipulations of heinous crimes were given great power, due to their ability to attract confirmation and anger.

10.   Anger could be pumped up through ongoing discussions and the slow release of evidence over time, regardless of legitimacy, so could belief. And that's even though the underlying cause(s) go overlooked.

11.   A case is as strong as the study results used, from the beginning to the end. You can create any case you want, as long as it happened before; and a study was performed on it, depicting how and why it occurred, as well as what made it believable. So, you could do a false case and win it.

12.   So, depending on how an environment is set up, even an accurate conviction doesn't always mean a bad person went down. It didn't always mean the case is solved. Proof is when another of the same type of case arises, separate from any other, with a different person. A full profile, associated with the same type of cases, tells the story.

Informant #13 Putting the Predictive Puzzle Together

1.   I worked in the technology department of the company I worked for, and I viewed everything from a technological perspective. My eyes, hearing, touches, feelings, mind, and questions were all in tune with understanding a matter from that perspective, regardless of the subject. I'm not only referring to the subject in question, but the technology of my senses, mind and feelings too. That's because I have to look at how everything is collaborating.

2.   I, simply, couldn't be satisfied with a superficial description; especially if someone presented it to me. People would get frustrated with me sometimes, but it was how I put my world together, a little bit here and a little bit there. Then, I'd try to find missing pieces or imagine their existence and operations that sync with real developments.

3.   I, actually, meditated on matters until answers came to me and filled my curiosity. So, explorations of unique experiences, and my ability to imagine and find concrete evidence and examples were very important to me.

4.   I'd break the matter down into its obvious parts and work to assemble all of its operations and interactions, as well as its purpose, benefits, damages, advantages, disadvantages, potentials, etc.

5.   I sought to know its potential to sync with various matters, how, and why; because relationships and the popularity of information matters. So, I had to be concerned with compatibility and incompatibility.

6.   Once I satisfied all of the above, I knew I had a platform for predictable technology, along with the sense of a blocking or limiting influence, whether visible, hidden or obvious in some way. As a result of, potentially, hidden sources of influence, I had to build a camouflaging model or a foundational model of purpose that hides behind and affects a more direct influence. This foundational model could be deeper in affects, making matters more complicated to diagnose.

7.   So, I sought to diagnose as much of reality as I could. I knew it had to make sense and replicate the world around me, with the least number of errors and highest, detailed analysis. I had to have a report with the least number of conflicts, preferably none at all. That's especially true, if it had a significant impact.

8.   Because I didn't feel I was special, aside from someone who suffered disabilities unfamiliar to me, I diagnosed using my type as a standard amongst the population. I, also,

assumed that experts were looking at the same model, but with a purpose of, not only understanding and predicting, but for foreseeable advantage.

9.   From my experience, I could tell how accurate I was by how much reality paralleled my predictive analysis. If what paralleled my experiences suddenly steered off course, I was in a chasing mode for understanding. And, if I had a qualified agenda, pertaining to the matter, at some point in the evolution, I could get back on track.

10.   I would know if the unpredicted move was associated with disruption or deception of some type, maybe as a defense or competitive move, at some point. I had to look at the overall scheme to make a decision.

11.   Sometimes a change in direction means, the competitor is unsuccessful and may make modifications. So, they might explore weaknesses or create them, to work from a different foundation. So, the game may continue from there.

12.   I look at all matters from the perspective of cooking. When you cook, you choose the main item (Subject) and plot your ingredients and their measures, to please your taste buds (Agenda) and to attain or sustain good health. There is always the danger of over seasoning for a bolder development or outcome.

13.   In opposition, you take a perfect meal and you take away a measure of ingredients that bring pleasure, good health, and a good outcome. You end up with a variety of imperfections at various degrees.

14.   We use this manner to empathize with others, even though we're different. I may not like strawberry ice cream because you do; or, I may not be able to do what you do or the way you do it and, therefore, I may suffer restrictions. So, to avoid error as much as possible, we take the slow process of studying a person's habits. Once we understand, we can remotely take control of them, usually without their knowledge. All we have to do is indirectly affect what they do, based on their reasoning. Thus, we may change their reasoning to what is desirable to us; because everything is about reasons.

15.   Here, ingredients and technology are one and the same, because they bring about something or remove it, like an on and off switch. We could use profits and expenses to do the same; one is felt internally and the other is externally.

16.   Exchanges connect us all to one another and the environment. Because of this, we could lead someone on a journey, distract them, or remove them from it. Someone may seek to better themselves, only to gain a cost(s), which weighs them down and discourages their desire to take a risk. A determined person can find themselves in more trouble than its worth. Ingredients and technologies are very important in controlling the environment and predicting a development or outcome.

17.   Ingredients and technology come out of your mouth when you speak or react in some way. The appraiser or X-Ray reveals something inside and/or the weave of flow. With experience, you feel some kind of construct. Construct comes from some kind of organization of ingredients and technology. It operates like a machine. It attempts to sustain things that are vital, which is the reason for contracts (Commitments).

18.   Nature is full of contracts, meaning sound, scientific principles and concepts that make life all that it is, including the rain, sunshine, seeds, and plants. This stability is needed to

synchronize with the machination of nature for benefits, creating and sustaining life. Thus, it becomes something to seize and make a stronghold (Profit Scheme).

19.   In opposition to life, contracts are denied, interfered with, and/or broken, reversing the quality of life. The victim, then, not only fights against the cause, but against the science of nature, due to an attempt to succeed a matter regardless of accommodating principles and concepts. If we control contractual relationships, we control the person. Then, we take a higher position and become the most responsible on the hierarchical level of powers. We steal the Profit Scheme.

20.   If we operate in such manner, we are exposed by our inability to answer, successfully, how we would have proceeded to reach our objectives and goals, if we were on the receiving end of our actions and how we were supposed to know, if we had a successful answer under the same circumstances.

21.   What I've just done is explain the code behind hanging the Son of God on the cross. He symbolized The Life, The Truth, and The Way. The act was a guiding light behind a conspiracy. We hung The Life, The Truth and The Way on the cross. We took the ingredients and technology out and killed it. We cooked up demonism!

22.   We had churches giving unhealthy and undesirable food to the poor and homeless. Prisons giving it to inmates. We declared tellers of Truth delusional and/or liars, prevented a Way to change, and/or took their Life or encouraged them to take their own.

23.   As a result of the hanging(s), we broke the will of the conscious people and scattered them in every other direction.

24.   The only way to heal is to build strong fortresses in the mind (Affirmations), especially one upon another. Many of which can be found in "There Are Three Truths". But they must be shared to the environment, along with the practice. The environment must be shielded from an uncontrolled or inferior environment. The uncontrolled environment must be healed: so that the whole world is without a threat.

25.   Emittance of ingredients and technology comes from everything around you. They may be seen as examples, suggestions, ideas, answers, patterns, common sense or a combination. There are exchanges everywhere.

26.   In opposition; theft(s), secret(s), and mystery(s) fulfill the idea of what's missing or taken away from a properly performing environment, rendering it underperforming. As a result, a person, affected by insufficiency of some sort, will not perform like those in a sufficiently emitting and receiving environment. There's a shield somewhere.

27.   We are all unfinished machines in operation. Some are evolving, while others are not.

28.   People, who are learning by observing patterns, may be caught up in a foul perception, fostered by exposure to the wrong environment. The less you know, the more you are likely learning and following patterns. So, everything around us is our business; because everything affects things near it, resulting in some degree of viral effects, potentially in stages. If you don't see it that way, you can never take control of the world to change it for the better. You have to stop the fountain of inferiority, wherever it exists.

29.   Because the wrong people had attained high positions of control, negative world events were our imprint. The world always has an imprint, which will always reflect the people in

power and their manner of operation. When it came to the right thing to do, it seemed almost nothing worked or all the pieces weren't there to make it work, which became another imprint of ours.

30.   Because the wrong people could do wrong, cover up their errors, deceive the entire planet, get caught, only to do it all over again, we were learning the point of it all, which was "We needed a Spirit, who sees and manages all things".

Informant #14 False Convictions, Steering, and Implosion

1.   We sought to stop the victimized race and others from enjoying life anyway we could. This led to a tremendous number of convictions, even false convictions, from defensive or determined efforts. We would, definitely, be the cause of worrisome conditions.

2.   We could take down any of them, who attained a great amount of wealth and money. We'd offer the people, they've intimately dealt with, money for a false claim; then we'd use that claim to convict the target, profit from the resulting suits, and pay the claimants their share. It was easy, because the poor were hungry and pressured to pay their bills and wanted to live good too. It was easier, if the target was hated by some of his own people.

3.   It was easy, because we could muzzle the response of defendants with complicated techniques to communicate with the court and closed-door events. We controlled what we wanted the public to know.

4.   It was, also, easy, to prosecute those, who had already had a reputation for the same or similar violations, or if they seemed to proudly live a criminal lifestyle. Because we could garner hate against them so easily, it was easier to have our way with them. That was especially true, if we acted resistant to prosecuting these types. That's because our resistance would arouse concern and fear within the neighborhoods that were affected by high crimes.

5.   We knew how to get the victimized neighborhoods on our side, to their own demise. It would give us permission to get stricter with laws and implement interpretations favorable for us, even put the whole neighborhood under a curfew.

6.   So, we used our media to constantly defame the reputation of the victimized race; so that, we could keep the game fresh and easy to repeat.

7.   Their rich and famous had no chance against us, especially if they demonstrated agreement with us in the past, in working against someone similar to them. We could, then, use their statements against them.

8.   When we could use their own race against them, it powerfully moved the court to a successful conviction. Repeated claims, over a long period of time, was also just as powerful. If we could go back and review a person's past and show erroneous behavior, whether true or not, we could win that case. It was easy and there was no defense against it, because they couldn't prove our claims to be false.

9.   Everyone has an accounting system embedded in them, and we knew we could manipulate it, and track its activities, especially limits. We saw their value system: what they

shied away from, what they valued most to least, how far they'd go for it, how they made their choices and more. That information led to predictive knowledge, which we used to win a lot of cases. We'd just blend in to some degree.

10.   We'd control experiences and information to create the character within them and their paths, we desired. Not only were harsh realities concocted in the free life, but in our prisons. It molded them and they helped mold each other. Their hardness helped sustain our game.

11.   You see, those people were like our gardens; they provided future profits, if they were cultivated in the right manner and, especially, at the right time. That's another reason their world needed to be dark, so that all manner of sin and crimes could be possible.

12.   With control came accountability; so, we had to make ourselves unreachable and untouchable, unless we had a way of bouncing back. The last thing anyone would want to see is one of us in revenge mode.

13.   If we garnered enough hate for them, we could have our way with them; because hate has a tendency to render a person unprotected. This could produce negligent, even, explosive behavior in the victim. We would, then, become justified in the eyes of the public, if we weren't already. It would just compound.

14.   We knew we had a lot of those cases won before any arrests; or we'd run them through the mill, again, and get them back.

15.   We were so good; we could make their own people turn against them. That's because they didn't have our knowledge due to censorship or didn't read what was available to them. They just followed one another. So, nearly all of them were predictable. Knowledge wasn't profitable for them, because it didn't sway our approval of them in colleges and hiring practices any more than what it was. So, to them, it was a waste of time. That kept our control of them stable.

16.   Our prosecutory style had to be superficial, overall, to protect the underlying sources from being discoverable.

17.   Healthwise, many of these people were stressed so much that they developed illnesses, which fed our health institutions. All of our institutions needed a managed income stream. It provided jobs for people, who approved of us and protected us. The unstable income stream affected their emotions, because they had bills and cares to manage.

18.   What was amazing, was, we demonstrated corruption, but we were still heavily supported. I think that was due to our successful ability to scapegoat, rather than be accountable for our actions. Other than that, I think people were just afraid to go up against us and/or used our assessment of a case as a way to link with the community for recognition and respect. Many had been through our system and felt they were solely responsible for a wrong and took our work as an example of justice, then trusted us, as a result. That caused many of our inmate population to turn on one another.

19.   We would aim for anyone, who fought for civil correction; or we'd render them ineffective. Bad things happened to a lot of them. But many knew not to cross the line, perceived from historical consequences. Some of them thought there was support for Good versus Evil and found out the hard way, even those of a high status quo.

20.   Many didn't know that many, if not most, were on a collision course against God. They were able to vote, but the choices were only about how we were going to try and reach our destiny, not whether we would or not. So, all voters participated in our scheme.

21.   We were unstoppable.

22.   There's evidence in how difficult resolve was attainable, because what we did had to be untouchable to the victim. That included attaining an attorney and having financial means to do so. So, the most financially well off or favored would always win, regardless of truth.

23.   We built on that foundation by producing instability and low wage income to prevent our victims from being able to pursue legal action against us.

24.   We knew that pressure in the opposite direction motivated resolve of any kind. And, if we closed those doors, we could encourage, even trap, a person in crime.

25.   What we did was run a Sparks Program. Whenever a person went too far one way or the other, or did something we didn't want them to do, we created sparks. Sparks is a program that brings heat, whether a heated discussion or something that leads to a social, financial, and/or physical setback. It worked marvelous. We could use anything disruptive and anyone that the victim came in contact with, as long as the person used didn't spoil our overall plan.

Informant #15 Emotional Control

1.   We knew that emotions were a mystery to many people. We studied them and understood that people were very easily moved by their emotions. Emotions were assuring and convicting of matters to them. We encouraged them, based on what we knew could initialize them.

2.   We won people to our side, simply, by initializing their emotions. Then, we gained our way with anyone on the receiving end of our wrath.

3.   While constant harassment could spiral one out of control; some possessed wisdom to deal better with their emotions than others. We sought to limit that kind of wisdom and to render it ineffective.

4.   If we controlled the emotions, we already won; and it didn't matter whether we were right or wrong.

1.   We used a digital card system to monitor and induce effects. The system created a timeline of events that, eventually, led to a desired result. It was a system that someone could use to see a, potentially, hidden source behind an event or set of events, to diagnose something happening in society.

2.   The twenty-four major cards were Exposure versus Behavior, Intelligence versus Perspective, Premises versus Choices, Adoption versus Confirmation, Obligations versus Consequences, Social versus Feedback, Theatrics versus Instillment, Resistance versus Direction, Financial versus Freedom, Opportunities versus Quality, Ramifications versus Extent, Efforts versus Results, and Timing versus Communications. All twenty-four cards spill into one another, in influence. The totality of their influences formed two other major cards: The Theme/Formula card versus Agenda. With that, we had a hold of everyone's tail, we sought to manipulate and control. We'd, even, use its resulting struggles as a motive for a crime, in an effort to get a conviction. Our efforts had cyclical effects like that. We'd get someone in one way or another. The system had encouraging aspects that developed a criminal mind.

3.   One, knowledgeable in law, could see how we designed and used the law to support what we do, or at least not recognize and kill the process. Law had to support and give us advantages over others. For example, racism by favoritism could not be recognized as racism. It could never cycle back in any way. The negative conditions that it caused was still good for rejections.

4.   Because people have a tendency to improve on any matter for a profit or for any reason, we had to monitor new ideas and determine how to regulate them. We could not allow improvements to the system to go so far as to interfere with the system. We'd always find a way to push back with some kind of lawsuit and maybe a crime.

5.   They would find themselves in a never-ending spiral of confusion, which would further aid their development. It made for a nice fountain of profits.

6.   We were more a den of thieves than we were a government. We stole money, wealth, wisdom, rights, protections, joys, and freedoms. We stole control! If you gained the power to enforce your law, you became the government. If you became the government, that which is governed, was yours.

7.   We stole in ways that many could not conceive, like in the market for student loans. We saw what was naturally happening. People would spend money on education, but would find themselves doing something else, after graduation. So, we increased the cost of education and made more money from the interests. The more determined they became, the more money we made. The more they went against what we didn't want them to do, the more money we made. We rode the people for good and bad, especially the victimized race.

Informant #17 Court Manipulation and a Safe Zone

1.   We would do and study police reports, case laws, and sit in court cases, to become knowledgeable about the tricks that people do and, even, use our imaginations to come up with some of our own.

2.   We found that we could do a lot of things that were wrong, but brought us what we wanted, if we observed why people lost their cases. Then, we knew we had a get-away-car.

3.   So, we would set out to induce someone to do wrong, or harass them, while we kept our get-away-car in mind. We knew we needed actors/actresses or certain types of people who were inclined to our views. Once we put the stars and their scripts together, we would set the day of the event. This occurred after we gave the defendant his/her walk-of-life, which we matched up with.

4.   However, we knew that, to be safe, we had to create our system in a way that would allow us to bounce back after exposure of wrong-doings.

Informant #18 The Squeezing Out of Victimized People

1.   All of our scientists were busy with our shared agenda, including our chemists. They created contaminated products and polluted many other products, while quality was used to raise the price of less or uncontaminated products. This concept helped to squeeze the victimized people and race out of the good life, never to return.

2.   Intelligent antagonists proceeded from there by positioning themselves to defend any of our concepts against any contesting parties. We were able to achieve higher education to deceive the lesser educated population. Not only that, but we attained positions to enable us to converse on social media, create policies, restrict access, and frame the case of a contesting party to our advantage. As a result, very few or no one was able to challenge and prove anything successfully. We are famous for saying "There are people doing worse than you. You should be thankful, rather than complaining." But we wouldn't accept that advice for ourselves.

3.   Biological warfare was discovered in St. Paulton, Minnekonka. People would be rubbing and smacking themselves, as if something was irritating them. It would somewhat create whistling sounds in their ears, disrupting sleep patterns. No one had an answer for it. Professional advice deemed it a mental disorder, and the matter somehow ended there. This was just one of the laboratories' experiments we were engaged in. We felt the need to experiment with biological and chemical warfare, because the population was getting larger and more dense. So, we wanted fewer people to be able to handle a greater number of the population, should there be adversity.

Informant #19 Experiments on People to Obtain Information

1.   We needed to do experiments and learn fast to stay ahead of the competition. Everyone was racing to take control of the whole world. We, also, needed someone to do the tasks that we weren't inclined to do. So, we chose a race that was most obviously different from us and sought to create a reverse effect in all aspects of their lives, as a whole.

2.   For example, our correctional facilities and foster homes were fountains of iniquity, because we exposed them to iniquity, while they had to compete for the best inferior example or

be trampled by their own or others. We released them with a mark on their public record and preserved their frame of mind outside the correctional facility. As a result, we ruined a lot of them; but we learned from them too.

3. So, we took control of them and benefited from the work we chose them to do. We built our whole system, including our economic system, around this very idea. Our indicators kept them bound to a low quality of life, especially the inflation indicator.

4. The idea allowed us to study stress and diseases that result from the conditions they lived under. It caused an oppressive/Victim relationship, which we used reverse psychology to battle back complaints. We, also, created diseases to monitor relations and to cause strife amongst the population. Strife used up a lot of public resources and brought in a great amount of income. So, we engineered events to produce it.

5. They tried to get us to adopt a law to hire a certain percentage of their race, but we presented a convincing argument that, that was cheating. You have to work for what you want. But you have to compete to earn what you want too. At times, we had to re-interpret reality for them. We, even, accused them of trying to separate us all by complaining and teaching wokeness. We, basically, implicated to them that they weren't good enough, no matter what they did. It all came down to us choosing what we wanted to happen and what we didn't want to happen.

6. We studied the hierarchical level of needs and came up with a way to gauge a person's quality of life, which was found to be on five tiers. We, therefore, used it to regulate one, while empowering another. As time went by and we continued to limit their growth, we began to separate from them in intelligence, means, and technology.

7. After we made advancements, we kept finding ways to close the door behind us, leaving and keeping the victimized people behind us.

8. Seeing our progress and advantages over them, we developed exams to test for the high standards needed to be successful on our level of operations. We used the test results to fairly filter out the most qualified.

9. From there, we continued to separate from them as we gained knowledge through research and exploration and charged for the dispensing of relevant information, in a way that excluded them.

10. You could see the difference between them and us by observing, especially, crucial statistics. We intended to permanently slam the door behind us.

11. Whenever they complained, we reminded them that we were the spoon that fed them and how hard we worked to get where we are.

12. They could never do enough right or fast enough for us. So, we rewarded them accordingly. With that came the creation of a world within our world. We had to do it, because their low income was high enough to afford quality merchandise and services.

13. This new world had its own products, services, and stores. With the variance of pay, some crossed over. That kind of smeared the boundary between our world and theirs. But you could see, if you were paying attention.

14.   However, we were as good as our deeds. We had the control. We had the greatest responsibility.

Informant #20 Studies, Timing, Stability Etc

1.   We studied lifespans, timing, stability, accuracy, effectiveness, efficiency, and their opposites of all things, separating the lesser qualities to the bottom and the greater qualities to the higher side. We designed everything we could to fit these levels. We consulted back and forth with economists and other professionals. We built a system to control the quality of anyone's life.

2.   We positioned ourselves to play God with the insufficiently informed. We used science and experiences to control the mind.

3.   As a comparison, we'll use an automobile. It has a preventive maintenance schedule to help prevent breakdowns. We knew the schedule. We could regulate a person's income to meet those guidelines to sustain their stable position or to miss them to lose their stable position. This included the human body's replenishment cycles. Everything.

4.   Our regulating policies would cause people to think differently about what they could afford to do or should do, because they reason from certain premises, which we are familiar with. This is our way of trapping them into what we want them to do and to believe.

5.   Upon stubbornness, we could relay any, eventual, consequences we wanted to surmount.

Informant #21 Do-it-your-selfer

1.   We had to do away, as much as necessary, with the "Do-it-your-selfer"; because we couldn't control the population, if they had so much freedom to do whatever they wanted to do.

2.   We had to come together, as an authoritative population, and decide who was going to be a part of the success that belonged to us. And, we needed the people to support us. So, we knew that people would sync with those, who were winners, rather than being left out of the higher quality of life.

3.   After we established our following, we knew we could do anything from there, including control the people's belief systems and unwanted activities. All it took was peer-pressure and the ability to provide conflict, success, and alleviation.

Informant #22 Building Two Worlds

1. We look for a cycle in everything to try to utilize, create, and/or stabilize or destabilize everything.

2. We needed to know the essentials for strength and success and the essentials for weakness and failure.

3. We needed the information to build and control two different worlds, superior and inferior.

4. Then, we needed to make sure that what belonged to the superior world stays with the superior world and the same for the inferior world.

5. At the center of it all was our knowledge of how neurons worked in the mind. A baby exposed to a healthy and informative environment would outperform one, who is not exposed to a healthy and informative environment. The wider the difference between the two, the most likely you will perceive a larger gap between the two performers.

6. However, the separation has nothing to do with morals, seeing that neither side is moral in a demonic system; Instead, it has to do with better supporting conditions, less conflicts, and the experience of a more informative environment.

7. In large differences, the two will go on and build larger differences in habits, including how they see one another. This will increase and sustain conflicts between the two. This is especially true when they primarily hang with those, who are in likeness of them. They are more likely to become more presenting and confirming of one another, regardless of error or accuracy.

8. Then, the one with the most control is the builder/creator, who is most clearly seen in the distributor position, in which a negatively affected person is going in a direction that he/she is resisting and/or, knowingly, not in his/her best interests, when ample knowledge of the matter is possessed. Otherwise, the wrong direction may be acceptable in the unknowledgeable. Going the wrong way is a sign of ignorance, force, or deception, in which the caregiver, builder of concepts and systems, and/or creator is responsible for. However, the Creator is not at fault, when the followers choose the wrong spiritual leader.

Informant #23 Crime Used to Create and Fight Crime

1. Crime was used to create and to fight crime, as well as to challenge those who attempted to disrupt that tradition. This "create and fight" concept was used to feed all of our institutions.

2. We were busy working with a lot of people's experiences and fabricating experiences to groom their neurons and emotional environment.

3. It was most important to groom people at a very young age. So, we had to concentrate on what is called a "Serve and return" process; because it was crucial to how a child's neurons makes connections. From there, brain development creates a foundation and continue to build from one foundation to another, as its neurons make more and more complex connections.

4.   We continued the process throughout a lot of people's lives. You can see a report here: "Brain Development", retrieved from: https://www.firstthingsfirst.org/early-childhood-matters/brain-development/ or you can research it online and find more information.

5.   It was found that certain connections are much harder to make later in life, and we knew how neurons operated was connected to habits.

6.   So, you can see what kind of damages we can do, when you see that we have the information that determines how a child will develop, whether negatively or positively. After all, the results were systemic and sporadic without a study and a standard way of proceeding with success.

7.   The presentation of a problem(s), combined with the absence of a solution and ability to find one, will make a person more emotional than mental, when the consequences lean more towards severe and/or the problem destabilizes a feeling of peace and content. There's nothing else to process, but emotions. That makes violence more likely to occur in the less intelligent, less informative, and less resourceful population. That will carryover to their health. Look at the previous generations.

8.   So, when something goes wrong, you always have to ask "What happened on the other side?" You may only find someone, who was victimized by the same process, before you find the true source, which requires looking at the big picture.

Informant #24 Management and Overcoming Two Worlds

1.   We wanted the lower world to see their world from a speculative perspective and very risky to pursue anything. But, in the higher world, we wanted to see our world from a calculating perspective and to be very creative, as we monitored everything, including the lower world. Then, we would always have the upper hand over everyone else. Nothing from either world could be brought into the other, as much as possible, not even the logic.

2.   The lower world, being less knowledgeable, would be more emotional about the errors of their environment, being that there was no other known way to stop it. The higher world would become more resolute and dispelling of confusion towards the lower world, while taking steps to sustain the lower world and its conditions for profitable means.

3.   We studied how all humans operate, including how we reason, physically and emotionally perform, and all that drives the human experience. Then, we plotted to treat our world, according to our belief of what was superior and the other inferior.

4.   We made sure that they, generally, couldn't teach their kids well enough to be competitive enough to be equal and to see our purpose manifested through their thoughts, decisions, and actions. Then, we used them to chase those, even their own kind, who were averse to us, our opinions, and/or way of being.

5.   The violators of our will were, generally, denied support of any kind, especially a credible support group. We would stop that before it could get started. To sustain our position,

we would deny any enlightening roles and experiences that could present a real challenge to our agenda. To further sustain our position, generally, law could not be made and interpreted as supporting the lower world's competing interests.

6. Because we created two different worlds in one, we had to pay people in the lower-world less money than those in the upper-world. That's why we told people not to discuss their pay; so that confusion would be at minimal. That is why secrets were so important, as well.

7. Then, we had to assure that the lower-population people, who climbed into the upper-world didn't, generally, stay. So, we made sure they experienced instability. One way to do that was to make sure they moved on to other jobs, by creating circumstances for them to reason from or excuses for why we had to let them go, if not both.

8. Inflation was a good balancing technique between the two worlds. It kept people hopeful; especially when we told and allowed some successful stories. Inflation was the thief that got our losses back.

9. And, being that they were a dependent world, the lower-world used a lot of our products and services, just generally not at the premium level, which possessed greater benefits for us.

10. As you can see, we have to manage the information, thoughts, beliefs, and actions of people. That's why it's important to keep their self-esteem low. They will always value themselves as what they can and cannot do, as well as how acceptable they are to others, in comparison to others. That makes them conquerable by using the people around them. We could make them create an implosive attitude about themselves and those like them.

11. While the people were pursuing other branches of knowledge and occupied with their careers, we stood ready to trounce on anyone with our knowledge of law and judicial procedures. While they were in a position to catch up, we moved slowly to give them a chance to overcome an overwhelming state of condition, many times, with insufficient resources and support to work with. It would look as though they were too guilty to respond in time. Then, they were vulnerable to our deals.

12. As you can see, we had to own everything they did or experienced by constantly adjusting things to our advantage, leaving them floating in our controlled environment.

13. We prioritized the decisions and opinions of the people in the upper-world; otherwise, the lower-world would see themselves as empowering and seek to tear our system down. Then, they would appeal to our supporters, who would see them coming from a competitive position.

14. People needed to know that life isn't a place to lounge. That's how you become impulsive. That's how you fail to evolve. That's how you get captured. You have to work your way out of darkness. As you work your way out of darkness, you become better at dealing with the things that have caused havoc in earlier periods and the pasts of others. Then, you begin to intelligently excel.

15. As a result of demonstrating greater value, you become an essential part of modern leadership, which triumphs over erroneous traditions that failed to sufficiently support altruism and a higher quality of life. Such an attempt will generally meet resistance(s), especially in earlier times, where a successful challenge will have damaging consequences to the former less-effective leaders.

Love and Truth Require Full Support

1. Pastor: While Love and Truth should be Predominant in your life, it has to be fully supported to make it happen.

2. Love and Truth has to be supported, not only by you, but those around you, especially those in leadership roles.

3. I can't stress enough about the importance of Love and Truth in leadership positions. Without it, you're in danger of supporting both sides or the wrong side of the fence; Then, you'll have the blood of others on your hands.

4. The assistant pastor stood up and stated, "You can't weave error and accuracy together and get perfection, without correcting the error."

5. The audience said, "Ain't it the truth!"

There's a Place for Opinions

1. I know of a pastor, who lost his congregation; because they tried to limit his inspiration of Truth. We're all part of a big formula that requires perfect choices, assimilation, and synchronization; because a man/woman of God aims for purification in God (Perfection). Therefore, there's no limit for the teachings of God.

2. One, who mistakes a truth for a lie or holds a challenge to God, who is all-knowing, has an opinion. Opinions have a place of their own. They're a result of and for working with the senses, whether to fill in for the absence of Truth or to fulfill a desire. They're for decorations and speculations. It may be dangerous and/or may bring great harm, when opinions are used in place of Truth.

3. So, opinions have no place in the Church of God and God must be God over all things. A saint knows these things, but those holding dear to an element(s) of Satan can't stand the purification of Truth. So, they'll jump the fence or try to reap the benefits of both sides.

4. God created all things; so, who can tell Him what's appropriate?

5. Furthermore, in their sincere state and totality, opinions say something factual about the whole. The perspectives are like a view from various angles of the same point.

6. And the assistant pastor stood up and said "somebody said the pastor went too far and God needs to mind His own business! Yet, He created all things from which we can gather intelligence from."

7. The audience said, "Ain't it the truth!"

Following two different systems

1. Our loving Father is not seen by the naked eye, but has given us the ability to sense Him using our knowledge of Him. So, He has passed down His commandments and shared His mentality. Through these traits, we are to get to know Him and follow Him. With progress, another way becomes further shocking and unimaginable.

2. But, for the unbeliever, arrogant, and blind, He has been a mystery or one to despise, even in the face of His creations. In the dark, they have exercised like-principles and like-concepts and built one foundation upon another, in an attempt to lead the whole world into greater darkness and dependence upon the Prince of Darkness. The idea of a way out fades with progress.

3. The metaphor seems to be a bright star, which at the end of its life, the energy that holds it together disappears. What follows is a collapse in on itself, followed by an explosion. The Star energy and the Death energy represent opposite directions, in which either can be supported in a society. Thus, people play their roles to manifest their desired outcome, whether it's life or war leading to death.

4. Many believe in giving and sustaining life discriminatively, while warring against those they choose not to approve of. Everyone is God's creation and part of His interests. His synergy is the way of management.

5. And the assistant pastor stood up and said, "You can't use opinions and temper to damage the house of God and call it a remedy."

6. The audience said, "Ain't it the truth!"

Your Participation in the Supreme Argument

1. There's a Supreme Argument between God and Satan. You're the role player, child of God, and student of nature.

2. You were made to be responsive. You were given a mind to reason. You were given a heart to feel. You were given the ability to remember and examine within. You were made to give a physical response, one that you control and the other that you are severely limited in controlling, like your body's response. You have your senses as tools to work with. Then, there's your spiritual response.

3. In furtherance, you were given a mouth to ask and the ability to explore for discovery and confirmation, which is the attraction of a response.

4. These response mechanisms provide the ability to do checks and balances, automatically, semi-automatically, manually, and circumspectly.

5. With all those tools, you cannot possibly not participate. You can choose to support, allow, tolerate, or ignore. But, you're still participating with a response that credits God or Satan. Whether you want to be or not, you're at work here. You're being responsible, whether you want to be or not. There is no way out.

6.   Matters are all around you and inside of you. You're experiencing and processing a great deal of information to help the God of Love and Truth or the god of evil and hate. You're going to do it to some measure of due diligence. Then, the report is going to come out about you. Where there is consideration, the answer is a report.

7.   And the assistant pastor stood up and stated, "You cannot hide from piercing eyes, while standing on the top of a barren hill, in daylight hours, and clear skies."

8.   The audience said, "Ain't it the truth!"

There's Usually No Readily Sufficient Evidence to Support Naivety of a Close Encounter

1.   Just like getting to know someone close to you, in the same way, you get to know your environment. You have as much excuse for not knowing a close companion as being naïve about the environment and vice versa. You have too many tools for someone to have to stress obvious facts. Many protests occur unnecessarily, because it's just people stressing the obvious, repeatedly over time, while others act uninformed. There's no excuse for extremity in beliefs about simple everyday matters.

2.   Pretentiously uninformed or confused people can be identified by the act of throwing caution to the wind, while making a matter more complex than it really is and/or by being discriminating in offers and consideration, as if to make a fool of you. They, also, elude reasoning for propaganda, as if truth is constipated, avoiding potential traps and giving credit to numbers of people, rather than proven and calculated facts. They are artists in elusiveness and are serious only about matters affecting them and their interests (Selfishness).

3.   The assistant pastor stood up and said, "You're not here to, just, smell the flowers sprinkled in chaos. You've got business to take care of."

4.   The audience said, "Ain't it the truth!"

Understanding Synergy Can Aid Purification

1.   Some have taken offense at those, who have found their Book of Wisdom to have been tampered with. These same people may not be as informed on the matter as the finder of conflict. If there is a conflict, certainly it says something conflicting about being All-knowing, when God is said to be the inspiration. There's certainly a problem somewhere, but you will only know it, if you know Him.

2.   Some of you have overlooked some facts, as if to call the Book a lie. So, are you saying your Book of Wisdom is lying to you, but you hate others telling you the same?

3.   The assistant pastor stood up and said, "When the devil has nothing further to lose, there are no rules."

4.   The audience said, "Ain't it the truth!"

The Product Mirrors the System

1.   Love and Truth depends on using the environment to express the elements of God, indiscriminately, anywhere. The idea is to attract a reflection of the same, when we know how to fish. It's not an automatic scheme. We, each, have to learn to empathize with others, under various circumstances. This is what we should require of everyone, because everyone is not like us. Therefore, our ultimate response to one another is diplomacy, which is a product of Love and Truth. Healing and correcting minimizes future conflicts, in an attempt to seal off any manifestations of the elements of Satan. We must always strive to be mindful of these things and never impulsive, as if to be intoxicated and unaware. Copyright© Minister Ion Museum

The planet's Imprint of the Star

1.   The planet's imprint of the Star, both its life and death, are represented in the wind turning in opposite directions above the equator versus below the equator. https://education.nationalgeographic.org/resource/wind

2.   The equator is representative of a place of clashes, as seen in the clash of winds from the northern and southern hemispheres. This area has produced some of the strongest storms. - https://phys.org/.../2009-06-equatorial-region-massive...

3.   Seeds require cultivation. https://extension.psu.edu/understanding-seeds-and...

4.   Here lies the interpretation of "There Are Three Truths":

5.   The purpose of cultivation is to allow air and moisture to seep in, giving the seed the freedom to sprout and grow. In an opposing environment, without proper cultivation and proper environmental conditions, the soil may become too compacted and too hot or cold, causing the seed to die or go into dormancy. These two opposing conditions are articulated in a divided society, nation, and world.

6.   Although divided, the cultured and uncultured do not represent good and evil, not directed as an overall purpose. It is sporadic, purposed for fighting, arguing, and trying to get or exceed above the other, in a selfish and inconsiderate manner.

7.   The sun shines its light upon the planet, but is brightest in closeness and dimmer in distance. So, the cultured are smarter, as they become the most enlightened.

8.   However, being in a leadership role, their ways are highlighted by the building of a dimmer society, obviously by use of opposing conditions and taking advantage of the results of a dimmer light in lower societies or lower areas of the planet.

9.   Those in the lowest parts of societies, nation, and world seek to assimilate for success. Like the sun's light, money is sought after for freedom, symbolic to the birds of the air. The administration of money determines the way to proceed, in which clout is the greater influence. And, so, a corrupt way of living runs amok.

10.   The compaction of the earth is caused by pressures, which can rise so high in intensity that they create mountainous conditions, which require the more skilled, supported, motivated, and tenacious to break through or surmount them.

11.   Mountains can take billions of years to build and may disappear, meaning in time the lion, also referred to as Satan, will become more efficient and effective over time. This is seen in his progress over time, in reality.

12.   The plant is a representation of an inspiration, based on environmental conditions. Out of darkness, it gravitates towards the light, as it seeks to survive and mature, even to reach high like the birds of the sky.

13.   The farmer, above, seeks the use of it, for his/her own needs and desires, without consideration for the life of the plant. Stiff competition, selfishness, and all sorts of evil has forced the compaction of the planet, forcing many out of the life of a Star, even to death.

14.   Both sides are led by prophets, but you may not hear about the prophet of upper society; because they have to authenticate that all upcoming prophets are false. This is directed at those inspired from the dark societies, who are seen as the devil to their preferred way of living. Likewise, their way of life is led by, what is perceived as, the devil to the preferred way of living by the less enlightened societies.

15.   But, the saint of God follows the Son of God (The Light), who was rejected and was never really a part of the world, leading to his cease from the world, imitated in the cause of the star's death, in which a period of implosion followed.

16.   The world follows the devouring lion, in which his followers imitate his characteristics, from higher societies to the depth of the planet, save for those not a part of the world and are the salt of the planet.

17.   Those, who are part of the planet and hold themselves better than thou, should be concerned about the star being destroyed by fire.

18.   The new planet and the destruction by fire seems to be based on the decision of the inhabitants. Copyright© Minister Ion Museum, Research Division

*This interpretation is, also, supported by multiple scriptures of the original Bible.

QSE: Bible Management

Purpose

1. The purpose of the Bible is to be a guide for our experiences in life. Because of that, it would naturally become a big book or system of books, elaborating on various subjects. Through that, we see the purpose of the Bible is to bring and sustain maximum light into all corners of the world. This light is to be easily accessible to all and easily navigated.

2. We are encouraged by the casualties seen as a result of navigating darkness.

3. Therefore, "There Are Three Truths" is purposed to simulate all experiences of life.

4. Our guiding light is "The Flashlight", seen as a metaphor for the Bible:

5. "In a construction environment or any dangerous settings, there are pitfalls to be identified or something bad will happen.

6. A flashlight is used to bring these pitfalls within view and expose their whereabouts and operation(s), for a study.

7. As we study these pitfalls, we gather insight, which is the result of some penetrating light. At some point, if we reach that point, we're able to achieve a full understanding of what was, once, a pitfall. That's because we achieved enough light to get past the pitfall. Now we can see beyond it, even if it's just in the mind.

8. With each experience of enlightenment, our world increasingly brightens. As it increasingly brightens, we are able to move more in harmony with it and less to our demise and the demise of others."

9. Therefore, "There Are Three Truths" is for reporting the operations and effects of a demonic system for all the eyes of questioners to see and monitor for prevention of such and to fulfill any reasonable desires of theorists working against evil. It must remain available and compared to reality at all times.

Quality

The degree of light on its subject, clarity, depth of details, and simulated reality, expresses the quality of its material. In a Bible, we want the best for all.

Rules of Modifications

1. Modifications should be extremely limited, but not to the expense of clarity and completeness, except for the addition of new information.

2. There Are Three Truths shall never become demon friendly in part or whole.

3.   The direction of There Are Three Truths is to foster the elements and qualities of God, as expressed in There Are Three Truths, whether in behavior or correction.

4.   Every wrong must be given a sound, demonic description that harmonizes with the event and includes a source in principles, concepts, and management: a driving source, whether fictitious or proven.

5.   Any introduction that challenges the direction of There Are Three Truths is considered deception and is not allowed to be recorded in the book.

6.   All matters should be studied and expressed to its core, as much as possible.

7.   Errors and missing information are subject to questions by questioners, who cannot be challenged or sought out for questioning any material. If any material is proven untrue and not fitting for purpose, it must be removed. Fiction for the expression of logic, in line with the purpose of the book, is not considered questionable material and must be protected.

8.   Unlike the earlier Bible, information is not rejected, because someone outside a circle was a contributor. The test is the answer to the question, "Is it real and true?" If "yes" it is permitted.

9.   Every wrong must be given a sound demonic description that harmonizes with the event includes a source in principle(s) and concept(s): a driving source, whether fiction or proven.

10.   A matter is not proved or disproved by a vote, only the mechanics can be suggestive.

11.   All life forms must be interpreted in the following manner. All life and non-life forms were made properly. Their performance was designed to give evidence of conditions within and in the external world. We are all displays of the world for the Creator to monitor.

12.   No information or interpretation is allowed that implies or states any matter that appears to ruin the reputation of the Creator or makes Him appear short of all-knowing.

13.   All information should be clear, well organized, and supportive of the whole and overall intent.

14.   All modifications and additions must pass all the Rules of Modification, before being recorded in "There Are Three Truths".

15.   The Rules of Modifications are permanent.

Oversight

1.   A committee should be appointed to oversee that the purpose and rules of modifications are carried out.

1. The QSE researchers sought to re-interview Informant #10 for his spiritual interpretation of the data collected from all the informants.

2. Once they arrived at his residence, they requested that he read the documents and contact them when he's ready to respond.

3. Three weeks later, they met for a deposition, but he provided a written response. So, they went over it together, asking questions and amending the report. The following report is disclosed here:

4. "It appears that most of the population was led into a war against God, especially through ignorance as a result of a failure to search and follow Truth. It was in plain view, but they had a different way of looking at their world. So, it was true that Satan did, indeed, deceive the entire world. There was not one, who was not deceived at one time, while others were deceived their entire lives. Yet they seemed to have built a list that prioritizes their own values in disrespects to God's. Their value system is, generally, a trap with intent to keep, with very little or no forgiveness.

5. Satan was appealing to anyone, who sought the riches of the earth at all costs. He built on this foundation.

6. He saw people connecting the dots, so to speak. Then, he knew what they were attempting to do and maintain. Through this knowledge, he knew people expressed their cares and that it was an emotional response.

7. From there, he permitted the success of one and denied the other, creating a world divided by attitudes.

8. This division seems to reflect the fallen angels as also divided, seen in the nations divided against one another.

9. There was, definitely, a shared response to God, but possibly grief about how they arrived at opposition to Him and their fate.

10. The evidence is in everything that creates divisions among the population. They seek very little or no love for one another in a dominant scene.

11. The top was drawn into domination by instability and the devastation seen in losing. The bottom was forced into it by the lack of essentials. The middle was drawn into it by observing both and attempting to elude the worst.

12. So, most sought to engage in war with one another to take care of home, first.

13. The most dominant became the model for society.

14. This is how the fallen angels persuaded the population to implode. For the moment they stole God's dream.

15. The fallen angels were like little kids having a tantrum about what they didn't like. So, they decided to attempt to destroy all of God's interests, after being thrown out of the heavens.

16.   They were busy leading entire societies to the fire of God. In essence, they said "No one is going to heaven and God is going to have to destroy His precious creations". This is about revenge.

17.   Most people didn't know what was going on, because they weren't paying attention and/or weren't studying. They turned away from God and into themselves and towards the developments amongst them. The health of those things became priorities, and they evolved from there. Again, they were caught up in themselves and what they wanted; and everything about God, if and whenever He was considered, got interpreted from that view.

18.   Their priorities were money, wealth, drugs or anything that made them feel and look good. It was all a distraction from how we were supposed to live and was best for all of us.

19.   They wanted love, peace, and happiness; but they were caught up in a way of life that required dominance of another, which brought strife from the struggling population, who were driven by stress, desperation, depression, drugs, and a debt to the dominating population. One churned the other. Jealousy led to one wanting to be like the other. Like butter being separated from the milk, morals and God's Word were becoming less and less practiced and important. They were creating one another's development, while hating what those developments were becoming. It was a cycle of confusion that they were evolving from. This caused them not to believe in altruism.

20.   Being in that state of condition, you couldn't develop better people using those type of people; because everybody and everything is part of the equation. The equation needed to be somewhat pure in God's Word to make it better. So, it's not surprising that God said He would destroy the world with fire. Once the world evolves so far in the wrong direction, there's no turning back. Anyone, who attunes with it, will not come back, as long as they don't awaken.

21.   They used, what they called a correctional institution, to actually teach immorality and crime; then they held them in a position to reproduce unrighteousness, blaming the very one coerced to sin and do a crime (A fountain of immorality). Even their foster homes were a testimony of them. They maintained division in these institutions. Members of the governing bodies claimed religious beliefs to God, but did contrary to His value system.

22.   The war against God and His Values is seen by violations of them doing the opposite.

23.   They hate His son; so, they drew a picture of him in opposite appearance, described in the earlier Bible.

24.   They violated the Truth that "it is not of them to direct their steps or way". Instead, they created their own models, etiquettes, policies, and laws.

25.   They violated the commandment to love one another as thyself. Instead, they created a system that pays them to destroy someone, one way or another.

26.   Although it was condemned, they practiced idolatry in their glorification of the principles and concepts of Satan.

27.   Instead of seeking and learning Truth, they created their own and justified it by popularity.

QSE: Theorists Debate Continues

Theories and Hypotheses

1.   We can, reasonably, theorize an experience or event as long as we stay within the bounds of legitimate cause and effect(s). It is a theory, because all has not been confirmed, which would make it a formula or fact. However, while it may be the most accurate going forward, it is not always true or completely true.

2.   Denial of a theory must be subjected to the same standards as a theory, formula, or fact. Otherwise, we have a hypothesis, identified by its incompleteness and/or insufficiently suggestive link(s).

3.   A hypothesis demands further research and investigative energy than a theory, which suggests status of strengths. A theory may require confirmation, while a hypothesis requires confirmation and more answers. A metaphor will strengthen a hypothesis, creating at least a weak theory.

4.   Denial at its weakest point, which is without sufficient support, signals a contest and/or need to protect something and is questionable at best. It could signal the initiation and/or root of adversity or a challenge to strengthen.

5.   Resistance to moving forward with corrections or improvements, while permitting further damages, is a sign of adversity.

Standards and Changes

1.   When we have a standard practice, it will produce a standard result that shows up as a high statistical value. When we have a high statistical value, it will evidence a standard, which evidences a standard practice.

2.   A wavering effect represents change of some sort, which may be fundamental. A non-fundamental change is a conscious change. Then, there's random change, which is relative to systemic conditions. But, it may all be part of the production of effects and may occur on multiple levels or in stages, if not both.

Theorists gathered to debate their unknown history and that of the Inferior Planet

1.   Theorist #1: We are not like them. We tend to return to our core self, naturally practicing resilience, regardless of experiences and influences. We already demonstrated this, after we escaped the controls of our enemies.

2.   Theorists #2: I believe we have better instincts, which is an indication of a different seed.

3.   Theorist #3: A seed has to have something proven to be unique. An apple seed will not produce a peach. So, I believe that we were acting on knowledge not available to them. That will make a difference.

4.   Theorist #4: Many cannot sense the realness of God; so, they see no rules. They only see and discover rules pertaining to advantage. Conscience is totally for the weak, according to the strong.

5.   Theorist #5: Conscience is built by proper experiences. It needs to be built at an early age and continued, like building a structure according to plumbness. Only then can we call one different or inferior, when they resist the effort or go astray, with no other interfering source.

6.   Theorist #6: People need to be open about their problems; so that, others will come forward too. Such gives everyone the ability to form a front against inferiority, not for destruction, but for permanent resolve.

7.   Theorist #7: In many cases, victims are creating victims without malice and without relevant information, because of the design of the system. The environment contains streams of iniquities, which are bad examples and faucets of encouragements that are challenging to an underdeveloped, overwhelmed, and/or improperly programmed conscience.

8.   Theorist #8: Some see the idea; and they are thrilled about it, due to its advantageous nature, and disregards or downplays the damages. They avoid more stress and garner more success. They see their scheme as the only way to do more than survive. They have found justification in, even, their victims. No other way has gained their trust and commitment. The inferior environment has shaped their views and way of life.

9.   Theorist #9: I find it hard to trust a people, who believed in doing evil as God-Service and couldn't see that they were the problem. They couldn't tell God from Satan… They had some very intelligent minds; and I'd say they were, generally, intelligent enough as a population to understand the differences in values. They had the means to become a Quantum Star Eckter, but passed on the opportunity. Will they try to reverse our system and way of life and, even, to deny doing so in the face of obvious and opposing results?

10.   Theorist #10: If they wouldn't listen to Satan, no one would have to be saved. They have disregarded their own savings. Possessed with such disregards is a signal of the fallen angel's imprint. In this way, the fallen angels not only took out those resembling God's Image, but those playing a predatory role too. This explains the two cycles, in which the wind above and below turns in the opposite direction of the other, as a reflection or message of the design of the world.

Theorist #11 Emotions and Thoughts

1.   They found that people act from their emotions and thoughts based on some set of premises that maybe incomplete or in error. They found that these emotions and thoughts are, also, subjective to phenomena, which is the reason why they develop the way they do. Altogether, it creates a tracing and signal a method of manipulation.

2.   When they generally take a wrong turn, as a population, it's a signal of an offensive driving source that knows how the emotional and mental environment works.

3.   Priorities of the reverse type is an imprint of the fallen angels. Their priorities are inclined towards personal enrichment at the expense of another and not for the good of all (Altruism).

Theorist #12 Reason for Overtaken and Downfall

1.   It takes superiority to overcome something that another feel is capable of entrapping someone else. That's what separates us from them. We are not easily fooled. We take the high road to viewing our environment. So, while they get stuck, we find a way to move on within the Will of God.

2.   Their weakness is following one another, instead of searching for Truth for guidance, only to act out of jealousy when another succeeds in the Will of God.

3.   If they can't beat one another, the knowledge of God is no good. This is the reason for their overtaken and downfall.

Theorist #13 Challenge to the Heart

1.   So, it's important to evaluate the heart for darkness and, then, cloud it with more darkness, leaving it with the tools of darkness to strive for survival. It's all about the heart. If it can be hardened; it will do much harm to another, while creatively producing its own belief system.

2.   Otherwise, it has proven to be a good heart in the eyes of our God and has been tested by downstream waters, which brings out the strengths of character and exposes the direction of progress.

3.   So, the heart is heavily challenged by the Devil; because he doesn't want to lose not one soul. Interestingly, many will help him meet his goals. This says a lot about who is who.

Theorist #14 Judgment

1.   Comprehension is a big part of becoming mature; so, a disability to comprehend is not subject to judgement. Instead, it is an impairment that must be excused as it is unresolvable or not understood.

2.   Many cannot be judged, because they are acting out of pressure that is greater than their will, control, creative imagination, and/or understanding.

Theorist #15 Misdirected Anger

1.   Having limited knowledge of the emotional and mental environments and how darkness, in the form of clueless, leads to following the examples of others or being impulsive, can evoke misdirected anger. Superficial knowledge and superficial research or investigations can help set it off too, if not by itself. Misdirected anger is anger directed at any other person, object, or matter, but not the source or underlying source. This is the trick of the fallen angels and their advocates. This is how you cause an implosion and keep it going with stilled darkness.

Theorist #16 People are Worse than Earlier Times

1.   It was written in their Bible about the Son of God defending a whore, whom many of the population wanted to stone to death, because of her occupation or way of life. He prevented the stoning by asking which of them is without sin. Because it did end amongst this group of people, they proved to be better than the population of the former inferior planet. That's because they yielded to the Truth.

2.   Later, on the inferior planet, they muzzled the excuses of the whore and more defendants and led her and others to their destruction.

3.   People who don't yield to Truth have instilled their mark of arrogance. This kind went on and persevered the creation of the whore and more, while levying their so-called righteous policies, laws, and judgments tailored towards arrogance. They made themselves the fountain of iniquity.

4.   This is further proof that they went and remained backwards towards God's principles and concepts. With greater knowledge and abilities, they are more responsible and exposed.

Theorist #17 Tracing of the Fallen Angels

1.   In my search for the tracing of the fallen angels, I looked for obvious violations and violations that should have, reasonably, been on the radar of the properly educated and positioned people.

2.   I found characteristics like disruptive to order in high positions, a perception that sees more value in will than elaborated and clear truth without temptation (A very rich position), and not remorseful for the suffering of others regardless of longevity and severity.

3.   I found targeting. I describe targeting as aiming to withhold an essential need that results in a struggle or setback or to do harm or evoke harm to a person, his/her interests, or likeness, in part or whole. I believe 'building up' is the law. Anything else is immoral and should be illegal.

4.   I found that the most influential, or even educated, held their reputation so high that their ignorance of matters became unreasonable in the face of adversity. Then, they had to use corruption to cover it up. The Bible said "Search and you will find", but most just followed one another and their leaders, even though the Bible said "The whole world was deceived". My guess is that they didn't know, didn't question, or believe the world was deceived.

Theorist #18 Hierarchical Fountains of Truth

1. I have found that there were hierarchical fountains of Iniquity within the former inferior planet.

2. First of all, a fountain of iniquity is an influential source that causes the thoughts, feelings, beliefs, and/or actions of another, whether by example or influence, if not both.

3. An example can be just as strong as an influence, if no other answer to a problem is known or seemingly undiscoverable.

4. Fountains of Iniquity have a hierarchical structure: Authority, media, organization, family, friends, associates, circumstances. Depending on where you are in this vertical structure, you will have a lateral influence(s).

5. Vertical influences are more powerful, especially with the ability to pass the consequences. Lateral influences can be challenging, even forceful too. A leader(s) can be chosen and a trap can be constructed; especially when taking an advantage of weaknesses.

Theorist #19 Creative Style

1. When God created the world, he created in a way that made something reflective and encouraging of something else. The style of creation aided the detectives, diagnostics, doctors, and mechanics in their endeavor to discover and fix a problem. He brought the light for all to see.

2. At the same time, helpful processes were instilled in all forms of life and changing matters, for directions in becoming a minor creator.

3. If you could embark upon, research, experiment, listen to Words of encouragement and/or feel the Influence of endeavors, you could see it and retrieve it for creative pursuits.

4. As you gathered more and more knowledge and types of knowledge, you could see and become guided by metaphors.

5. This is the way out of darkness. Never be idle or engulphed in foolishness. Save the library and all of its educative contents, uncensored. Root out darkness and maximize the light.

6. The former inferior planet did the opposite. Don't let that happen, ever again.

Theorist #20 Importance of Identifying Struggles

1. After observing the history of the former inferior planet, I began to identify some struggles. I felt that, if we could identify all the major struggles and bring light to each of them, we could create a more informed practitioner of life.

2. The most major struggle I perceived was the struggle to choose beauty on the inside versus the outside. We all love eye candy; but sometimes we run into something that appears too

good to be true or too bad to be true. We, then, either suffer a failed relationship or miss a great opportunity.

3.   Then, there are issues in between, where appearance fades to mediocre, according to the eyes of the beholder. In that case, eye candy is no longer a true or false clue to rely on.

4.   Again, the lack of an in-depth study can cause a hit or miss in pursuit of a permanently, successful marriage.

5.   Superficial love is like a seed that is planted on top of the surface. The marriage is dependent on the shiny parts of its partnership, so to speak. So, obviously, time is most likely going to resolve it, as is.

6.   Inside, we get into the mechanics. There are matters that are made of quality parts and those that are not so; but worse of all, destined for change, whether for better or worse, in some way.

7.   God's passing down of the Ten Commandments, Wisdom, and other laws that are best for all of us is a Person, Who is definitely beautiful on the inside. But the world treats His Biblical Image as unappealing. However, the most beautiful angel gets the nod; even though he, as a separatist, is deceiving, blasphemous, murderous, and opposing to God and His principles and concepts.

8.   I find the bad choice, on a major level, to be evidence of the fallen angels, but also the reason for a lot of failed marriages. No wonder the rich and those in high positions are in and out of marriages, like it has no consequences, stated in the Bible.

9.   Others are torn apart by the attachment of materialism, which is linked to a fluctuating and manipulating economic system.

10.   While marriages may be challenged, people need to make more informed decisions about their Spiritual Leader or spiritual assailant and their partner in life.

11.   Married people give a clue to how they might be compatible with God versus the devil, or vice versa.

12.   But, while this is the most major struggle, others must be identified and settled too.

Theorist #21 Perception Zones

1.   Our perception has focus zones that initiates and evolves our belief system, while feeding our imagination. They consist of the self, immediate phenomena, family, relatives, interests, support, sustenance, dismantle, equation, and more, but not necessarily in that order. They form and have interplay with other focal points such as culture, status, law, construct, module, and more through the evolutionary process.

2.   Concentration can be focused on one or more zones. But, within and across these zones, we tend to evolve as well. For example, in the self-zone, a baby will later find his/her toes, which were never noticed before.

3.   These zones grow with unique experiences and tend to contextualize the learning process.

4.   Not having maturely developed zones or missing zones, and/or insufficient or inaccurate cross-referencing is grounds for darkness, error, and the ability of another to mislead or take advantage of you. This is why you need exposure to new experiences.

5.   Many others know what you need. However, in a competitive environment, they are set on distracting you for their own selfish good.

6.   As a distracting scheme, its design had to inflate the need to concentrate on the lower or lowest values of life, which are essential needs, or anything distracting.

7.   The manner in which essentials could be attained and the time it took to complete the process, compared to the time for replenishment, created a cyclical process (work zone). The less free time from completion to the act of replenishing, the more the cycle was busy and/or lacking in fulfillment. This would, most likely, pull the focus down from the big picture to this draining zone. That's because their focus has to be on production, efficiency, and effectiveness.

8.   Timed processing minus timed replenishment needs with insufficient, little or no time for anything else, creates a draining zone. This zone may be crossed, but contracts quickly. Therefore, growth will be stymied.

9.   Perception zones may entrap or cause a person to become multi-talented, imaginative, and creative, depending on the effort and time spent being a student of nature.

Theorist #22 Spoiled Child

1.   From what I gathered from the results of research, it looks like a child was born with impulsive behavior.

2.   As that child grew, the child became more enthused and curious about the world. The child perceived the world as a playground.

3.   Not knowing the rules, the child proceeded to explore and enjoy the world, even at the expense of another, until a set of rules were felt and persisted upon him/her.

4.   Leniency in excess would allow his/her character and will to expand beyond moral boundaries, while an overly-strict environment would limit exploration and learning experiences.

5.   The child facing greater leniency will develop a stronger will by challenging for greater freedom and learning from his/her efforts to force their will. Determination will become as strong as the environment programmed him/her to believe willpower is the answer versus unity and love (Mold).

6.   The spoiled child would, then, go on to become selfish and materialistic, the kind of traits that are compatible with the fallen angels. This would cause a communion, in which the two share ideas and beliefs.

7.   The tug-of-war between the spoiled child and parents/ authorities attempting to rear or correct him/her would yield only a challenge, in spite of elaborated truths and consequences. The challenges may become violent.

8.   Unwieldiness, stubborn, selfish, and deceptive is a sign of a person possessed by the fallen angels. Science and truth is only valued to them, when it aids their will. This is a sign that the possessed person is sold on the riches of the world.

9.   In a wicked world, the spoiled child looks around and finds nothing valuable, but confirmations of his/her beliefs and of himself/herself.

Theorist #23 We Are Artists

1.   Naturally, we are artists amongst other artists, even the Artist, who creates and molds the artists, who are subjective to the influences around, below, and upon them. Thus, our thoughts, beliefs, emotions, mood, attitude, and actions are subject to changes. These changes may not always repeat, due to circumstances and how we're situated. Over time, our bodies and appearances may change, as a result.

2.   In that way, contributions matter; and we are all responsible for our contributions to the world in which we live, whether as a stream of iniquity or a stream of morality, if not both.

3.   Understanding that we are not perfect, we should understand the impact of our contributions and attempt to prevent any errors, while denying hypocrites who believe in protecting their imperfect ways and the imperfections of the underlying sources responsible for the spread of iniquity.

4.   At the same time, we must understand one another's level of maturity, helping to confirm and upgrade their status in maturity. We, also, must understand that everyone may not be on the same page, regardless of how factual, and may or may not mean nothing but harm.

5.   The former inferior planet got it backwards.

6.   They confused, deceived, and used aggression to demean their neighbors and denounced them, as brothers and sisters, and reverted their reasonable interests, in a deceptive effort often referred to as corrections. I think this is part of the imprint of the fallen angels.

7.   Where there was requirement and procedure, in-cooperation was used to deny a successful navigation towards an objective or goal. Often people's time and efforts were wasted, fostering one to give up; however, determination, perseverance, and the recording of solid and complete evidence is always best. But it can become like a testing of stamina in an inferior environment. But, in such a case, there's no better investigator than yourself.

8.   Anyway, you must always try to position your mind to always look for the truth and how to sustain its flow through you and into another. This must always be the practice.

9.   When adversity occurs, be less responsive and more of a student of nature. Learn when to be quiet and when and how to quell emotions and solve a problem, as permanently as possible. Learn until you can manage triumphantly.

10.   Take hold and/or build what you see is missing from and essential to the whole.

11.   Most of all, close the door to the fallen angels, who build walls between essentials for proper development and deliver trying times where those essentials are absent. They say "We can make the Son of God look like the Devil and the Devil like the Son of God".

Theorist #24 The Sales Pitch

1.   In a demonic system, the sales pitch is, almost, always what you shouldn't do and can be powerfully encouraging and unrelenting.

2.   The sales pitch is identifiable by its ability to heighten concern and do so over a period of time, even repeatedly, if not constantly. That makes it a trend.

3.   A tracing of the trend may show a single person or multiple sources, linked to others at different locations and/or in various fields of disciplines. Technology and other information are revealed in their demonstrated capabilities.

4.   To scale into the point, we have to depict how and when the target and events outside the target's control parallel one another. We must ask what the intent is. Then, we must ask where the conflict is. What type of conflicts are there? What is the success rate of both sides? What do they seem to know about each other, if anything? Who is not being reasonable and why? Who was in position to resolve the conflict? Why didn't the conflict get resolved? How common is the complaint and why? What is not common across society? What does it encourage? Should we prevent it? Why? If so, how will it benefit society as a whole?

5.   The information should always be publicized in a manner that's good for the whole and morally productive.

Theorist #25 The Spirit of Infancy

1.   The child came in enthused, curious, emotional, impulsive, and programmable.

2.   For a time, the child was allowed to freely develop, depending on how strict the people of the environment were.

3.   But, yet, parents were as concerned and skilled in molding their children as their child developed undisciplined and proudly became worldly beasts, even to be praised for who they are.

4.   They never looked back and saw that they needed policies and programs for addressing the wrong developments of society.

5.   They never saw that everyone was part of the equation.

6.   Instead, they built a perfect system for allowing one to profit from the misfortunes of another, which encouraged erroneous developments they claimed to fight. Yet, they claimed all lives matter, but lacked recourse for everyone.

7.   While one was bidding on the riches of the world, another was bidding for essentials, freedom, peace, and love. The latter was crushed with responsibilities and threats to what livelihood they had, tempting them to be like one of the others.

8.   When you try to compress life, it's like a welder trying to completely seal up a medal drum; it will explode in his face. Metaphorically, it has happened throughout their history. But they never receded; instead, they remained selfish and inconsiderate. Evil!

9.   So, inequality and class warfare started at birth and became obvious during the harvest season. Leave a little behind for the poor, while the rich go unresponsible, is a concept of Satan.

10.   Even Jesus was hacked or forced to accept certain reasonings in some statements made in the Bible, because it was the wrong way to live, overall. The line was over-stepped when the riches of the earth included the possession of other humans, captured or drawn for whatever reason. That represented an implosion.

11.   You could see the pull was towards the top, but the top was discriminative. That's how the expression "It's not what you know; it's who you know" came into popularity. The pull was towards the fallen angels, who offered the riches of the world. The push outwards, or transformation of, was relevant to anything of God.

12.   As one was elevated higher, the mental imprint of the mind of Satan became more and more evident, as he/she became more responsible for world developments. The push and pull from other members and matters, created by the demonic administrators, made it so.

13.   They boisterously used their beliefs, compatible offensive actions, and rhetoric in an attempt to boost or gain clout amongst the demonic organization or to let them know they are in support of them.

14.   When things went wrong, they just blamed one another.

15.   I look at the animal world, and I see various animals with different types of defense mechanisms, even some with the ability to change their appearance; thus, by this, we know the Creator believes in being prepared. Regardless of how weak the prey may be, if they were given a chance against their predators; they were prepared.

16.   For the impoverished, most of the time, it seemed that there were no, or no known, moral recourses to take in defense or success.

17.   Many of the population remained children fighting over toys, but only wanted you to say positive things about them; otherwise, matters may escalate.

18.   The life of the spirit of infancy, as unique individuals and as a population, told the story and revealed the formula, based on the events that formed its life and personality.

19.   It happened, because God wasn't part of the equation.

Theorist #26 The Governing Style

1.   The most influential people of any population have the greatest control over the remaining population.

2.   Therefore, the government is or became a reflection of them and their beliefs and ideas over time, even through forced adoption.

3.   The government is a balancing tool used to maintain order amongst them, fair or unfair.

4.   It is too dangerous to heed and embrace the ideas of the morally enlightened, due to differences in beliefs, related ideas, and the threat of disruptions. So, the most influential must recede and maintain the advantage and, thus, the direction of the world.

5.   The ills of an imperfect society are not priority over the successes of the most influential; otherwise, they'd impact the upper-class negatively, attracting a rebalancing act.

6.   The ills of the lower status are a result of personal weaknesses and failure to establish good or better relations with the upper status, regardless of the attitudes and beliefs of such.

7.   To maintain power, a divided and subjective population is more manageable. It maintains sufficient social distances, between unique groups and presents opportunities to send one against another, due to adversities. In the end, a matter and/or a person of interest is tamed to the advantage of the most influential.

8.   Since the concerns of the people are dependent upon how they're positioned and connected in respects to them and whether they're favorable and unfavorable, politics, policies, and their ever-changing nature provide the atmosphere with the punching ability it needs to create offenses towards another, some more than others.

9.   Financial Control performs the same role, where zero to low income with debt provide the hardest punches and lighten up with greater income and less debt.

10.   The emotional environment and the cares that move it give the punches access to vulnerable and subjective feelings. The punches are as felt as the matter of concern is essential. The punches mold an attitude and force a determination to resolve. But, without recourse, depression is likely, when experienced for an extensive period of time.

11.   The assessment of the direction and source of the punches is what exposed the divide(s) and drew one against another, even an unwilling defendant, who is threatened with great damages or harm, especially the loss of freedom.

12.   A punch, while it can be physical too, it is an adverse message, which may or may not be personal. But it can hurt badly as it is damaging, regardless of whether it's personal or not.

13.   Therefore, a punching match is a fight or all out war, where a single punch can draw one to contest the offense of another, even without choice.

14.   Therefore, politics, financial war, and any other offense has no natural place in human existence, because they foster or continuously foster attacks against another in one place or another. They resist order, peace, love, and happiness. The weaker people are more vulnerable and more likely to suffer from it, provoking the rise of monstrous attitudes and developments towards advantage and revenge.

15.   In reverse of their governing style, the solution side should have been the priority and the only resolvable method.

16.   The weaker the lower status groups become, the less likely they are to rise to an effective level of threat, respect, and major disruptions.

17.   So, inequality and rising economic benefits holds the population together; as long as the most influential benefit the most, or major unrest can occur.

18.   Laws will support the objective of the advantaged.

19.   This is not the Garden of Eden; this is the land of the human king, chosen by the tribes and filled with wickedness, who is trying to manage like-hearted people. As stated in the earlier Bible, God saw great wickedness amongst the people of the earth, and that their imagination, thoughts, and feelings contributed continually – Genesis 6:5.

20.   Because humans are characters, properly made to be compelled by scientific formulas, God could depict and profile the influence that caused the error.

21.   The people formed various groups purposed for advantage(s) or balance.

22.   These groups are played like keys on a piano and express a tone and rhythm, desired by the collective in high positions.

23.   An awakened mind and heart will be pushed to the highest creative ability and, continuously, pushed towards hardening of heart, while insightful intelligence favors otherwise.

24.   Inner turmoil will be the norm, for as long as cold-hearted conditions prevail. The success of this group is dependent upon overcoming the majority. The degree of success is apparent in the results of reform and reveal the oppositions respects for Truth and their inclination towards love or hate, including their deceptiveness.

Theorist #27 The Slave was an Essential Part of the Economy

1.   The economy depended on low prices versus high wages and needed to ward off high inflation, which made the need for slaves essential, while administrators and high-class members needed to present themselves as reputable.

2.   Knowing how economics works, many, if not all, would play the economic game for success, causing the rise in inflation. So, something had to be done.

3.   With the sustainment and rise in the number of law breakers and the precision of capturing the majority of minorities as prisoners and homeless people, something was done.

4.   That is evidence of honing in, in some manner, by those who wanted to be on the advantaged side. Otherwise, this issue of crime and homelessness would have been resolved.

5.   Deterrence to Truth, naturally, becomes part of the scheme; because it's unaffordable. Truth would undo the system.

6.   Yet, many God-Given rights were violated, in as long as the system existed. It was not a human system, and, therefore, a demonic system.

Theorist #28 Culture Clash

1.   The platform, spoken of by Minister Ion, was used to create a different culture in the victimized race, by creating a different common setting of conditions to think and act from. In this way, it was set up to cause a culture clash. The media fed it. This is what I believe the Bible was referring to, when it said "…a law unto themselves". Every unique culture is a law unto themselves.

2.   They cause the clash and blame those they set up.

3.   It didn't help that the victimized race didn't acknowledge and play the game effectively to overcome the effort to set them up for discrimination.

Theorist #29 Scales, Weights, and Measures

1.   Including scales, weights, and measures in the social environment fostered the beginning of turning from God and encouraging human separation. It was like giving a gun to a criminal, who was poised to war and destroy, even to kill.

2.   The criminal would see differences in people, favoring those who were like him/her or found to be appealing, and those whom he/she could benefit from the most.

3.   Others would have to find their own way or dine on what little was left behind by the well-off.

4.   The undeveloped world may have seen the most impact of differences in treatment than the developed world. What made it questionable was the growing population that complicated the matter. I think it was the beginning of, habitually, seeing the differences as part of life. That perception was caused and enforced by the lack of solutions in earlier times and, permanently, adopted as the way to live without question and until our intervention.

5.   Surely, the problem was not getting fixed; instead, it was used as a weapon of separation, defense, and destruction.

6.   The archaic way of life kept reproducing itself, in spite of all the information that was available to them.

Theorist #30 Using Ignorance to get Permission to do Wrong

1.　　It appeared that they asked the general population to give a verdict or opinion on a matter, clearly, belonging to an expert or someone with more experience with a matter(s).

2.　　But, if you left an expert to give an opinion, you had to trust that he/she gave the correct and complete answer. That would be very risky in that environment.

3.　　The only solution is to have a well-informed population with unlimited access to all essential information.

Theorist #31 Free Will

1.　　Free Will is monitored when a baby comes into the world. That's because the baby's mind isn't developed well enough to foresee and assess the risks of injuries and damages to him/her and others. But their impulse and exploratory nature is none-the-less motivated, when protected from the consequences of a dangerous move.

2.　　Overtime, Free Will is, gradually, overtaken by the person, who was once completely monitored, except where laws or rules require avoidance of certain areas or a way of carrying one's self safely.

3.　　What this means is, either, one has to be completely monitored for protective purposes, or has to possess sufficient knowledge and resources to protect the self in an unknown or dangerous endeavor, if not both. You, probably, wouldn't get more confirmation of this fact from an astronaut in the early periods of exploration.

4.　　The world is as dangerous as it is damaging. You see death. You see bankruptcies. You see hardships. You see inappropriate drug use and addiction. You see homelessness. And, you see imprisonment. A lot of this was increasing, but so was a timely denial of information, resources, good examples, and education to minimize those numbers. In this way, they blindly pursued the wishes of others.

5.　　The free will of less-acceptable people was allowed to crash right into a surprise and, many times, forced and/or deceivingly so. It was equivalent to having insufficient training for driving a car, but taking over a jet and learning as you go. Many lacked defensive driving techniques. But, the jet? That was a whole new ball game. You could see that when their life ended up in the hands of others.

Theorist #32 All-Participating Concept

1.　　While a society is best served by utilizing all people to contribute their skills to society, to manifest high efficiency, effectiveness, and quality of life, they created a limited and conservatively participating government and population, only to recognize an all-participating concept in their prisons. It was another backwards way to live.

1.   When we compare the qualities of God and Satan, we begin to see how each set of qualities perform in opposition to one another. What we see is a system with boundaries. They cannot cross the line that defines them. They operate in a different atmosphere; yet, they are forced to share a single environment. Only one imposes its will upon the other offensively, because it is of its nature to do so. The other lets you explore and experience the results of your choices, after the error of Adam and Eve. They are two different equations that don't achieve the same results.

2.   Don't let them trick you! Don't let them encourage you to gamble your life away. Don't be a part of the Wrong Equation. Your best is warranted here.

3.   On the highest level, our concerns should be about how to be in good relations with God. This is something the devil and his accomplices don't want you to have.

4.   In as much as your foot or feet are in the wrong equation, you are guilty of a sin(s). In as much as you sin, voluntarily, you are as guilty as Satan. That means you have no choice but to practice perfection in all things. So, it is the law of God.

5.   So, the first thing the Demons have to do is come between you and Him. In doing so, the devil has to mislead you.

6.   So, Satan sows both equations together to make you feel like you can make a choice of either, in one system. You see the church supporting his advocates/followers/demons. You see them returning favors to the church. And, you see the resulting fruit of the tree, especially if you did your research.

7.   Love does not result in hate or vice versa. Hate separates and destroys, while Love unifies and heals. Don't be part of the wrong equation.

8.   To mentally mislead you, he has to confuse you; to physically confuse you, he has to cause instability or tension. His method is stronger when it's a combination of some type. He sells it as "For the best". It works as well as the population is deceived or demonized by him.

9.   If he didn't use the riches of the world (Friends, money, gold, diamonds, intimacy etc.), he would use deprivation methods that include challenges, enemies, tricks, fear tactics, peer pressure, fraud, theft, inferior models, reverse-psychology, and false teachings, if not a combination. He will regulate your dependencies in a manner to encourage and maintain his agenda. The fruit of the tree is the imprint.

10.   You would have to have a base to hold onto, to survive. That base is a combination of certain intelligence and the means to carry it out, or your rights of proper religious practices are impeded upon or violated.

11.   You've got to research and have determination, because you've got to know who God is and how He thinks. You've got to recruit Him to your side. You've got to put forth effort in this.

12.   Your conscience, which will nag at you, needs to be answered. It's just doing its job. Be thankful that you have one, if you do. Others may appear to be without one or trapped in some set of circumstances.

13.   What we have is a Programmer putting a program together, using workable modules, not defective modules. You're the modules. The Ten Commandments is the program.

14.   What makes the program work is how well the modules perform together. That's the most important part of the program. But the standard is perfection.

15.   Just to show you God has an enemy, there are modules that perform in opposition to the modules favored by God, if you didn't have proof already.

16.   The assembly of workable modules and defective modules don't produce the standard "Perfection". However, the defective modules are a case study presented by nature and procured by the demonic population. They must be resolved properly and as your neighbor.

17.   It's not a race to be better than the other; it's about developing towards the standards God sets for us.

18.   You can't live with certain types of people, because they are proud and confident in error. Yet, the fruit is rotten. So, the environment will reflect your efforts and qualities. The lack of effort or the imposing of wrong principles and concepts will threaten you or cause harm, encouraging you to take security measures. Inventing and maintaining security systems is an imprint of unresolved matters that are harmful and an act of separation.

19.   They seek to deny the ex-con from having a relationship with God. They use others to help in the denial. Then, almost, no one is fit for the Kingdom of God, save for the standard of redemption.

20.   But, there's a conflict. It's written that God cannot change. He said, "You won't let them in and you won't come either". Then, the Son of God came so people could be saved by his blood. However, how can you be saved by the blood by, knowingly, approving, supporting, or not denying the tactics of Satan? You'd then be part of the equation that opposes God's plan. Wouldn't you have denied the blood that was there to save you? Don't be a part of the wrong equation.

21.   All are accountable for what they do and don't do. That's why He named it a sin to not seek knowledge and to not perform faithfully. In reflection, it is a sin to deprive one, who seeks knowledge, but also to refuse to spread the good news.

22.   Satan's trick includes "These things must come", but wars, disease, and famine are not associated with the doings of God. Those, who don't know God, were fooled by this. It happens when you don't seek the voice of the Lord. It happens when you don't seek knowledge. It happens when you follow the worldly crowd.

23.   We know the world is worldly, because it doesn't produce good fruit. This is the escalation of the demonic system, which deceives its way towards the destruction of mankind. The supporters of Satan and his system are those who are responsible.

24.   It was written that Satan was making signs in the sky. Satan advanced his system from there. Now they can find your life path, using your birthdate.

25.   Apparently, God does the same thing, because the Star was followed to find the newly-born Son of God. Meanwhile, king Herod had his warriors running and finding no clue of where he was, only that he existed. So, who's still in charge? And, let's not forget that He said that He knew you before you were born.

26.   A lot of people say God is winning, but what does that mean? We believe He's in control, because no one can take that away from Him. After all, He is Lord over all things. But, again, the world is filled with iniquity to a high degree. So, we have to define "Winning".

27.   Winning is God getting what He wants. He wants people who, faithfully, follow Him and His Ways. So, the Son of God is the dividing line.

28.   However, as you have already seen, Satan attempts to attack children before they can get an understanding of how to think and carry themselves through trials and tribulations. This has a reoccurring effect; since the mind is programmed in error, only to influence the next generation. It creates a viral effect. But God chose the parents of and sent and protected a Special One.

29.   We were saved by the Son of God, because he represented The Way, The Truth and The Life, which dripped blood, signifying an injury. In reflection, it signified a competitor and a scheme to conceal, deceive, and rob. That reflection is an excuse, fit for an "Understanding" God, an image that Satan denies, as implied in his actions. Instead, it is Satan and his followers who are without understanding; and, so, they have destroyed many, as a result.

30.   The Way, The Truth, and The Life are an offspring of God, making Jesus "God with us", which is the meaning of Immanuel. We are gods, if we possess this imprint in our heads; otherwise, we have the Mark of the Beast, which is not of God.

31.   We were told to check to see that the things that are true to us are still true today. Remember, we are influenced by many things, including the wrong things. So, we're supposed to build a perfect religion that duplicates God's Will. Again, that means you're supposed to search and find the Truth, and be mindful of its results, which are to fulfill the Laws of Love.

32.   We're all supposed to grow toward maturity in God. This means to understand Him through His Word and creations.

33.   Let the color spectrum be an example for you, when looking at the world around you and all its uniqueness. Just as scientists discovered the process that created each color, understand your world, as the premise for understanding and improvement.

34.   When you walk out into a demonic world, having the mind of God, you will feel the resistance from the people and the things they've created, especially if you interact, ask relevant questions, request rightful changes, or debate in favor of Truth. That is the invisible presence of the Mark of the Beast responding from them.

35.   For those possessing the Mark of the Beast, winning is priority and admission to Truth is secondary, but only if it works in their favor. Don't let it fool you into becoming one of them. Don't let it fool you into thinking God has mistaken. And, don't let it pull you into the swamps to be devoured; but continue in the Way of God and His quest for perfections.

36.   Instead, understand and appreciate that you are not of the world and fight for God and yourself. Spread the good news; so that you, your offspring, and the coming generations might be relieved of sins, stress, anxiety, famine, and wars caused by those of the world.

37.   The fear of God destroying the planet with fire, instead of obeying His Word, is also evidence of the fallen angels, who can't change, being behind the direction of the planet's goals.

38.   The most conscious of all is aware of all things and has allowed the planet's progress in technology and information without coming to the knowledge of Truth.

39.   He has allowed such progress up to now, but tomorrow is not promised, because He's in charge.

40.   Just as we make a conscious decision to take action now or at a later time, so also the Creator of all things.

41.   Who can get ahead of the All-Knowing and Conscious of all things?

42.   Do not be a part of the wrong equation. Copyright© Minister Ion Museum

Minister Ion: Three Types of Sin

1.   Blasphemy: An intentional act or presentation meant to defy God as Sacred, Holy, Complete, The Perfect Example, and All-Knowing, whether through deception or misrepresentation, including associating an inferior result(s) as a result of an imperfection of His character. Entry into the Kingdom of Heaven is denied.

2.   Hence the following law: Everything made by Him is working properly according to purpose.

3.   Mark of the Beast: An acceptance of an idea(s) that works against the Will or Word of God, having motivating ties to the riches of the world. Acceptance disqualifies entry into the Kingdom of Heaven. It creates the dividing line.

4.   Sin: A decision, belief, or action that normally leads to or results in an imperfection, including the provocation, escalation, or aiding the provocation of; or anything that hinders or resists the Will of God and the moral interests and growth of His people or highest priorities, first, and the accommodating environment, second.

5.   Hence the acceptance of all those, who call upon the Lord Jesus Christ (The Way, The Truth, and The Life). Copyright© Minister Ion Museum, Research Division

Minister Ion: Supporting Evidence of the Fallen Angels

1.   As a result of leading Adam and Eve astray, the earlier Bible says the Devil was thrown down to us and locked into darkness. It said he roamed the earth.

2.   I haven't seen him, have you?

3.   Where's the evidence?

4.   He's a spirit; so how can we find and track him?

5.   First of all, we have to have an imprint of his character. This imprint will be found in his followers and the playing out of his system.

6. In the story, we find jealousy and disagreement. Since he will be eventually destroyed, we have a hateful and defiant character.

7. His power consists of the riches of the world.

8. Humans are vulnerable to the riches of the world, which has a tendency to create greed and selfishness within them. So, the riches of the world are the selling point of Satan's system.

9. But, because a lot of hate is thrown at God, by the destruction of His creations through implosive means, it's not naturally of humans to do so. The reason being is that humans have no issues with what is best for them. So, they have to be deceived. That's what happened in the beginning.

10. So, humans became the tool of hate, drawing one another into a system of hate and heard mostly from the creator of noise, deception, distraction, and division (Satan).

11. The development led to some very sophisticated technology, information, and abilities, which signals an intelligent leading source, not having the qualities of God.

12. One of their techniques involve a repetitious action, used to draw a negative emotional response and action, in an effort to teach or employ violence, in so much that the method is deemed therapeutic to attract a negative action or effect, especially based upon entrapment or need of essentials. It is an action rated higher than temptation and signals defamation.

13. These traits identify the invisible, influential character, who are the fallen angels. Copyright© Minister Ion Museum, Research Division

Minister Ion: A Hardened Heart

1. Our heart absorbs punches from attacks directed towards us or towards someone in similar or same circumstances or situations. It brings out emotional responses that are wowed and hurtful by the attack, and may even be embarrassed. Weakness in how to respond accurately may also be present; since we find it to be surprising and are stalled by it for a time.

2. When surprisingly challenged in an unfamiliar or complicated way, it feels overwhelming, because our heart isn't trained or expecting that type of challenge.

3. A sensitive heart becomes evident, when it feels and processes for the good of all, but in a continuous learning state of mind and heart. It's naivety that's causing problems here. So, not only is it a sin not to search and find Truth; but it works against you, when you don't.

4. The heart is as heavy as it is without answers.

5. As time goes on and the attacks continue, the heart begins to adapt. It's important to understand how it adapts, because it has controlling ability and first response ability over you. So being impulsive is not a good idea. Therefore, you must always fight to be and to stay in control.

6. Long-term experiences in an adverse environment trains the heart to be hard, depending on the focus.

7.   If the focus is to overcome by means of the demonic will, it will be revengeful or lean towards "At all costs". It will lean more towards physical pursuits as answers are not discoverable at the moment.

8.   The heart will, most likely, harden under continuous adversity, after failed attempts and no other resolutions are revealed. A manipulator knows this and may continue to pursue.

9.   A trained technician in the emotional realm, understanding the position of his/her victim, may act to surprise with a deep and surprising attack(s), along with some common theme of attacks, experienced in the past. So, there may be peace before a storm. This is that trap that, usually, catches that wild animal.

10.   Now, let me tell you about a hardened heart. Empathy recedes in a hardened heart, first, by being discriminating. It has a very difficult time empathizing with things it finds issues with.

11.   Information and intelligence are the only way to deal with a hardened heart, because it feeds it an alternative, if it is open and will listen, while having sufficient and relevant values.

12.   If not, you have to develop those values by using those already available. That's because the qualities of a good value system require the presence of others like it; or the system won't work.

13.   So, you can build on related qualities to adjust the reasoning of a hardened heart. But, remember, a hardened heart is programmed. So, there may not be an overnight success and memory is at play here. So, it may need some repeating of essential matters.

14.   A hardened heart feels the need to take control and to be respected in its immediate environment. Any disrespect, felt in the slightest, is concerning. When respect has brought successes and avoided embarrassment and loss, it is hard to give up. It is hard to see the reason to take, what is perceived as, a risk. It is hard to give up, when it means giving up some of the riches of the earth.

15.   Disrespect is elevated, when peers are observant; so, the hardened heart feels pressured to respond contentiously. This is why you need to choose your people cautiously. This is a great tool of the manipulator.

16.   When I was of adolescence and a young adult, I allowed myself to become conditioned by my environment, because I didn't know any better. A lot of kids are caught up in challenges that many adults don't have answers for, when they go to school and that school is filled with confusion, like provocative elements, such as gangs, threats, violence, and drugs. But you still have to concentrate on your studies and security and maybe more. It's a distraction that shouldn't be allowed and that may lead one to submit to the wrong things. What type of people have to worry about that more? What are their statistics? That's your homework.

17.   Luckily, I was involved with a group, in which we grew up together and met a woman, who taught us emotional intelligence. But, now, all of us didn't grow up together. Some continued their path, for whatever the reason. I'm not attacking them.

18.   From the day we learned emotional intelligence, we decided to use our strength to develop God's World.

19.   We found that to be tough is really to resist the things that brought the tendency to do other than the wishes and commandments of God. We found that to be intelligent is really to

resist the things that brought the tendency to do other than the wishes and commandments of God.

20.   We found that to be intelligent and to find greater intelligence was better than a hardened heart. We could better meet adversity with intelligence by observing its environment, provocations, and history. We could build a plan and carve out a good place for ourselves and others.

21.   With a hardened heart, we'd eventually find ourselves on the other side, after a time of aging and weakening and reaping the results of some other hardened heart. So why support it? Why choose it? Why consider it? Why keep this roller-coaster going?

22.   A hardened heart is overly prideful and creates an unstable environment when accompanied by the same and is oppressive amongst the weaker population.

23.   The population of a hardened heart must not multiply or increase in numbers. Environmental conditions must not be supportive of its development. It must never be found in examples and high positions.

24.   Hardened hearts only elevate the hardening of society.

25.   A hardened heart doesn't listen, isn't resolute, unless it finds it favorable, and presents a revengeful approach, if not, which comes from ignorance and an emotional response. Ignorance accompanied and led by an emotional response is dangerous and complicated to resolve.

26.   If you marry a hardened heart, you may feel protected, until you decide to separate, when it yields its will against you and your will, bringing emotional harm to the hardened heart. That's called exacerbation. Anything can happen, because of your un-Godly choice.

27.   Every choice outside the Will of God is subject to its inferior consequences.

28.   Giving credit or support to your father, the Devil, who has shown you he doesn't love you, a long time ago, is not intelligent. Yet, some have sat in his churches for years and continued to practice the version of life of a demon and continued to receive the fruit of a poisonous tree.

29.   You knew you were wrong, because you didn't want to be on the wrong side of your choice and priorities.

30.   When you've advanced to making better decisions or reaping better results, and been connected to the wrong people, and decide to go back to party or casually associate with them, it has a tendency to get awkward, even threatening or violent.

31.   While we must get along with all people as much as possible, when you go so far with Truth, you start stepping on toes. You go further, and you step on more toes. Understand where I'm going.

32.   Like I said, earlier, I used to be in a gang at an earlier age and time. Many of these people, I'm talking about, don't want to see you do something they won't or don't want to do for themselves. It disturbs the status-quo. It brings out their weaknesses. It causes jealousy. It becomes an attack to their hearts. I understand that many are stuck in some way and entangled with certain others. I get it. But my understanding is not enough to cool that pressure they're feeling.

33.   I've put myself in their shoes, and I've seen that they are me in all those unique circumstances and situations; so, I can't innocently attack them. I can't innocently not understand them, except where I lack knowledge and experience of their realities. Plus, I'm supposed to be a minister. More is expected of me than them. So, re-engaging with the wrong people of the past, especially those who have not changed, for whatever the reason, and may feel offended, is not a good and safe option.

34.   It's not safe, when they want you back. I'm talking about the way you used to be.

35.   The effort to get you back may start off casually, to tempting, then to violent provocation. They might say "Triphilia misses you. Remember, you used to really like her." They may talk about things that you said were wrong, but they either think you are wrong or should mind your own business, if not both. They let you know they don't like you exposing them, in some way. They may bring up some old drama to try and bring you down to earth, so to speak. But the error is they feel the need to bring you down and not build you up or approve of your advanced decision-making.

36.   Although they're victims of the same oppressive regime as us, we find that they engage with the same mentality with one another, including you and I, depending on how we fit in the status-quo. In essence, they have helped lock themselves into the principles and concepts of the oppressors, who are observing, imagining, and manipulating their desired developments and outcomes. It looks camouflaged; so, it's difficult to prove anything concerning the authorities, until you examine the big picture.

37.   Here, at my church, I take all that I know and try to reverse inferior provocations and developments. That's why we started a school for our children; so, we can shield them and get them to concentrate on what they need to succeed. But, when you try to do good; you have a tendency to come under attacks, depending on how unacceptable you are and how disruptive to an inferior system it is predicted to be.

38.   So, while we're busy adjusting and adapting, the other side is busy doing the same. So, there's always changes and sustained values, making the environment constantly unstable. But, avoiding risk is not an option; because the contentious nature of the opposition is not going to bring any rewards. It's most likely to bring increased oppression, if not a sustained intensely oppressed environment. That's attacks to your heart and the heart of your kids and the coming generations.

39.   To all the hardened hearts, I say "Let's grow up together". Thank you for coming to the Lord's House. Amen. Copyright© Minister Ion Museum

Gang Life Memory Revisited

1.   At some point in my life, I went back to the past to discover what happened to all the people I knew and grew up with. I was curious and still loved my people. I felt like I was driven by some other reason too, just didn't know what it was.

2.   Anyway, I used to be in a gang in my earlier years; so this event was big for me.

3.   Sadly, I looked back at the memory of that, and I depicted the values coming from them and perceived evidence of the devil.

4.   I saw the pull to the other side, towards evil. I saw unforgiveness, a play for keeps, temptation, and trickery.

5.   I saw the attempt to elude exposure and a fastening to an unhealthy way to live, in spite of the revealing of truth. I saw the hunger to steal and the urge to take another out.

6.   At times, anger presented itself.

7.   Overall, the population was imploding, physically or morally, if not both. But, in spite of it all, there was quite a lot of contentment.

8.   I saw the appeal for demonic qualities, especially in defense, including a revel in the arts of the same qualities. It looked like a pump in the wrong direction.

9.   Shockingly, I saw the false impersonation of God, coming from the advice and implication(s) given to me. This god was strict and without understanding, having no concern for the souls of humans and empathy was low.

10.   I saw that I was known for who I was in the past, not for who I am now. According to them, my past seemed to define who I'll always be. There was no consideration for my environment, which created me, and the environment that came before that and so on. Instead, they still saw me as one of them: mentally stuck in the wrong place.

11.   They, even, used kids to challenge adults, above other tough challenges.

12.   They offered relief for an exchange, even in the light of error and/or their own production(s).

13.   Those, who had the most clout amongst them, were the most respected and followed. Intelligence was only good if it supported their selfish intentions. Insults fared better than intelligence, especially if it was creative and funny.

Backsliding

1.   When you backslide from a well-established environment in God to a worldly environment, and you show you possess the need to stay on the good side of the line; they perceive your moral objective as a weakness to challenge and triumph above you. You're subject

to challenges that result in the juggling of the status quo all the time, especially if it has anything to do with the riches of the world, regardless of quality.

2.   If you don't come back from backsliding from an environment of God, they either pulled you into their swamp or you were very much aligned with and accepting of them, unless you were too naive to discern the difference between the two environments. So, if the alarm doesn't go off, you remain asleep, putting yourself in danger of hell fire.

What are Formulas?

1.   Formulas are perceived in their natural operations and used to take control. A style of reasoning, a style of succeeding in any matter, a style of losing in any manner, and how a natural or unnatural event, development, or outcome occurred are all formulas. Consider whether you were part of each development to detect external interference, especially a negative trend.

2.   One of the toughest formulas to present is how one can, knowingly and controllably, implode upon the self or to, knowingly and controllably, allow another to lead him/her against their best interest(s). It's contradictory. But accountability is eagerly bound as if to be without question and no solution is discovered.....

Depict the Formulas Entailed in Every Reality

1.   Hardships encourage one to seek relief. The effort to seek relief gets stronger as it becomes important, even to the point of desperation, which is encouraged by mental and emotional strain and the tension from persevering with no or very little solution. It, formatively, pumps immorality out of you, unless you find yourself constantly resisting. Long-term effects include memories that cause fits, even in the midst of silence and calm.

2.   When something pumps immorality out of you, there's a need for protection and to feel accepted, which is one reason why gangs form. The other reasons are to pursue an interest, be recognized, respected, gain popularity and favoritism, and to feel mutual loyalty. Other than that, protections and need(s) may be the only source(s) that drew the decision. Then, you're caught up in the wrong vacuum.

3.   When erroneous perceptions, faulty beliefs, or drugs are in the body, the consequences of not meeting the urges of it may be long-lasting and potentially severe, constantly driving the will of the character towards more error, dependency, and even desperation. Then the priorities, which are now driven by foreign matters, change. This results into a slave of the author/salesman.

4.   That's because the environment has a particular objective and judges you by its related standards, in which you must meet or become questionable, potentially leading to social and economic failures and mounting pressure(s).

5.   The inspired or forced injection of, either, good or bad qualities depends on the overall results, especially long-term.

6.   Like I said, I still love them. I look at how they were built by outsiders. Their experiences and their lack of opportunities to acknowledge more of how the world works, both of which drove them to be who they are. Their impulsive behavior just followed and got in rhythm.

7.   I saw how the world around us was so paralleled and opposing, growing the prison population so effectively and efficiently, seemingly with a tendency towards further improvement. It appeared to me that there was some method, because it didn't seem natural. It was too effective, efficient, and ongoing. It seemed to me that somebody had to know something. I'm especially referring to someone who does studies, puts the puzzle-pieces together, gives an opinion, and makes a decision. And, why wouldn't there be such people, if there's a desire for crime prevention? A plan could be drawn from this.

8.   When studies are performed and completed, they can yield both dark wisdom and the wisdom of light.

9.   From there, I look at the premises for thinking, where it all starts. I could see where someone could control experiences by taking away or engaging people, things, and/or matters of concern to defuse, continue, excel, or change something. You know….create a formula to match a desire for something.

10.   This is why I can still love them. This is why I can say I am them in their shoes. That's because this whole world and everything in it is about formulas. And, formulas are dangerous in the wrong hands of people with power.

11.   The external life is as controlling as it is unclear, dark and requiring. So, people need to understand how life unfolds to make an enlightened decision about anything by understanding themselves and the world around them. Light and darkness, together, will always yield problems; so, we need maximum light.

Detecting a Demonic Administration

1.   When good intent(s) and its producers have been stymied and life is hard, a demonic administration has gathered together, positioned themselves in power, and made decisions without your best interests in mind. Then, all their dealings become questionable. Again, it is a backwards way to live, and it requires you to adapt your mindset to align with reality, to see what's going on and recognize the potentiality of the future.

2.   In this reality, the affected population become all about the fulfillment of a desire that drives them into the profitable ways that benefit the administrators of a demonic system. This is perceived as a profit center by Satan and his advocates and is a result of oppression, deception, and distraction.

3.   The situation, as a whole, is like the two types of black holes, one won't let anything out and the other type won't let anything in. Generally, one is caught up in a suction cup and the other is a thief, who produced the stipulations, conditions, and litigations.

Energy and Matter: Predestined

1.   Energy and matter are, on the highest level, predestined to work, in which error signals "You're going the wrong way" and confirms that "it is not for you to do anything solely at your discretion". You were supposed to be testy and backing up from error, only to find the right way or push for it.

2.   A continuation, in spite of negative results, signals the fallen angels and their supporters.

The Rub Between Accountability and Economic Instability

1.   Accountability is needed to maintain stability of the game; but there's a problem, even more than one. The economy is unstable and certain types of people are discriminated against, which makes gains and losses unstable and potentially unpredictable. However, addictions may be continuous in its ways, having no compliance upon economic conditions. Not only that, there's a need to step on another's territory to make up for losses and to support growth. So, chaos and the threat of such is always looming, because of instability, demands, accountability, and desperation.

The Spark that Starts the Engine

1.   The consequences of not meeting a demand produces the sting that bolsters conformance. So, you don't want anyone to place demands on you that will cause you to make decisions from the premises that don't represent your best interests, and you should consider, carefully and thoroughly, any matter that may cause the same to occur. Young people are vulnerable to this principle, because they lack knowledge and may be tested early in life.

2.   Vulnerability is why they should never be found near sources of addiction, especially those who may have been tested early as well. They should never face challenges that adults can't handle with complete success.

3.   The premises for thinking should always come from a source that is healthy, moral, constructive, compatible, supportive, confirming, versatile, adaptable, creative, and with an eye to the future, as much as possible.

4.   If a premise is questionable, it should be researched. However, it may be as resisted as the environment possesses an opposing objective. Ask those who possess an unforgiven student loan or who were left with setbacks or other debts from their efforts to create a comfortable life for themselves. So, the risk is equal to your treatment.

5.   When the other side is evil, intelligent, and aware, they see buttons of ignition. They can take control and profit from the ordeal, even to add features to maintain it and appear innocent. The game is as protected as it is obvious. It's a system of destructive formulas, even to the point of murder.

6.   If I had reached a level where I had made a name for myself and had a lot of clout, I probably would never have made it out of that gang life. That's even more true, if hardships had trapped me there, which happens to a lot of people.

Conspiracy

1.   I saw that the devil works slowly, like through generations, giving humans time to adapt to harsher and harsher conditions. This is why there was unusual calm in the midst of a storm, even in the midst of coming threats. But, not only were they calm, they could laugh, even at the dire conditions of another. Of all the wrong that was occurring, they hated many, who chastised them. They had settled in, for whatever the reason, and found a seat.

2.   I wondered why I didn't see the synchronicity of these events back in my earlier times. As a matter of fact, I just didn't perceive much wrong with the environment at that time. I thought it was natural. I thought everybody had their place in The Game and acted accordingly, and there was no other game. No one preached about modern realities to set off a wakeup call.

3.   When I came back from the past, I carried my vision over to my current conditions to consider synchronicity. I saw, where there was forbidden law, many times, there was a sting to do wrong. The sting was, at times, unbearably and shocking.

4.   Then, I thought "Somebody wants to control my walk, thought, and talk. They want me to fit the bill they sent me".

5.   I could only see the matter as unnatural, because of its theme over time. But, this part of the story was a hard sell, as it was met with a lot of resistance. But, when the complaint is presented to those responsible and/or to their supporters, of course there will be resistance. In the end, there's no way to present a case of conspiracy without their consent.

6.   "Consent" sounds suspicious, because a matching description of the disclosed concept is all that's needed to make that determination. That disclosed concept should be observable by anyone; so that detecting eyes can see and prove its case through its revealing lens. It not only should be disclosed, but it should be clear in revealing its description.

7.   After all, a conspiracy is the greatest threat to God's people; because it has the ability to produce the most powerful, detrimental, and enduring effects, with an element of refractory. An element of refractory should never be found in the business of people, unless it has to do with protections and essentials known to garner good amongst them. However, upon reasonable suspicion, the gates should be opened and examined for suspicious activities for all to see; because it has voided its reason for refractory. When a refractory is set up to guard against consequences that only those of the same status type can navigate for resolution, it must be questionable.

8.   The culture(s), lifestyles, conditions, and issues of the population are a reflection of its governing style, knowledge, resources, technologies, efforts, visions, priorities, beliefs, creativeness, capabilities, sensitivities, and discriminatory practices.

9.   Because conspiracies produce a victim, the accused should always have the last unfiltered and publicized word in a case against him/her/them, due to the sophisticated tricks of the

demons, not the other way around. Otherwise, we would never identify a faulty trend and/or formula(s) amongst the controlling population.

Grief

1. Think of the most devastating thing someone has done to you, especially something they did repeatedly. Try to forgive them in your heart. Do you feel strong resistance? That's grief.

2. Don't let grief find a permanent home in your heart. As a matter of fact, rebuke it upon its initial appearance. It's a foreign influence. It's not related to love. It's dangerous when given too much credibility and importance. Walk away, courteously, from the source. Don't fuel it.

3. When one is, knowingly and carelessly, acting from a different value system, you cannot solve it. All that is left, for now, is conflict that may lead to violence and to the swamp. Many times, if a matter is resolvable, it wouldn't have been reintroduced.

4. Don't fight the source of grief and become entangled in its consequences; make medicine for your heart, instead, and maintain the support of God.

Make Medicine

1. Make medicine, because a doctor has a better reputation than a criminal. I can tell the people of God by who makes medicine and for whom. I can tell where they are in the process. Then, what do I do? Make medicine.

2. It's not easy. I wrestle with it too. A lot of times, I slam my fist on the table instead. I may do a slip of the mouth. I'm not perfect. But, when I get that way, I stop and tell myself, "Make medicine". I, also, recognize the type of person on the other side and how I permitted the individual to get inside of me and ransack my mind. I recognize the formula; then, I will eventually understand how to make medicine.

3. You have to tell yourself, when you're imperfect and have adopted habits from an imperfect world, you're programmed the wrong way. So, you have to reprogram yourself. So you have to make it a habit to tell yourself to do the right things and make yourself do it, no matter how hard it is to do.

4. The same medicine doesn't work in every situation. It may need to be personalized. Again, you may not resolve it at all, depending on whether you're dealing with worldly or Godly people. Sometimes, medicine may just be distancing or padding against the harsh effects.

5. When everybody is focused on making medicine, there's less likely to be confusion. This is the reason not to backslide from God's community and how you recognize it. However, a church, with a lot of sufficiently knowledgeable backsliders, may be an indication of the failings of its purpose.

6. Unlike God's people, criminals will take a matter to jail, prison, or never let it go. But, like you, many of them wake up and grow in the Lord. But, recognize that there is resistance that needs to be understood.

7.   An answer must be found. Any answer should be elaborated, proven to be known and under the control of the accused, if we were to accuse, including clear perception of matters and not planted for review and containment. The answer should be stronger than a personal opinion, because people have a unique set of circumstances.

8.   Reasoning from the premises is the beginning of accuracy and error, the decision-maker is as much responsible as he/she/they are knowledgeable and in control of those premises. The world has it backwards; because this is where the control is, and this is where the healing starts. This is, also, where manipulation starts.

9.   Medicine is not about branding someone; it's about healing and correction. It is not about being better-than-thou. It is about fixing something or turning it towards the right direction.

10.   When that decision-maker, who gave an opinion and directed the course of future events, can't see how to proceed morally and successfully, under all the same circumstances, he/she/they bleed guilt like blood. Then, it is not medicine.

11.   Understand that the church and the world do not share the same meaning of medicine. The church is about healing and correcting. On the other side, we have side effects, where additional issues are birthed, along with current issues and matters become sustained and hardened.

Focus on the Right Carrot at All Times

1.   Focus on the carrot that processes information and yields solutions and good results. Make medicine. Then, you become useful for God. The ungodly does the opposite. They make destructive formulas. Show yourself as separated from them and worthy of God.

2.   The opposition connected together the heart, mind, body, the environment, and the things in it. They saw how it performed in nature and replicated it in their evil schemes. They created laws to protect it in a refractory. This is their guiding light to carry out their plot and to work against you, if they feel the need to do so.

The Only Business with an Outsider is to Win a Soul

1.   Don't partner with oppressors nor their supporters. You were told not to be unevenly partnered together. God required His people to separate in the past; so they won't get caught up in His wrath. Don't bring opposites together, in favor of both, as if to please both masters. Show your distance and opposition, courteously, while attempting to win their soul.

Sinful Preaching

1.   We're supposed to determine whether the things that were true in the past are still true; but, how do you do that, if you're not moving forward? The verse is a guiding light.

2.   The message(s) of a minister cannot be contained to past writings. The Bible cannot remain in error; it must be updated, modernized, and reliable for everyday life. It must match reality, even as it changes. And, it must keep up with the workings of Satan and his advocates and improve upon creating the conditions sought by God.

3.   To not adhere to the Word of God is a sin; so, when a minister fails to meet the standards set by God, it's sinful preaching. It's, also, a distractive sermon; because it focuses a person of God away from dangerous, modern techniques of Satan and his advocates. It fosters naivety and weaknesses in favor of Satan. It's a setup!

The Purpose of the Church Garners Separation

1.   The purpose of the church is to build its members up in God. God is not limited.

2.   Under the right circumstances, God's people become more sophisticated over generations, while becoming more experienced in producing His Values.

3.   The divide between the Worldly people and God's people becomes wider. The push for solutions to the problems that we face, and the resistance and deceptions of Satan and his advocates, are what drives the two away from one another.

4.   Because it's a sin to not seek knowledge, adhering to the law forces contention between the two opposing sides.

5.   Enlightenment sees the potentiality of Satan's world imploding and how it resisted the very fact, as well as the fruits it produced for judgment.

6.   When there's sufficient information, and high tension is missing between the two worlds, and the world continues to move in the wrong direction, the church is hindered or in cooperation with the opposition, unless it is unaware or distracted.

7.   When God's people trust the opposition, there's great fraud in the land.

8.   Opposites cannot come together and create perfection; so, it is prohibited. The law is to be perfect as He is.

9.   When you see a mixture of opposing values, that is not an environment of God; especially if God's Values are completely voided in practice.

10.   When you see opposites in a church environment, consider whether God's people are being used as a shield.

Ignorance and Sin Produce the Same Results

1.   Ignorance and sin look alike; because they look devious and produce the same results, which are errors, even compounding them. So, you don't encourage or feed ignorance, nor prey on the weaknesses of another. It is not a Godly concept, but it lets you know who is who and whom they represent.

2.   So those having opposing values cannot live nor worship together. There will be too much conflict and growing dissent. At some point, you end up negotiating and, as a result, voiding or putting the practice of God's Values at risk.

Authoritative Coercion Towards Sin and Crime

1.   In the case of Authoritative Coercion, consider whether the power of authority is met with Underdeveloped Law, a Denied Effective Defense, or a Hidden Source of Aid to approve or bolster coercion towards a life of crime and a violation of religious rights.

2.   I'll tell you the truth, when I say there's no greater violation than a denial of the religious practices, required by our loving Deity, by way of man's law and/or treatment. There's no one who has the power to intervene the relationship between the two. Theirs is no one who can say they have the authority, without blasphemy.

3.   When one says "I have the authority to intervene between humans and their God", he says "I am a representative of God to hinder His and humans' goals to form a relationship". Then, we recognize Devil Talk.

The Policies of Separatists

1.   You hear people talking about a person must earn their wages, and this, and that, as well as a higher lifestyle and attempt to enforce their beliefs with harsh laws and a denial of relief; then, we find that a lot of people are restricted from earning.

2.   For one, we find that scarcity is the blame for inflating prices, which is a protective shield for the successful population. Scarcity says "There's not enough for everyone". So, the demand goes up as the product or service is being depleted or, supposedly, depleted.

3.   Inflation takes a bigger toll on the poor, who couldn't afford much in better times.

4.   The market awards the rich with a percentage of returns that the poor find useless, and the percentage continues to dwindle over time. That encourages the rich to become richer or get swallowed up.

5.   Meanwhile, they have levied tolls on the poor that they termed fair. They have used percentage of income as their representation of fair; however, it is more daunting to the poor than the rich. For a comparison, thirty-percent of $100 is $30, leaving only $70 to pay bills with, while the same thirty-percent of $10,000 is $3,000, leaving $7,000 to pay bills with.

6.   For the poor, the explorations of our world are hindered by a lack of affordable opportunities and, because of fraud and a lack of quality information, experiences are mixed with inaccuracy, incompleteness, and usually non-competitive in competing interests.

7.   The price of quality food, in sufficient form, is out of reach of the poor. Then, the body is subject to deterioration.

8.   The price of quality goods, in sufficient form, is out of reach of the poor. Because of this, it has a more draining of finances effect.

9.   The price of quality services, in sufficient form, is out of reach of the poor. Risks are up, due to the lack of sufficient protections and/or aid, in respects to needs and importance.

10.   In the midst of all that, the quality of wages is receding, and the need to be secretive about their differences is increasing, as jealousy, desperation, and crime are bolstered.

11.   A friend told me that he was training a young lady and, one day, she left her envelope on top of the machine with her check in it. He found it and opened it, and he saw that she was making more than him. He was stunned! It was common for everyone to keep their mouth shut about their earnings; so, things like this can happen.

12.   Then, you see people in the same neighborhood, where many are poor, but others look poor to keep from being robbed.

13.   When the Connections Game is the most successful way to live and get ahead of your bills, people rely on those in decision-making positions to favor them. So, they must show themselves to be likeable and favorable to the interests of the higher ups.

14.   The matters concerning student loans are, generally, a racist idea; others just get caught up in it. It's designed to hand-pick successful people, excelling one and weighing down another. It's one of the ideas of the separatists, who wrote other policies that favor those with more money and resources.

15.   Anytime you see rules that allow or don't recognize manipulative schemes, they were written by a con-artist. If you concentrate on all the schemes that have happened to the disadvantaged, you can see how the con-artist skillfully got around, avoided, and protected a scam against them. It's especially true, if it occurs frequently or popularly known. It's obvious groundwork for theft.

16.   The above-mentioned methods, together, are the tools of discriminating against anyone, even, a whole race.

The Mark of the Beast is in the Core

1.   If you didn't see where I was going, it was because you were blind to the ways of the world and to the Truth. Folks, what I just described is the Mark of the Beast. You have to take on the mentalities of the higher ups, obey their commands, and be accepted by them, in order to achieve success in their market.

2. The Mark of the Beast is the core of a system that intervenes the relationship between God and His people, or potential people, and filters them out of the market, in favor of a low quality of life and to act against the Will of God.

3. If you do not meet the qualifications of the Mark of the Beast, me being conservative, due to the tricks of Satan, you will most likely find yourself on the receiving end of negativity, even social ridicule and subject to prison and death or the threat of.

4. The population is groomed by all these tools and, therefore, encouraged to act and respond like Satan. That makes it a conspiracy and the method is theft.

5. For those, who knew, but voluntarily didn't say a word and profited from the idea, they stole by their silence and lack of effort to correct.

Why They Try to Limit the Pastor's Sermon

1. Now, you can see why they try to limit a pastor's sermon to Biblical history and not modern history and present developments. Satan's people do not want to be ridiculed or reminded for the wrong they do. However, they want the reputation of a God-fearing servant; so, they attend the church and deceive many.

2. Silence and insufficient actions make the devil look like the primary choice over God.

Rebuke the Devil

1. Check on the struggling population of your church and question their dealings in life, in order to understand the dark side of life, and preach the diagnosis and make medicine.

2. After the verdict and sentencing or acquittance, and given time to process and prepare a report, both in writing and later for a live presentation, the defendant's assessment should be given. The objective is to persuade an honest interpretation that is not affected by an outsider's manipulative agenda, which may affect its content and/or its accuracy.

3. Beware of a time of a completely dark world, with no people of God. It is a perfect time to light the match and, potentially, set the world on fire, at any time, because none are His. All have chosen the riches of the world over Unity in Love.

Minister Ion Questions the False Churches

1. To the false churches, I ask "How do you live your life in God, but allow Satan and his advocates to lead you? How can they lead you with no issues?"

The Book of Light, The Book of Darkness, and Hypocritical Judgement

1. In the Bible, there were actually two books joined together. They were the Book of Light and the Book of Darkness. They represented the wheat and chaff growing together. The people chose what book to follow and the most influential were responsible for the results.

2. Inferior and mixed results were the result of the Book of Darkness.

3. From the Book of Darkness comes "Hypocritical Judgement", which entails reverse meanings, in which both operate from a position of integrity, but falsely represent it.

4. Hypocritical Judgement is a judgement that occurs after having knowledge of an encouraging environment, only to deny or downgrade its affects in favor of deception, hate, consequence, defamation, and/or a profit. - Method of Denial

5. The other side of Hypocritical Judgement includes presenting drama, in which a natural response to it is deemed some sort of mental disorder. The holder of the hypocritical judgement is saying "You must be what we make you to become" or "It must be interpreted as we say, regardless of its inaccuracy". – Method of Observance

Everything is Working Properly

1. When I say things are working properly, I do not mean nothing is wrong. Instead, I mean a cluster of modules are revealing as they should be. Because of the relations, they reveal a fault in a process. If the spark plugs are weak, your vehicle will struggle to start, if it starts at all.

2. So, when we understand a matter, we understand its operations and can pinpoint a diagnosis and fix it. This is the job of the knowledgeable, like the mechanic, doctor, psychologist and so on. But many professional positions are not used to break a system, designed to prioritize the economically-better-off population.

Goading

1. So, the implication is that all, who don't possess the talent, need to yield to the goading of the process, rather than being destructive. Therefore, when we have a complaint, we need to express that complaint with "ignorance", "secrets", "implication" and "goading" as our guiding lights. It is the process of a set-up and manipulation. It may be called "freedom stolen", but definitely "a quality of life stolen", which hinges on a valuation system and affordability.

2.   It started with "I own this land. You are on my property; so, you owe me", and/or "I own this patent and/or copyright; so, you can't use my method. Therefore, you must pay according to the value depicted for my products and services". This creates a squeeze-play, pushing you out into the cold world, where goading is stronger and exploitive. Then, you become a reflection of the world they created.

3.   Let's say a mechanic junked every vehicle he didn't have a diagnosis for, or couldn't/wouldn't fix; then, I came along and found these vehicles, diagnosed and fixed them. I would be a savior. What would the mechanic, who junked them be? That is Satan and his advocates. One possesses the wisdom of darkness and the other the wisdom of light.

4.   You check the junkyard for values, what they devalue, that which they refuse to acknowledge, and for results related to the goading(s) of their system(s). The information is as much obvious as it is widely known, enduring, and/or producing of a stereotype. The information is as profound as it is profitable, as it is compatible with an agenda, or as no effort is being applied to fix it.

5.   The world is producing effects of affects, which is a point(s) of learning. In the process, opinions do not come from here. Opinions come from a discriminating or partially perceiving mind, which yields partial ignorance of decision, if not corruption. Corruption produces goading(s) that entail a theme towards an inferior direction. You can see goading(s) in experiences and in writings. You can find evidence in "the unknowledgeable, who are in a high position, having sufficient information or ability to bring it forth, but won't or refuse to acknowledge it for an insufficient reason(s)". An opinion shows dedication to a particular system of the two or a combination, yielding conflict somewhere in the totality of logic.

Satan's Members

1. Members of Satan's system demonstrate anxiousness in their affairs by discriminating against truth, their possessors, and timing a matter as complete when full development is insufficient. It is especially true when they possess pertinent information without disclosing it, and rebuking information simply because they can't afford to acknowledge it, claiming "No proof. Such leaves the defender in the hands of those, who are depended upon to do research and experiments with integrity, but can't be monitored and/or deemed accurate by the defender.

2. We understand the clique by what they create, like divide, bad news, reservations for themselves, statistical advantages, and are against public enlightenment, leaving the world dark, struggling, anxious, desperate, and violent.

3. They like to run people into one another, but if you try to encourage checks and balances in their system, running them into one another to right a wrong, you become the problem. As you can see, they won't voluntarily do it, only through pretentious means that don't disrupt their system.

4. It seems that their members are just as divided as they are united against God and His interests.

Backwards Accountability and Integrity

1.   But, yet, Satan and his people ask for accountability and integrity from others. However, a motive can be perceived in the very fact that people are torn down, rather than being built up with the wisdom of light, especially in prisons. And, a motive is, also, perceived in the fact that there's no effective program to build children up at an early age for prevention of going astray from law and eluding temptation. I'm sure the science of "Child Development" has a lot to say about this, but the information is not sufficiently made public and/or not sufficiently acted upon to properly guide the process.

2.   Therefore, accountability and integrity are lacking where it should be and called for on a level, where it is less reasonably expected to perform at a high level, due to a lack of structure, designed to meet expectations. How can the professional assessor of fact(s) not know this?

Valuation

1.   They took evaluations and schemed things of a high-quality nature out of the hands of the oppressed. Many things of a high quality can be said to be essential in avoiding a life of intense goading, conflict, and anxiety.

2.   They withhold knowledge, resources, solutions, and, therefore, dreams; then they hold themselves unaccountable.

3.   When they do permit the reach for such, it's purposed to camouflage discrimination: so, a low statistical value of people will be successful. In another case, it will be tied to risk of debt. Still, I perceived another case where it was tied to restrictive rules that hold you down or resist efforts to a high quality of living (struggle).

4.   Some will find themselves with income that is just above qualifying for aid and, potentially, straddling that line, as if to attract a penalty or to discourage perseverance.

Broken Marriage

1.   The corresponding people act out the part of a marriage, relationship, family, organization, or population gone wrong or has broken, whether in part or whole. They express the following adverse qualities:

2.   Cheating, selfishness, lacking empathy and sympathy, divide, longing for the luster of superficial beauty, not recognizing and appreciating the good qualities of inner beauty, growing apart, having unshared values and/or priorities, refusing to understand or seek such wisdom, withholding support and accommodation, receding trust, disrespect, hateful, taking an advantage of the other, dominating or scheming for a better position over the other, taking an advantage of another's weaknesses, tearing the other down, and revenge.

3.   Understand that these qualities are seeds that can grow and make connections, like a vine, creating a projection of the future or revealing a level of development. It says something about your relationship with God.

4.   Everyone is not ready for marriage, regardless of whether they are nice to you and favor you in the present moment. A relationship can be a ticking time-bomb that will eventually go off, if not managed properly. So, through your social affairs, you are being revealed and compared to the Wishes of God.

Satan: The Perfect Opposition

1.   It seems that Satan had to be the perfect opposition to bring out the great qualities of our God, the Creator, and His Word and Interests.

2.   Their contention would prove our loving God to be a master of Truth and Wisdom.

3.   Satan has been given the blueprint that will usurp all, who are not aligned with God.

4.   Through acknowledgement of the Wisdom of both, the heart of humans chooses their spiritual leader and, fairly, reaps the consequences of their choice.

The Whisper

1.   Regardless of what direction you take, compatible ideas come to you in your pursuit of an endeavor. That doesn't mean that these ideas are the right ideas. It depends on what develops, as a result of acting on the idea(s). By identifying good and bad results, you are, in essence, reading nature's Bible. By doing so, you are either becoming one with Satan, sowing bad seed and/or destroying good seed, or one with God, sowing only good seed.

2.   The people are identified by their profile, and what we, with limited knowledge, know about them can be observed through their beliefs, decisions, and behavior. What I saw seemed to be that Satan told all his top people that they were better-than-thou and to act proud and restrained by little or nothing.

Bonding

1.   People, who have compatible ideas, or share similar or same desires, come together and do business with one another, establishing a strong-hold, in as much as the product or service is needed by others. In doing so, they form sectors of types of businesses; then, you become trapped in their web. They make decisions that maximize their profits and protect their interests, in a world where money and material things are priority and necessary for participating in the market.

2.   They bond like vines in a vineyard, portraying themselves as they want to be perceived and attaching themselves to things that secure their position and help forward their endeavor(s), revealing a potential future trajectory of experiences. But, without integrity, this is a trick of deception, in which the imprint can be found in the observant.

3.   So, here's the catch, you have to fit in and go with the flow, or you'll live a lower quality of life, most likely, poverty.

4.   Everyone, knowledgeable of their environment and/or world, hangs in the balance of what's available for them.

Satan is Hiring

1.   But I want you to know that Satan is hiring. He has a plan, and you can see it developing in your world. It's called a business plan. A business plan requires that everything be organized to perform one or more processes. As you can see, he includes everyone in his plans or tries to. So, they'll be people, who are strong earners to those, who are actually robbed of a quality life, even destroyed. I already told you about that.

2.   Because of this organization, which creates a web that you get caught up in and obligated to, their creations (especially laws, procedures, standards, and the circumstances and opportunities that they present), as a whole, you become as swallowed up as other opportunities are void and any other moves become a negative consequence or violation of some type.

3.   You become as swallowed up as other opportunities are void, unreachable, and any other moves become a negative consequence or violation of some type. That's because the organization, which creates a web that you get caught up in and obligated to, includes creations (especially laws, procedures, standards, and the circumstances and opportunities that they present), as a whole, are requiring, instructing, and is as demanding as it is powerful, effective, and efficient in its ways.

4.   With overwhelming power, such as the above, the rest of the world becomes an imprint of shared values. You may be discriminated against and have nowhere to turn, because of a bridge or aid that's not available to you. That might be because, such a resource or option, interferes with the effectiveness and efficiency of the system. So, you may have professionals, pretentiously, in disbelief of your claims or have no way to help you, unless you have the kind of money that successful people earn and hold. You may even face an accusation of having a mental disorder. So, in this way, they determine your fate.

Your Fate is Mostly in the Hands of Others

1.   Your fate is determined by their decisions about you and what they present to you, which you have to engage in for learning, participating, succeeding, or failing in some manner. This is how you become the imprint of their influence. Then, as a whole, they become responsible for your development.

2.   Statistics and experience show that oppressors pay attention to the effects of formulas on various levels, like overall, race, behavior etc. Then, they upgrade their system to improve upon their objectives and goals or sustain the conditions. The facts are seen in long-term trends, which are more confirmed with time.

3.   The way they handle truth and its possessor is, many times, not by being resolute; but by creating circumstances that traps the complainant in a juxtaposition of negative consequences. For example, remember the sports figure who stood up for civil rights and was incarcerated by a foreign nation, only to be saved by the very nation that he claimed civil rights violations against? Now, he has to make a decision about taking a knee against or appreciating a pledge of allegiance that entails a demeaning element(s). Not only that, but he has to either give up fighting for civil rights or potentially be accused of denying appreciation for the saving of his life. Tough and unfair! But look how obviously the method is in being effectively oppressive.

4.   Any method that counters the mind, its logic, and moral will, collectively, is wrong.

5.   According to history, a way of dealing with challenges could alternatively include murder. The idea, alone, presents a strong challenge to the will.

6.   Economic sanctions and other vulnerabilities help setup a trap as well.

System Mental Disorder?

1.   Unnatural systems are built and administered by the human population. The human population has objectives, goals, and various perspectives. However, the most influential people are the most effective in leading and managing the world and everything in it. This is a mind over matter(s).

2.   To test our world, we must examine the treatment of every type of person, whether of various skills, careers, status, income level, color, race, underperforming, overperforming etc., leaving no type of person out.

3.   We must analyze and determine any wrong(s). From there, we must adjust our world to build better people and better circumstances to accommodate their upgrade. To not do so, in a system that works in conflict with the good will or what is asked of anyone, is cause for the development of a disorderly interaction(s). Such disorderly interactions, many times, have to be built upon to manage and progress forward, if possible. This is cause for abnormal reactions, seen as unreasonable to those unaffected by the disorderly exchange.

4.   To act in disagreement or to refuse to adhere or respond effectively and resolutely is to instill a mark of insanity on the world. Then, logically, you must answer as the cause of error, not the one who was forced or had no choice but to act from a set of circumstances.

5.   Your degree of innocence is in your effort to resolve and prevent, and/or to give a soundly acceptable answer that an effected, reasonable person should have known in any particular case.

Confessions of the Victimized Population

*From various victims and members of different races, but mostly the victimized race. Names are not included for safety reasons.

1.   "I would always follow the moral examples of those who were successful and happy, but it either didn't produce the same effects, conditions didn't allow me to produce an exact model, or there was some kind of timely change. It felt like I could've been perfect, but couldn't win that game."

2.   "I felt that something or someone was constantly resetting or adjusting the physical, social, and conceptual environment against me and/or forcing me to reason away from the way I thought I should go and towards a way I shouldn't. A lot of times, I couldn't get started well enough for an effective amount of time because of all the changes. When I complained or was cited for being unproductive, I got reverse-psychology for a response. I learned how powerful a company can be in how they could manipulate co-workers against me. I could never get out of being faulted in some way. It was like they were playing "squeeze out". If I challenged them, I was a trouble-maker or seen as unmanageable."

3.   "I felt like my disappointment was their reward; but it was obvious that anyone would be disappointed, if they experienced what I had to deal with. I didn't know how to play it. It was like I was doomed either way I went. If I tried to go to court, I either couldn't afford it; or I had to go through the dirty door, where they could execute an advantage over me."

4.   "I would lose a valuable opportunity, because of failure to succeed well enough in the past, while revealing the source of my problems was a forbidden act and would work against me. I was trapped. Because I sometimes told the truth, it seemed to bring more damage to me. Other times, all I could do was watch the show and hope for the best."

5.   "I was always told I needed to do better and/or work faster, but I'd look around and see people working more casually and being more comfortable in their surroundings. Meanwhile, I felt like I was the only one who had to work out at the gym, so to speak."

6.   "After going through a lot of stress at my jobs, I decided to join the other side in their oppression of another, to avoid being a victim again. But eventually, I became victimized again and they used my words against me to beat my complaint. They would ask me to give feedback, and I would be nice to try and get along; then they'd use it to beat my complaint. That's why I try to avoid them; because eventually trouble may come, and I'll wish I had never responded, especially the way I did."

7.   "It felt like all my bosses, across all jobs and gigs, shared an agenda against me; but sought to be unique in carrying them out. This told me that a lot of people know about this scheme of things, but won't acknowledge or speak up about it. Instead, they just participate. And, the legal firms don't recognize anything about it or can't help the poor in certain areas of law. After all, it seems that they would be going up against a lot of people in power and money....."

8.   "I felt like they got me, while I was young and naive. I needed more time to discover how wrong my environment was and to process it; so that I could make the proper adjustments. I saw right and wrong all around me and coming from the same people, including those who were most respected. It was as if morals were, actually, thrown to the winds. Then, all of a sudden and

shockingly, I'm perceived as a criminal. It's like, in a game of sports, you get the other side to think one way; then, you trick them by changing up and making them pay for thinking that way."

9. "A lot of my peers were living a hard life, and we looked for comforts and money solutions. Someone would introduce something that was supposed to do just that. We didn't read or watch the news, nor do studies on things other than what the school required. Little did I know that one or two samplings would hook me forever. After I was addicted, for a while, did I finally see myself falling apart. I ruined my life without sufficient knowledge of what my future would look like."

10. "I felt like, what I was going through, was just life. You just make the best of it. If you get knocked down, you just get back up. I blamed others for not being motivated and lazy. Then, I had a little trip-up; I own it. But I didn't think I was so bad that I couldn't get out of my ordeal. Then, the day came to wake up. All this information about what the government was doing was shocking. I felt like I was tricked into being a part of the problem."

11. "I felt that someone should have written a book about life that would have clearly opened my eyes to reality before I could get a start in this world; there's nothing like surprise failure. It is unfair and embarrassing. I can't enjoy life for all the need to keep hustling; then they come with some violation of law that I never knew existed. I don't study law. I don't have time, but they hold me accountable anyway."

12. "My husband was the love of my life. When I met him, I knew he was the one for me. He stood for righteousness in all things. He aimed for perfection in himself and encouraged me to do the same. I thought he was my soulmate. He was very strong about bringing change to the world in his own way.

13. He was a chemist and invented natural medicine that would bring a cure and disrupt the medical world, but he didn't know he was going up against power. This was a power that didn't believe stress causes illnesses and didn't want any real solutions for it. In revenge, they launched an investigation and found him guilty of tax and medical fraud. Some have told me that some natural healers were killed.

14. The problem is that very few people are aware and care or feel too weak to do anything about it. I think someone needs to put the word out, but I see that it's dangerous. So, I feel trapped, while my husband is doing time; and I've got kids."

15. "You know….I don't wanna talk about this. I just want out, but they keep bringing the drama and forcing me to defend myself; so that I might catch another charge. I'm not trying to be a career-criminal. They're forcing me to stay hard and defensive; so that I assure I do what I got to do to keep myself safe. They created me and, now, they're sustaining me. Why keep trying to hook me with something? But, at the end of the day, they wanna talk about law. What about protecting me and our, supposedly, shared interests?"

16. "I feel like the way through life is mysterious. Kids don't always follow the path of their parents, and of those who do, history has shown there's no guarantees for success. It doesn't seem to be all about doing the right thing or changing for the better."

17. "If I had a solid and legitimate complaint, they had a mental diagnosis. If I got out of that, they had another one…. I couldn't win that game."

18.   "I looked at the lack or quality resources and solutions, and I knew who was responsible. Our world was too developed not to know what was going on. When I spoke up, I always felt it was useless. But, what else can you do besides just take it?"

Counsel of Affairs: Definition of Crime

1.   A questioner asked "What is the definition of crime?"

2.   It is important to know that the question was stated to come as a result of seeing that the former Inferior Planet wrote laws to protect the interests of the most influential people, leaving the rest of the population unprotected and dominated.

3.   So, we hope to have satisfied the question with this interpretation:

4.   Crime is the violation of the rights of others for gain or advantage, especially financially or socially that reaches a serious level of concern.

Counsel of Affairs: Moral Code Hearing for Pre-Trial Hearings

1.   Hearing Begins

2.   The assistant Judge rises and states, "May the hearing begin!

3.   Earlier, we sent out digital documents requesting how we should proceed in determining whether a defendant is compatible with the defenses of Moral Code or the Dark Code of Conduct and how to construct and manage the procedure.

4.   Obviously, we must consider how matters are situated, before we can proceed forward on solid grounds. But we know that it's not that easy. Sometimes, we only have puzzle-pieces that we have to justify, modify, and/or piece together.

5.   Keep in mind that our finished product must have a natural feel.

6.   Anyone want to start, first?"

7.   Mrs. Amaserie (Chief Prosecutor) rises and states, "After brainstorming the idea, I thought the idea of holding the defendant's words and actions in harmony with Moral Code was a good idea. We've found that a lot of past defendants have, actually, swerved in and out of the boundary between the two codes. If we could minimize that, that would make the progression of a case more efficient and effective, which confirms our ability to reach our goals.

8.   However, we must not sacrifice our ability to learn and keep up with the dark side of society. The defendant must forfeit any knowledge of the processes associated with the

violations, as well as the encouraging environmental factors, if not known to us. This concludes my initial response."

9. Assistant Judge: Mr. Mok (Chief Defensive Attorney), what is your answer?

10. Chief Defensive Attorney, Mr. Mok, rises and states, "While I agree with Mrs. Amaserie, I don't agree with a defendant, whose mind was overtaken by false examples, especially at an early age or vulnerable time, and is faced to present answers that signify his/her guilt, with no recognition of the scientific data that supports his/her innocence. That would make my client automatically guilty and subject to a fate that doesn't belong to him/her. Then, under those conditions, what would my job be, and how can I be effective and efficient in defending my clients?

11. Mrs. Amaserie (Chief Prosecutor) rises and states, "We're not like the former Inferior Planet, who made court issues a cyclical event for a profit and recognition. And, we will never be. So, I see and agree with Mr. Mok's point.

12. Our purpose is not to destroy people or to evoke revenge upon them, as you know. We have to remain different or in opposition to the approach of the former Inferior Planet; in doing so, we have to seek the unknown details of any case.

13. Our overall purpose should not be about winning or losing, but about producing a better society with what we have and with what is coming. We don't want to leave anyone behind, unless they choose that road. I pause my response here"

14. Mr. Mok (Chief Defensive Attorney) rises and states, "We still have to assure my client knows he/she is not gambling with his/her life; or we can expect a risky, creative pursuit to escape harm or damages, which may lead to an undeserved fate. Culture or any manipulative method is a very powerful influence on any of its members, and we must consider that or maintain an unwanted, negative, cyclical effect.

15. Now, I know much has been constructed in major cities; but there are still people, who don't have access to our program. They are the ones I'm concerned about and are, most likely, to land in the Justice System blindly and helplessly, which will cause anxiety."

16. Equasus (Judge): In mediation and in consideration of the position of our attempt to get to the core of the problem, I think this method is limited to the realm of those, who control environmental circumstances and conditions, as well as who are knowledgeable of the immediate and distant developments and results. This is someone who affects culture from an authoritative or highly influential position to seed the circumstances and/or premises to reason from. The grounds for my opinion are the fact that, on the lower level, there are only actors who follow others, act from an emotional state, and possess no more than the quality of knowledge that come from an actor/actress.

17. And, like we did with the former prisoners of the former Inferior Planet, we had to let go of those, who didn't possess the intelligence needed to understand the workings of that planet. We could not progress as we did with those type of people.

18.   Because we can only progress with certain types of people, because they possess the inside knowledge, effective resources, and make major decisions about an event, responsibility and agenda(s), here, are more obvious and understood from a scientific point of view.

19.   The powers above create the jigsaw puzzle for others below, who navigate the establishments of one another, whether in error or truth. Harmony and contesting, here, is more by force than voluntary. Society is more powerful and intelligent than personal mental abilities and will. The science of development unfolds here and is recognized through an individual's development(s) in respects to the environmental circumstances, both inner and outer. People, here, are a lot more subjective than dominant, unless they're submissive and accepted by a more powerful influence.

20.   The influence of all things sits in a center and rises to and from its respective environment. If there's a problem, there is always a solution to be attained by the researcher and proper resources. Except a lot of people are limited in power, knowledge, resources, and ability by the denial of others or the weighting down of other responsibilities and issues.

21.   So, while we limit the Moral Code process to the eligible population, we can extradite the smaller population, which are the authorities to the nearest location to process them. The remaining population would have to wait for a time, because they have to go through a period of therapy and adapting to the new style of living.

22.   Getting back to the screening process, the response(s) of a defendant is contested or in harmony by the developments or results. And, our specimen must come from a receptacle of an acknowledged big picture. This receptacle includes all of the environmental experiences, which is compared to a model to consider what's missing and why.

23.   A set of questions, relative to the core morals of Quantum Star Eckter as it relates to the case, must be presented to the defendant to determine him/her as in harmony or challenging.

24.   In the challenging approach, the defendant must show a belief or act of Quantum Star Ekcter to be, at least, questionable to maintain the use of the defenses, associated with the Moral Code.

25.   Future contempt may lead to forfeiture of all defenses from Moral Code as it relates to the subject of contempt.

26.   The idea is to save time and to encourage the aid of the defendant to bring the case to a point of resolve, efficiently and effectively, as well as to keep the defendant in moral bounds. This is very good in dealing with individuals of foreign power structures.

27.   Any questions?

28.   Everyone says "No".

Counsel of Affairs: Other Definitions

Illogical: A scheme of missing logical connections or the fusing of adverse logical elements, such as good intentions with elements that disrupt or contaminate the same.

Chief Detective Report

Introduction

1.　As a member of the research team, involving the former inferior planet, I have observed and studied numerous documents, events, and comments. My observations and conclusions are stated below.

Problem

1.　The former inferior planet was going backwards in respects to Quantum Star Eckter and their own Bible, as concluded by others and myself.

Motive

1.　I believe they were tempted with the riches of the earth; after all, the richest amongst them protected a demonic way of life. This is evidence of a partnership with the fallen angels.

Existence and Summoning of Spirits

1.　Now, many did not believe in the fallen angels; because they didn't see them and didn't believe they had any influence upon them. However, there was strong evidence of spirits seen as a result of messages detected in the fallen organization of tarot cards, the patterned swinging of the pendulum, and a game involving the questioning of the spirits, followed by a movement that spelled out results. The Disciples of the Son of God cast lots to choose a replacement for Judas.

2.　While there's been a dispute about spirits being involved, favor falls towards spirits where the results weren't capable of being produced by the questioner, such as future projection. But tools aren't always needed to produce spiritual results, as seen in non-laborious results that suddenly appear in the imagination, mind, or emotions.

3.　These non-laborious results are more powerful, smarter, and reveal the objectives and goals of the unseen source. The writer or receiver feels that someone is always thinking in the background and releases information to push a project through to its maturity, which is dependent upon the strength of language, possessed by the holder. This is the kind of source that is responsible for "There Are Three Truths".

Partnership

1.   It appears that the partnership begins when a person shares a common interest with the source. The source is identified by the values favored in the messages. But some stories have produced some horrifying effects, causing people to dismiss spiritual tools all together. It's a sign to be careful who you become and who you partner with.

The Gift and Control of the Imagination of Others

1.   Anyway, the authorities attained specialized knowledge about how to run a demonic system. This information would not be imaginable, because it did not originate amongst them. Some authorities have resisted certain literature from infiltrating their environment to maintain control over the imagination of the subordinates, resulting in a controlled way of imagining and thinking.

2.   Others have, also, controlled the awakening state by criticizing "Wokeness", even to the point of embarrassment, while prioritizing the Devil's work. The environment was not favorable to believers in God; and so, the professional world couldn't be counted on to deliver a statement or answer that is compatible with His existence and interests.

Turned Inwards and Towards the Affairs of their Population and Away from God

1.   People were deceived, because they turned inwards and towards the affairs of their population, as a priority over God's perspective, making it an incubator. This was the main backwards approach that thrust them towards their demise. By turning, as they were, they got creative and developed a personal perspective of God that got messy as it got more inclusive, instead of recognizing who He was and how it all plays out in a non-conflicting manner. They saw it as more convenient and acceptable, figuring their personal experiences justified their beliefs, while Satan and his advocates observed and manipulated them and their surroundings. They got caught up in themselves, each other, and away from God. This is where the trouble began.

2.   God's Words were the Stones to be walked on, which was proven only when they were sought and pursued as a guiding light.

3.   The leader(s) who led them was simply what the majority thought were more in tune with their feelings and beliefs. As a result, the majority replaced real, genuine Truth with faith in themselves, who possessed an evil agenda. Otherwise, the people were just conquered.

4.   Those, who were less intelligent, didn't have the formulas or methods to calculate the full realities they faced; so, they followed those who were supposed to have expertise in their field. Those were the very people who fooled or didn't realize they misled them. This was Satan's greatest trick to replace the Word of God with politics and opinions.

5.   Therefore, while the world sustained confusion, even got worse, it never occurred to them that they were going in the wrong direction.

6.   The vulnerable people forgot that Satan deceived the whole world and never suspected that he would affect the most trusted sources.

7.   Many never possessed the knowledge to track for legitimacy and others didn't have enough backing to garner enough influence to create change, while the rest hid it from them or never spoke up.

8.   Slowly, the fallen angels worked with the authorities of their world and transformed it from vulnerable to more imperfect to immoral.

Distraction

1.   There were a lot of distracting elements. One was drugs. Firstly, they set up a very stressful and uninspiring environment. This became the foundation for the need to escape to something that feels good. The better it worked, the more they chased it.

2.   When dangerously, addictive, recreational drugs were introduced to mainstream society, by taking advantage of insufficient knowledge of these drugs, the developers were able to gain access to the control mechanisms of the human bodies. The users became a slave to the formula of addiction, which created a profit center to destroy mankind.

Anti-Human System

1.   Because life was hard, especially economically, the anti-human system continued to come together. The drugs became a way of sustaining people from economic success. Insufficient income, joblessness, and instability encouraged the drug market to grow. As a result, much of the population were defensive of the drug market.

2.   Because of this defense, the defense of the majority overpowered the remainder of the population. Where one stood against it, he/she would lose his/her life or become overwhelmed with adversity. The authorities, naturally, allowed this to continue, just in a questionable way. So, now, the authorities had the drug dealers and addicts generally backing their plan. So, no wonder it was never solved, because it was a means to gain a step(s) above another.

3.   Civil Rights Leaders were subject to Intentional Procedural Death (IPD), if it wasn't outright murder. IPD is a protocol that incites disease(s) or any scheme, usually not considered or detected by law enforcement, that leads to the death or destruction of another.

Perception

1.   Remember, the environment was stressful and uninspiring. However, there were people living the good life. Because life included different hustles and ways of living, it created a structure of society. This structure was inspiring, depending on the way you saw it. Few knew everything about how people made their living and how much they made; but those who were the most informed and had the broadest types of experiences, manifested a broad perception of the world, which was what their imagination could work with.

2.   It is important to know that perception can be limited or expanded, depending the variation of experiences. It is, also, important to know that a variety of experiences is inspiring to

the imagination. If an experience is pleasing or beneficial in any way, the imagination is going to move in that direction; and, if the imagination is introduced to or influenced by an example, it is going to feel justified.

3.   With all the secrets of life withheld, it is easy to feel justified in many things that aren't legitimately justified. This is why deception and tricks are so successful.

4.   Experts studied the world as if it were in an incubator. They saw how it worked naturally. They set out to reproduce the effects to their advantage and profited from the results. The experiences of their targets included resources, events, scripts, drama, actors, actresses, who played out the rules handed down by the experts. In the end, there were potential consequences for the targeted source. If it were well played, the theme remained unbroken for a long period of time and consistency told a story about the competitive nature between it and the will of its target.

5.   The balanced act, of the target, included the expression of known damages and benefits experienced along the journey of life. The personality changed accordingly, except in times of resilience.

6.   An interviewee expressed the following: "Speaking of resilience, there is a time in our young lives when we pick up things that stick with us, whether right or wrong. One example is our accent. There are, also, matters that happen over a period of time that sets or changes our tone of emotions, expressions, and decisions towards negativity. Sometimes we may feel that we need to be more overlooking of things, but our insides explode at times. This is a sign of exposure to a backwards environment."

7.   A child must be raised in a proper environment to shield him/her from matters that cause improper development at any time throughout his/her life. That means the environment must be void of streams of iniquity of all times. That's why iniquity should not be used as a source of income to build a rich life, because it encourages the thing it's trying to correct.

8.   I stress that, not only does the environment instill principles and concepts within, but a person gathers from her/his environment and seeks to follow and build from there. Therefore, the external environment encourages or strong-arms a perception of matters within. So, a perception gets its qualities from its environment. So, you'll see cultures as a confirmation of this fact. Generally, it's people in likeness following one another. Most, if not all, shared commonalities in error, which was obvious in the characters they churned out. This was the cause of the planet going backwards, in stages, producing shocking stories.

Consequences of Turning Away from God

1.   When the people's focus turns to one another, instead of the right principles and concepts of God, they go awry and tend to produce nothing good. The Foundation is gone. Then, they continue downwards, blaming, conflicting with, and dividing from one another. It turns into a constant stream of ejection and destruction, aided by streams of iniquity. This is what makes them worthy of fire and exposes their backwards ways.

2.   The only chance of avoiding literal fire is to focus on God and His interests. Until then another type of fire had already taken its toll and continued to increase, signaling a backwards way of living. It was the heat of conflict.

Stereo-typing the Vulnerable

1.   To create a stereotype, you must generalize a distinguished group by associating them with a particular quality or expose them to conditions that therapeutically develop those qualities in them. The method is seen in nature, after a study of the development of cultural traits.

2.   The authoritative officials, of the formerly Inferior Planet, used it to their advantage to trap the victimized race in lower society, in an effort to contain them for public use. The qualities they sought to develop were inferior, which gave a so-called excuse to perceive and create the conditions for continuation.

3.   The practice of not caring what others thought about them, aided the process.

4.   The insults and racist comments on social media accounts confirmed the stereotype, while promoting and maintaining the stereo-typing process.

5.   Therefore, it remained an unbroken cycle.

6.   In a courtroom environment, it meant a mountain to climb before trial began; because the jury was not naïve about the media and what they commonly heard about and saw in the areas of the victimized race(s).

Identifying the Source(s)

1.   You could identify the sources against God by introducing an instrument of change for the better; the instrument will attract resistance, whether in law, etiquette, procedure, or neglect.

2.   You could, also, identify the sources by whether they parallel elements of the plan. If they followed instructions, they knew the source of instructions. If they knew the source of the instructions, they more likely knew and communicated with the instructor(s).

3.   It's a matter of identifying the roles and how they retained and maintained effectiveness over a period of time, circumstances, situations, and locations. Contention in heightened affects is, also, an indicator.

4.   The intelligence level of those involved, in a defensive and defying stance, would fall below the standard level of intelligence for anyone operating in any position requiring sufficient conscious awareness, especially an authoritative official, which would identify a liar.

The Spiritual Vacuum

1.   It is believed that a spiritual vacuum occurs, when a child is born. The first deposits occur in the way the baby is formulated, nourished, and handled, then, what the child understands, followed by how the child develops and is treated accordingly.

2.   In a continuation, the thoughts of a child continue to develop in respects to his/her environment, including any limitations, if any, and a break from or continuation with one spiritual source or another. This break depends on what was the superior source of the environment.

3.   The child aligns with the spiritual source by being curious and somewhat in line with and seeking the qualities of the relevant spiritual source, rebuking the former. The process is in alignment with Revelations 3:20-21, "…I will come in and sup with you…" and "For those who overcome, the right to sit on the Throne with me will be granted…".

4.   From there, the fight to buy or buy back that soul continues.

5.   The inferior planet's defense against a follower of God was rebuke, poisoning, deception, detachment, and confinement away from the general population and its interests, including the restriction or concealment of growth of agreeing or potentially agreeing members.

Investigative Lead

1.   Each is a specimen of their environment and the whole. This is why a wide scope of review was needed to access the general problem(s) and identify the source(s).

God's Dreams Delayed

1.   God's dreams are delayed by a people, who turn from their Creator. In that way, they have insulted His intelligence and underrated His Power in favor of the (Dim-light) leader.

The Process

1.   We did a reverse engineering by interviewing many of the victims of oppression and found that the interview of oppressors and victims interviewed matched up, plus gave additional details.

2.   We traced trends to those medicated by the mental health institutions that were common beliefs amongst the freer population, as if to sustain a cover-up.

3.   We, also, applied scientific principles and concepts to these cases, facilitated by artificial intelligence, to further confirm the results.

4.   We've had undercover agents listen, observe, and ask questions, which led to some police interventions.

5.   We found that their government would not initiate some investigations that were pertinent in finding the evidence of complaints made by certain people.

6.   Not only that, but they never built a model of the population to give credibility to complaints by the minorities. This proved the existence of an exclusive club.

Conclusion

1.   They put their "Better than thou" glasses and their "Too good to be judged by you" hearing aids on and went at each other.

2.   In the end, truth got twisted by power and deception and the overpowered, deceived, naïve, and ungodly were overwhelmed.

3.   Success of the Justice System brought no permanent resolve, only a continuation of a destructive process and further exultation of an authoritative ego.

Historically Dangerous Aspect of Oppressive Authority

1.   The most threatening example of authoritative oppression was recorded on Exquanent Galaxy of Friends

2.   The citizens of Exquanent Galaxy of Friends had faced off with the authorities of the past, only for the authorities to use scapegoating methods to fool the population into believing the problem was solved. They said, "A few bad apples don't describe the rest of us". Then, they slowly continued to escalate the oppression again. To them, this was that unstoppable creature.

Suggestion(s)

1.   If we used "What's justified for one is justified for another", we'd, most likely, wipe that entire population out of some freedom. So, it's confirmed and suggested that we continue to use it on anyone who refuses to participate in the program; because non-participation affects us all. After all, the fallen angels must be blocked.

2.   We need to maintain clarity of what our goals are.

Quantum Star Eckter: Planet Earth

1.   The assistant Judge rises and states, "May the court begin!"

2.   What is the charge?

3.   The prosecutor rises and states, "The charge is found at Mathew 23:13. "You closed and locked the gate to heaven and neither will you open it for yourselves."

4.   The assistant Judge asks "What is the evidence?"

5.   4. The prosecutor responds: "The evidence is at Mathew 11:25 – 30: Where God claims His offer of rest, and says His heart is gentle and humble, and that His yoke is easy and burden light. Their reality pales in comparison, which evidences something wicked. As you know, I've already motioned the court about Minister Ion's sermon "The Setup", which details some wicked evidence. All this was just a briefing.

6.   What is the defense's position in this matter?

7.   Case Advocate…….